THE
HOMOSEXUAL
IN
AMERICA

THE HOMOSEXUAL IN AMERICA

A Subjective Approach

by

DONALD WEBSTER CORY

introduction by

Dr. ALBERT ELLIS

GREENBERG: PUBLISHER

New York

to Howard
A filosofia è necessario amore

Table of Contents

Part IV. CULTURE

Part V. ADJUSTMENTS

Part VI. OUTLOOK

APPENDICES

Introduction

There are many legitimate methods of investigating sexual phenomena. Thus, G. V. Hamilton (*A Research in Marriage*) and Alfred C. Kinsey and his associates (*Sexual Behavior in the Human Male*) have used the face-to-face interview technique to arrive at important sexual data. Katharine B. Davis (*Factors in the Sex Life of 2200 Women*), Lewis M. Terman (*Psychological Factors in Marital Happiness*), and the present writer (*A Study of Human Love Relationships* and other papers) have utilized anonymous questionnaires. Bronislaw Malinowski (*The Sexual Life of Savages*) and Margaret Mead (*From the South Seas*) have done anthropological sex investigations. Richard von Krafft-Ebing (*Psychopathia Sexualis*) and Magnus Hirschfeld (*Sexual Pathology*) have made medical studies of sexuality. Sigmund Freud (*Basic Writings*) and Wilhelm Stekel (*Sexual Aberrations*) have employed psychoanalytic techniques of study. Frank Beach (*Hormones and Behavior*) has devoted considerable time and effort to physiological sex experimentation. Mario Praz (*The Romantic Agony*) and the writer (*The Folklore of Sex*) have analyzed literary works and other mass media to explore and unravel human sex attitudes.

One method of sex investigation which has been relatively little employed, except in fictional form, is that of first-hand, subjective exploration and appraisal of one's own sex behavior and attitudes and those of one's partners. Havelock Ellis used this technique when he observed his own sex activity—particularly his nocturnal emissions— and (anonymously) reported this activity in one of the volumes of his *Studies in the Psychology of Sex*. Freud also employed this self-study method in presenting, in an open or disguised form, much of his own dream and self-analytic material in the course of his psychoanalytic writings. But by and large, the gathering of human sex data by means of the investigator's objectively and subjectively observing his own and his fellows' sexual behavior, and then frankly and fully presenting his observations in non-fictional form, has been a rarely used fact-finding technique.

Fortunately for the general reader of this book, and for students of human sexuality in particular, *The Homosexual in America* is an excellent example of what may be gained from a subjective approach to the problems of sex behavior. Writing with amazing frankness, and basing his material squarely on his own and his companions' sex experiences, Mr. Cory has given us a remarkable document. Within the covers of a single volume, he has beautifully managed to convey his own feelings about homosexuality; the feelings of many other typical and non-typical homosexuals; and the feelings of heterosexuals toward present-day homosexuals. Moreover, without pretending to be statistical or factually comprehensive, Mr. Cory has given us a large amount of factual material about American homosexuals, and has intelligently explored many of the most important sociological, psychological, cultural, religious, and other problems that now exist in regard to homosexuality. Many of the ideas he has brought out in the course of his book are original and stimulating; all of them are worth serious consideration.

I cannot, naturally, agree with all of Mr. Cory's views as they are expressed in *The Homosexual in America.* Just as he, as he frankly states, is prejudiced by his homosexual predilections, so am I prejudiced by my heterosexual ones. Consequently, I cannot quite appreciate some of the alleged social, political, and other individual and societal advantages which Mr. Cory claims for homosexuality. As a psychoanalytically oriented psychotherapist, moreover, I must also take issue with Mr. Cory's pessimism concerning the possibility of adjusting homosexuals to more heterosexual modes of living. As a social scientist, I should have preferred to see Mr. Cory put greater emphasis on the psycho-social contradictions which arise from the homosexual's trying, simultaneously, to fight the persecutions of heterosexual society and also to subscribe to the puritanical and anti-individualistic attitudes of this society in which these persecutions are rooted. As a sexologist, I find myself in distinct disagreement with some of Mr. Cory's expressed and implied views about the natural inherency and compulsivity of homosexual drives, once these drives are aroused. As a psychologist, I wish that Mr. Cory had placed even a greater stress on the multiplicity of the causes of homosexuality.

This, however, is not my book, but Mr. Cory's, and he is certainly entitled to his necessarily biased views on homosexuality—as I, presumably, am to mine. Let me say that, considering his honest espousal of homosexual leanings, his biases are remarkably few, and his ability to accept modern scientific views of homosexual relations is unusually high.

To comment on all the excellencies of *The Homosexual in America* would require a detailed summary of the book; and that, I take it, is not the function of this introduction. Suffice it to say here that Mr. Cory's book is noteworthy for its well-warranted indictment of our smug and sadistic heterosexual persecutions of homosexuals; for its acceptance of modern psychoanalytic thinking while resisting the temptation to go overboard into ultra-analytic symbolism; for its stressing of the problems of minorities other than homosexuals; for its full acceptance of the environmental, learned causes of homosexuality; for its intelligent and broad scholarship; and, above all, for its author's insight into his own limitations and biases.

All told, *The Homosexual in America* is by far the best non-fictional picture of the American homosexual and his problems that has yet been published. It is *must* reading for all inverts and for everyone who wishes clearly and fully to understand the question of homosexuality. It is a decidedly serious, honest, discerning, moving, and creditable piece of work. Even those who most violently disagree with its views will find this volume to be stimulating and worthwhile reading.

Albert Ellis

June 1951

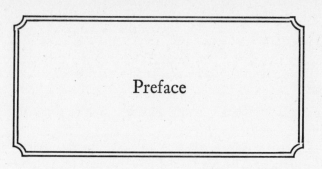

Preface

This book is the result of a quarter of a century of participation in American life as a homosexual. I am convinced that there is a need for dissemination of information and for a free exchange of argument and opinion on this subject. It is my belief that the observations and viewpoints of the homosexual are as essential as those of the psychiatrist, the jurist, or the churchman in arriving at any conclusions on homosexuality. The psychiatrist can never hope to meet a cross section of homosexuals, for his patients are only the frustrated and the maladjusted. In the same way, the experience of the penologist is limited to the homosexuals who run afoul of the law. The subjective approach of this book is intended not only to supply a reflection of the broader and more typical group, but to permit the expression of the opinion as seen from within that group.

The viewpoint espoused in this book is my own. I can speak for no others. But I believe that the majority of homosexuals will be able to identify themselves with the thoughts and experiences related in many sections of this work.

The scope of my work is intended to include only the male homosexuals, as I could not bring a subjective approach to the problems of Lesbianism. Here and there, where the subject of female homosexuality is pertinent to an understanding of my theme, it is mentioned, but not thoroughly analyzed. In the discussion of portraits in fiction, and in the appendix which gives a check list of literary works on this theme, books on Lesbianism as well as male homosexuality were included.

As an acknowledged homosexual writing for a general audience, I have felt compelled to use the language which I would employ were

I speaking to other homosexuals. The terms I have used in this book are necessary to a subjective study. The uninitiated reader will therefore find that homosexuals are called *gay*, heterosexuals *straight*—words in common usage in the world in which I move, and words which I discuss in detail in my chapter on the language of homosexual life.

The material in this book was gathered from original study and personal experience. I have leaned heavily on a few sources and have acknowledged their work. I am indebted to a young attorney for a remarkably complete study which he made for me of homosexuality and the law in the United States. The facts discussed in a chapter devoted to this subject were corralled by him, but all opinions are my own.

This book is, in a sense, a spiritual autobiography. In a work of this type the facts of a man's life are of secondary importance, the thoughts he espouses are of primary significance. However, I am writing as a homosexual and therefore should like to acquaint the reader with my own background. Since my early adolescence, I have been aware of the homosexual problem. My first awakening was the bewildering attraction that I felt for a young man a few years my senior. I had never been taught that there are men who are attracted to other men; no one had attempted to seduce or to tempt me. I only knew that I felt a drive, of a vague and troublesome character, toward gratification with one other person. I wanted to be near him, to embrace him. For two years after my first overt experience, I remained completely ignorant of any facts of homosexuality, and thus it came as a deep shock to me when, as a senior in high school, a teacher drew me aside, engaged me in conversation, explained to me that there were people who are called inverts.

In the years of later adolescence and early manhood, I studied myself and those like me, delved into every volume of literature which might shed light, sought to understand why I could not be like others. I was deeply ashamed of being abnormal and was aware of the heavy price that must be paid if anyone were to discover my secret.

I traveled through many stages in the years that followed. I struggled against my homosexuality, sought to discipline myself and to overcome it, punished myself for failures to resist sinful temptations. But the struggles did nothing to diminish the needs within me.

Then, revolting against the struggle, I developed many friends in homosexual circles and alternately felt myself trapped by a human tragedy to which I could never adjust, or blessed as one of the élite of the world. At times I would feel that only defeat lay ahead of me, and at others I planned to throw off the yoke of secrecy, openly proclaim my temperament for what it was, and live a full and complete life in unison with another male.

But love with another male, I was to discover, was not easy to achieve, and passionate infatuations that seemed permanent were torn asunder after only a short period of time. I participated in several erotic friendships and courtships, many times hoping that at last I had found the permanence of love. A friendship of a rewarding character developed when I was sixteen, lasted for two years, but ended as others were to end later. Then the passions endured only a few months, and then a few weeks, and I was scornful of those who would use the word *love* to describe such relationships.

Homosexual love, I told myself, is a myth. I would never find a man whom I could love. There would always be the short-lived affairs, and then each would go to new and unexplored fields. It appeared to me that I faced a life of dissipation, a hopeless dead-end. Where could I turn?

At the age of twenty-five, after determining that I was capable of consummating a marriage, I was wedded to a girl whom I had known from childhood, a lovely and outgoing person, who brought deep understanding to our union and who shared many interests with me. I resolved that marriage would be the end of my sins, that I would sever my ties with the homosexual circles and with my dear friends therein, and build what appeared to be the only life that might be fruitful for me.

I was not long in learning that marriage did not reduce the urge for gratification with men and that I could not have the energy and peace of mind to continue a fecund career while I was in constant struggle with something that was living within me. I needed my former companionships, but I would not allow myself to admit, even in the silence of the thought process, that I wanted them.

Compelled to solve the problem and convinced that the only way to solve it was to rid myself of the homosexual urge, I visited a well-known psychoanalyst, who assured me that I could be helped.

Gradually, as the long analysis proceeded, it became apparent to me that he was going to help me overcome my feelings of shame, guilt, remorse, rather than overcome the impulses which brought forward these feelings. I fought bitterly against this plan. I wanted my shame and was proud of it. In fact, I needed it. But my battle only served to prove to myself, with the doctor's aid, that shame and guilt were props that I had been using to make possible a continuation of the homosexual life I claimed to be in revolt against. By feeling guilty and remorseful, I exonerated myself of all responsibility, proving to my own self that homosexuality was a compulsion carried out against my will; and this exoneration made it possible to continue the very same homosexual life. But the price I was paying was severe.

Today, after many years of a successful marriage, with a happy home and with children, and with a firm bond of friendship that has developed with a man who has been an inspiring person in my life, I sit down to relate what it means to be a homosexual. This is not the thinking of a bitter and unhappy person. It is the accumulated experience and outlook of one who has been through the struggle with himself and with society.

Before concluding these prefatory remarks, I should like to mention an objection that has been raised to the assumed name over which this book is being published. If you have the courage of your beliefs, I am told, why is it necessary to hide behind the mask of anonymity? Why not sign your name, as have a few others, and be willing openly to defend the views you so militantly espouse? In reply, may I point out that other people are involved in every man's life in addition to oneself, and I do not feel justified in subjecting those close to me to possible embarrassment or injury by associating them with views they do not share. Moreover, I am convinced that, in the present cultural milieu in the United States, the pseudonymous or anonymous writer can be more outspoken than one who is willing to place a signature on a subjective analysis of homosexuality. It is not merely that I and others would suffer, but this book would suffer, and therefore I must refrain from the open acknowledgment of authorship.

I hope that my book will enlighten, that it will bring understanding on the part of parents, brothers and sisters, friends, and teachers. I hope that it will contribute something toward ameliorating a deplorable social condition and that it will give encouragement to those who, being homosexual like myself, are seeking the answers to the many questions they face in life.

I thank all those who have read my manuscript, in whole or in part, for their many valuable suggestions.

                                                    Donald Webster Cory

May 1951.

Part One

SOCIOLOGY

Chapter 1

The Unrecognized Minority

In recent years the world has become extremely conscious of minority problems. Upon industry, government, and indeed upon society as a whole, there is a constant pressure to recognize the rights of minorities. Usually by biological accident, sometimes by intellectual choice, many people find themselves outside the pale of the mainstream of life, unable to enjoy the benefits of civilization side by side with their fellowmen. Their plight is recognized; one constantly hears that human rights must be granted, regardless of race, religion, color, or political creed. The attitude toward minorities has, in the opinion of many, become a touchstone by which the progressive character of an individual or a nation may be judged. Minority rights, many contend, have become the challenge of this century; they are regarded as the corner stone upon which democracy must build and flourish, or perish in the decades to come. The lack of recognition of the rights of dissident and nonconforming minorities is the most distinguishing characteristic of totalitarianism.

The struggle for advancement by groups that are denied their place in society at large takes place simultaneously on two levels. It is a struggle that is fought by those who, voluntarily or involuntarily, are in the ranks of the few. Almost without exception, they believe that they are deserving of full freedoms, and they strive to achieve them. They have an awareness of their problems that follows them without cease; their escape is only occasional, momentary, and fleeting. They see life as divided into two seemingly hostile and irreconcilable camps; and seldom do they stop to inquire of themselves whether they display toward other minority groups the attitudes they demand be shown toward themselves. On occasion one discovers the rare individual of such stature that his attitude of deep sympathy for all human beings transcends his own identification with a group of people.

At the same time, the minority is not infrequently strengthened by the activities of some individuals from the dominant world who, whatever their motives might be, identify themselves with the aspirations of a group without being a member of the group. Their entire philosophy may be libertarian, their endorsement of the outcast may be prompted by personal, psychological, humanitarian, intellectual, or other experiences. But what matter the motive; history judges the deed. And history has taught them that the many cannot prosper while the few wither; that the majority cannot achieve a true happiness in a world in which a minority is deeply condemned.

Out of these majority-minority relationships grow literature, protest, search for change. The more articulate describe what it means to live as a member of the minority—the blind alleys and the dead-ends . . . the discrimination . . . the sneer, the joke, the abusive language . . . the humiliation and self-doubt . . . the struggle to maintain self-respect and group pride. As these people describe and protest, their voices are complemented by those of the allies found in another world, people who can never fully know the psychological impact of a hostile culture on those whom they are aiding, but who are peculiarly well situated to further a cause without fully understanding it.

The minority question has been studied exhaustively in recent years. Attention has been focused on the Jewish people in Germany and elsewhere in the world, the Hindus and Moslems in India and Pakistan, the Catholics in Ulster and the Protestants in Italy, the Negroes in America. Nor are religion, race, and color the sole aspect of minority problems; the rights of Communists in the Western democracies are debated, and rights for non-Communists in the Eastern European states are demanded. The privileges of atheists on the one hand, or Jehovah's Witnesses, on the other, fall within the scope of the study of minority problems.

It is my belief that another phase of the minority problem is demanding the attention of America. We who are homosexual constitute a minority that cannot accept the outlook, customs, and laws of the dominant group. We constitute a minority, and a unique one.

Some will protest against the classification of the homosexuals as a minority, on the grounds that the term usually encompasses ethnic groups, and that the latter constitute a number of people grouped together by act or accident of birth. Even the religious minorities are not exempt from the fact of being grouped in this manner, inasmuch as religious creeds are generally passed on from parents to children. However, such a concept of the minority, aside from the narrowness of the considerations, is significant only insofar as it emphasizes the involuntary and inescapable nature of group belonging. As I shall show in a section of this book devoted to the genesis of homosexuality, and as is conceded by psychiatrists, the fact of being homosexual, and therefore of belonging to a group, is as involuntary as if it were inborn, despite the fact that it is not inborn; and as I shall demonstrate in my discussion of therapy, the fact of retaining homosexual desires, whether one indulges or suppresses, and whether or not a bisexual adjustment is made, is virtually as ineradicable as if it involved the color of one's skin or the shape of one's eyes.

It goes without saying that there are some fundamental differences between homosexuals and the conventionally recognized minority groups. A minority, according to a rather narrow definition, would be any outnumbered people. But, in its broader connotations, a minority group must consist in the first place of people who have some important trait in common that not only unites them to each other, but differentiates them from the rest of society. Group psychology, writes Sigmund Freud, is "concerned with the individual man as a member of a race, of a nation, of a caste, of a profession, of an institution, or as a component part of a crowd of people who have been organised into a group at some particular time for some definite purpose."* From this definition, it can be seen that not only Christians and Jews, Negroes and whites, constitute groups, but Communists are a group, deaf-mutes are a group, as are physicians and psychoanalysts. But a minority group, from a sociological viewpoint, must have another characteristic, and that is its lower or unequal status in society. The physicians would therefore not be a minority, in such a sense, and it is even possible for the minority group, as has been pointed out, to be a numerical majority, the classic example being the South African Negroes.

* Sigmund Freud, *Group Psychology and the Analysis of the Ego* (London: International Psycho-analytical Press, 1922), p. 3.

By such a definition, the homosexuals are a minority group, consisting of large numbers of people who belong, participate, and are constantly aware of something that binds them to others and separates them from the larger stream of life; yet a group without a spokesman, without a leader, without a publication, without an organization, without a philosophy of life, without an accepted justification for its own existence. In fact, there is surely no group of such size, and yet with so few who acknowledge that they belong. And, were it not for social pressure to acknowledge, or for biological ease of identification, would not other minorities likewise lose a large portion of their groups?

Many have written about this problem. There are hundreds of books: novels, sociological treatises, statistical studies, psychoanalytic critiques—some of them worthy contributions toward the building of a literature. Yet, with but one or two exceptions, no one has stopped to relate in simple terms, not couched in fiction, what it means to be a homosexual. Seldom has anyone ever told the sociologists, the legislators and judges, the novelists and psychiatrists—except in confidential conversations that can never become part of the public domain—what it feels like to be a homosexual, living with a constant awareness of the existence of something inescapable, and how this affects every aspect of life, here, today, now, in the middle years of the twentieth century in America.

What are the problems a homosexual might meet, the accommodations he makes, the compulsions he carries, the conflicts he seeks to untangle? What do we homosexuals think of the origins of our problem, of the search for an answer, of the laws and the blackmail, of the desirability of marriage, of the novels about our group? What sort of a philosophy of life are we seeking, do we find life hopeless, are we defeated and dejected, or is there an answer that some, or many, have found? Do we want to be what the world terms normal, have we made the effort, what is our experience when we try? Do we acknowledge our inclinations to family and friends, do we develop friendships outside our group, and what are the attitudes that we encounter?

Delving into these questions, I find that fundamental to all answers is an understanding that the dominant factor in my life, towering in importance above all others, is a consciousness that I am different. In one all-important respect, I am unlike the great mass of people always around me, and the knowledge of this fact is with me at all times, influencing profoundly my every thought, each minute activity, and all my aspirations. It is inescapable, not only this being different, but more than that, this constant awareness of a dissimilarity.

Sometimes, perhaps as I lie abed in the morning, fully awake but not yet ready to rise, or as I sit and relax in a soft chair in my home, and drop the newspaper to the floor and close my eyes, I am able to retreat into myself with only my own thoughts, and I am overcome by a peculiar wonderment. An insatiable curiosity grips me as I yearn to know what it would be like not to be a homosexual. My imagination wanders madly, and I conjure up images that are inspired by art, poetry, drama, fiction, cinema, and personal acquaintances. I bring into my fantasy the heterosexuals I know, in real life and make-believe, and I persevere in my efforts to identify myself with them. To add to the realistic aspects of the fantasy, I picture myself making condemnatory remarks and harsh judgments. But it is all in vain. It is outside the realm of my wildest flights of fancy. I am powerless even to capture a dream image of another world. If I were not what I am, what pursuits would occupy my pen, what problems would occupy my mind? I do not know, for a state of existence in which I would be like others is utterly beyond my conception.

To my heterosexual friends and readers, who find outside the realm of their comprehension the desires that I always carry within me, I can only state that I find their own sexual personality just as much an enigma, just as foreign to myself, and beyond the powers of my imagination. To be transformed suddenly and as if by magic into the body and consciousness of a heterosexual—what would I think, know, feel, desire? My failure to be able to reply is more than an inability to imagine; it is a frightening fantasy from which I recoil.

I know that I cling to my entire personality, and that sexuality is basic in this personality and can never be relinquished. But sometimes I would wish to be normal—and I shall use this word in its usual connotation—just for a brief period. I would like to know the freedom from the anxiety of being the outcast; not merely to enjoy the pleasures of a relationship with the opposite sex, but to be free of the compulsive sexual urge that drives me toward my own sex. But, although I should like to experience such a freedom, it would be only to return to a gay world which I can never surrender.

Freedom—is this what I have been seeking? Is this what stops me for a moment from arising, as I hear the clock tick away on the dresser? Is all the past, I sometimes ask myself, a faraway dream? After all, I am a free individual, and at this moment no driving urge has me in its captive power. The body is momentarily void of yearning, has no conscious desire or anxiety. The homosexuality that has dominated it for so long seems to have departed during the turbulent unconsciousness of sleep. I am free of the bonds and the chains and the countless difficulties. I stretch my arms, push away the blankets, take another quick glance at the clock, and to myself I laugh. I cannot help but mock at my own folly, enmeshed in dreams and revelry as passing time bids me hurry to work. But with what clarity I recall the mind of a quarter of a century ago, the youth in his teens who would awaken with this new-found freedom. I would jump for joy, look with pride at myself, find a self-respect that had been lacking, and I would proceed to breakfast, my face radiant with smiles. A conscious feeling that I was not a homosexual would remain with me for perhaps a few hours or through the greater part of the day, until the inevitable doubts would assail me.

There was the occasion when I returned from a short winter vacation of skiing, tobogganing, and other delights. For five days my eighteen-year-old body had been consumed with athletic activities. Occasionally I would look at a friend and say to myself: what if he knew? Other than this question, sex was far from my thoughts. The first morning at home, I awoke, fresh and energetic and anxious for studies, and became aware of a curious exemption from any urge for a companion. A phrase came to mind: *adolescent tendencies*. Adolescence was now behind me, and with it I had left the secret thing. I smiled to myself and said, almost aloud, "I am a man."

The feeling that I was free—for so I termed it—was then rather frequent. That morning I felt particularly confident that it would not be transient. The cold has purged me of things sinful, I thought to myself. At breakfast I was remarkably comfortable with my family. How much more worthy of love I would become if I were really rid of this abnormality. After lunch I began to take seriously the free feeling. I passed the young men at college, and none excited me. I sat with students and teachers and looked particularly at the one whose presence had until that day been unpleasant because of the very fascination it held for me, but there was no evocation of feeling. The next day the freedom remained; it began to dominate my thoughts. Deliberately I put myself to test after test, but without arousal or desire. A curiosity came over me, at one point, to know just once again what the attraction to another male was like. The idea was eluding me, and I both feared and wished that it would never return.

A third day of a strange peacefulness, and I imagined myself disclosing the secret of the past to friends, teachers, psychiatrists. Imaginary conversations took place in my mind: I was relating my experiences to friends, and to a history teacher whom I had not seen for some time. Then, as I entered my home on the evening of the third day, I closed the door behind me, walked past the telephone, and stopped for a moment. My hand reached out and I knew that I wanted to call William, an acquaintance with whom I had had a recent intimate relationship. To tell him that I would be interested in seeing him no more, I said aloud, but my heart was now beating loudly, and I knew that it was a transparent deception. I paced up and down near the telephone, then proceeded, without making the call, to the kitchen, but I had lost my appetite. I awaited impatiently the end of the evening meal; then, excusing myself, I went to one of my hangouts. That night I found a companion much older than myself, and when I had left him I returned to seek another. Late in the night, alone in my own bed, I cried, but I had learned a cruel lesson, and one worth learning. No teacher but life itself could have convinced me that homosexual passions do not come and go at will, but cling relentlessly to the last breath of life. When I awaken today and feel devoid of the drive that has dominated my personality, I smile and merely await its inevitable return.

As I sit at a concert or engage volubly in a conversation in the office or at home, or as I look up from my newspaper and glance at the people occupying the seats of the bus, my mind will suddenly jump from the words, the thoughts, or the music around me, and with horrible impact I will hear, pounding within myself, the fateful words: *I am different.* I am different from all these people, and I must always be different from them. I do not belong to them, nor they to me. On my side of the chasm that separates me from the moving millions, I wonder who are my hidden companions. Is it a friend's secretary in an office, perhaps keeping a secret even more firmly than I imprison my own? Is it a married colleague or a cousin, here for an occasional evening, speaking in soft tones and well-enunciated words that lead me to suspect? Or the stranger sitting opposite me, engrossed in a book even as I am supposed to be in a newspaper? His eyes look up from the pages, and they meet my own, and because we retain each other's stare for a split second longer than one ought, I feel a sense of comradeship. To my mind, at least, if not to his, a bond of belonging has been established, although each of us goes his way, never to see the other again. Have I imparted to him, even as he has to me, imaginary pleasure; has he, like myself, received a feeling of mutual understanding?

I am different, I say to myself, but I know that my being different is not the same as that which members of other minorities feel. Are we not all different, a friend in puzzled sympathy asks one day. Is not each of us a part of some group, whether of religion or race or color, that does not keep step with the dominant majority? Do not the Jews, the Negroes, the foreign-born, the Southern Catholics, the atheists stop to state that they are different and that they must always be different from other peoples?

The analogy is weak. We homosexuals are a minority, but more than that, an intensified minority, with all of the problems that arise from being a separate group facing us that are faced by other groups, and with a variety of important problems that are unshared by most minorities. The ethnic groups can take refuge in the comfort and pride of their own, in the warmth of family and friends, in the acceptance of themselves among the most enlightened people around them. But not the homosexuals. Those closest to us, whose love we are in extreme need of, accept us for what we are not. Constantly and unceasingly we carry a mask, and without interruption we stand on guard lest our secret, which is our very essence, be betrayed.

Sometimes I find myself drawn as if into a net by the abuses and sneers of the hostile world. I hear the vile joke or the calumnious remark, and must sit in silence, or even force a smile as it were in approval. A passenger enters an elevator and remarks, "When I come out of a barber shop, I have a feeling I smell like a fag. I better watch out or some goddam queer'll pick me up on the way home." The operator laughs, and I find myself forcing a smile, joining in the humiliating remark that is, unknowingly, directed against myself. And, leaving the elevator, I resent neither the passenger nor the operator, but only myself, for I had debased my own character by giving tacit consent and even approval to the abuse of which I felt I was personally the victim.

Where is your self-respect, where is your self-pride, I ask. How do you dare to say that you are proud of what you are when you allow the epithets of the enemy to go unanswered, when you turn the other cheek out of cowardice and not Christianity, when you even join—as so often you find yourself doing—the hostile camp?

It is not only shame at my own debasement that demoralizes me, but a great wave of self-doubt that is infinitely more difficult to cope with. Am I genuinely as "good" as the next fellow? Is my moral standard as high? Are my ethics—before my own self and my own Maker—as defensible as those of others around me?

Or am I actually what they call me? Despite myself, for I know that this urge is not of my creation and that I can neither efface nor over-come it, am I a degenerate, immoral, and lecherous character, a dis-grace to the mother who bore me and to the little girl and boy who call me Daddy?

Society has handed me a mask to wear, a ukase that it shall never be lifted except in the presence of those who hide with me behind its protective shadows. Everywhere I go, at all times and before all sections of society, I pretend. As my being rebels against the hypocrisy that is forced upon me, I realize that its greatest repercussion has been the wave of self-doubt that I must harbor. Because I am unable to stand up before the world and acknowledge that I am what I am, because I carry around with me a fear and a shame, I find that I endanger my confidence in myself and in my way of living, and that this confidence is required for the enjoyment of life.

In fact, I must ask myself whether the life that I lead is an inferior one, and whether those who practice it are inferior people. Is there justification for the loathing with which mankind regards us? Nothing is more demoralizing than that I must even ask myself this question. And, though adamant, on an intellectual level, in my negative response, I find it difficult to reconcile self-pride with cowardice, abnegation, the wearing of the mask and the espousal of hypocrisy— in short, with an outward acceptance of the mores of the hostile society.

Retired into the intimacy of the homosexual circle, I find that it is
only with the greatest of effort that an individual can acknowledge
with words a tendency which he can so openly express in action. And
when words are chosen, there will be euphemisms, a semantic choice
of subtle synonyms that express the same thought, but with cushioned
impact.

The trepidation to acknowledge extends even to the presence of
those who have already discarded the mask. In the course of my
studies I meet many individuals to whom I relate my own homosexual
experiences, and although I am perfectly aware, not only by observation but by previous knowledge, that I am discussing these problems
with people who share them, I find that I evoke intelligent participation in the conversation, a deepfelt understanding and sympathy, but
seldom a frankness. Guarded is each word, and I look in vain for the
admission. And why? Surely not out of fear, for there is no possible
harm that I can do. Not out of lack of necessity, for how much more
freely could the interchange of ideas take place if there were mutual
confidence. In my opinion the individual is unable to bring himself,
even in the presence of the most sympathetic ear, to say, "I am a homosexual," because of the impact that such a sentence has on himself, as
a result of the total activity and attitudes of the hostile and dominant
group.

It is not only out of fear of rejection by others, strong as that fear
surely is, that homosexuals are stopped in the paths of self-expression;
and it is not from fear of consequences, real as the latter may be. It is
due to the fact that self-expression means self-acknowledgment, and
this in turn requires a rejection of the opinions of those who despise.

The prejudice of the dominant group, seen everywhere and displayed in countless forms, is most demoralizing when we homosexuals
realize to what extent we have accepted hostile attitudes as representing an approximation of the truth. Here and there, in a book, a
sociological document, or a psychological treatise, there will be a
justification, but it does not negate the overwhelming weight of
antipathy. A person cannot live in an atmosphere of universal rejection, of widespread pretense, of a society that outlaws and banishes
his activities and desires, of a social world that jokes and sneers at
every turn, without a fundamental influence on his personality.

That influence I find to be complex. First, there is what can be characterized as self-doubt, but this in turn evokes its own response, which comes out of the need for self-acceptance. The reaction against the world which insists that we are inferior beings is the search for a fallacy in that thinking. Some of us may take refuge in the involuntary nature of our predilections. Inferior or equal, whatever the verdict of the world may be, we are homosexuals in spite of ourselves. How, we ask ourselves in amazement, can a world condemn an individual for being what he was made to be? Despite the widespread view to the contrary, we homosexuals are utterly incapable of being other than what we are.

More than that, if we are to believe in ourselves, we must reject the entire theory of the inferiority status which the heterosexual world has imposed upon us. And therein we find a reaction common among people who live in a special minority category: we create a new set of beliefs to demonstrate that our gay world is actually a superior one. For some reason or other that few of us stop to investigate, we come to believe that homosexuals are usually of superior artistic and intellectual abilities. Everywhere we look, we seize upon outstanding examples of brilliant people, either in our own circles or in the public domain, who are gay, or are supposed to be gay. How is it, we ask ourselves, that our friends are always outstanding among their business associates; that members of our group frequently graduate from universities with the highest honors; that at least four of the giants of modern French literature were sexual inverts. The list could be continued, although it includes only those recognized; what of the many who have achieved success and have hidden their secret even from those who share their burden?

Whether or not there is a factual basis for this belief in our own superiority is of secondary importance. Whether illusion or reality, the belief exists, and it stems from a desperation, deeply imbedded in people who find themselves despised by the world, and who require a belief in themselves in order to bolster an ebbing confidence and enable themselves to function in society.

Thus the homosexuals constitute what can be termed the unrecognized minority. We are a group by reason of the fact that we have impulses in common that separate us from the larger mass of people. We are a minority, not only numerically, but also as a result of a caste-like status in society. As I shall demonstrate in these pages, our minority status is similar, in a variety of respects, to that of national, religious, and other ethnic groups: in the denial of civil liberties; in the legal, extra-legal, and quasi-legal discrimination; in the assignment of an inferior social position; in the exclusion from the mainstreams of life and culture; in the development of the protection and security of intra-group association; in the development of a special language and literature and a set of moral tenets within our group.

On the other hand, one great gap separates the homosexual minority from all others, and that is its lack of recognition, its lack of respectability in the eyes of the public, and even in the most advanced circles. It has become a sign of worthiness to take up the cudgels for almost any minority group, except the homosexuals. One is a "hero" if he espouses the cause of minorities, but is only a suspect if that minority is the homosexual group.

As a minority, we homosexuals are therefore caught in a particularly vicious circle. On the one hand, the shame of belonging and the social punishment of acknowledgment are so great that pretense is almost universal; on the other hand, only a leadership that would acknowledge would be able to break down the barriers of shame and resultant discrimination. Until the world is able to accept us on an equal basis as human beings entitled to the full rights of life, we are unlikely to have any great numbers willing to become martyrs by carrying the burden of the cross. But until we are willing to speak out openly and frankly in defense of our activities, and to identify ourselves with the millions pursuing these activities, we are unlikely to find the attitudes of the world undergoing any significant change.

Chapter 2

Hostility: Its Hidden Sources

It is apparent that the condemnation of homosexuality is today almost universal. In some communities and in certain lands, the severity of that condemnation is greater than in others; while in a few circles, particularly among the most artistic and intellectual, on the one hand, or among those most in rebellion against organized society, the hostility is less pronounced. Occasionally one encounters an attitude not so much of tolerance but of actual acceptance, but this is rare. Whether organized society passes laws and enforces them, or effaces such laws from its statute books, is important, although secondary to social condemnation. The basic problem is the hostile spirit pervading even the more permissive of modern peoples; and this spirit of censure can be traced back many centuries, although it has not been universal.

At least sporadically, states Westermarck, homosexuality probably occurs among every race of mankind; to which we might add: and at every stage in man's history. A few observers have denied its existence upon their return from foreign lands, but it is likely that practices of homosexuality were being kept secret, itself an indication of a moral judgment.

Homosexual practices were found in abundance when European travellers studied the lives of the American Indian tribes. Men were discovered dressed as women, acting as wives for their warrior-husbands, performing all of the duties of the household, and accepted by the women of the tribes. Renunciation of one's own sex was a tribal ritual of the Chukchis, and the youth who voluntarily performed this renunciation took a husband. The shamans, or high priests, were usually effeminate, and gave evidence of being homosexual. They were regarded by their tribe as magicians, having supernatural power and the ability to interpret dreams.

Early travellers and explorers found homosexuality in many of the Malayan Islands, in New Guinea, the Marshall Islands, Hawaii, Tahiti, New Caledonia, and Australia. In her studies of life in the South Sea Islands, Margaret Mead found homosexual practices among adolescents prevalent and free from condemnation, but such practices seldom continued after the youths matured.

In some of the primitive cultures a homosexual prostitution thrived. In others a warlike fraternity of men in which sexual relations took place was widely accepted. Native communities in Australia (before the conquest of that island by the white man) went through all the rituals and taboos of marriage between a man and a boy, such marriages being characterized as "exceedingly common." The Japanese knew no punishment or public opprobrium for the homosexual until the influence of the West was felt, and the male Japanese who loved a man, it is said, was considered more heroic than the woman-lover in the great era of chivalry of that Empire. The Chinese were likewise free of any attitude characterizing love of one's own sex as wrong, until the influence of the Christian world became dominant. It is possible that the Chinese people considered homosexuality an effective means of controlling the growth of the population, and it is from China that one traveller returned with the famous remark that he had never heard a Chinese say that homosexuality was bad, except for the eyes.

A great mystery surrounds the homosexual in early civilizations and among primitive peoples. The Scandinavian rulers were harsh; pederasty was a form of sorcery, and sorcery was a supreme crime. But the Mexicans tolerated, permitted, nay encouraged the practices, even attributing them to their deities. Tribes have been described in which the acquisition of a boy-wife was a great honor, a prize of the first magnitude. But others despised the pederast, even stoned him to death. Where communal opinion veered toward disapproval, the passive homosexual (playing the so-called "female" rôle) was the object of the greater contempt.

The literature and history of ancient Greece show that homosexuality thrived, that it was fully and completely accepted by the people, but that it was seldom the exclusive channel of love for either man or woman. For the Greeks, pederasty was a noble form of love. It was linked with courage, devotion, sacrifice on the battlefield; with athletics and physical prowess. It was a glorification of both strength and tenderness. Plutarch pointed out that love of youths was found in the greatest and most warlike of nations, and among the greatest and most warlike of heroes, and Plato said that an army made up of lovers and their beloveds, fighting at each other's side, could overcome the whole world, even though these lovers be a mere handful.

In Rome, during the most successful days of the Empire, homosexual love was glorified by the great poets. Catullus wrote a love lyric to Juventius, whose "honeysweet lips" he sought to kiss; and Vergil, Horace, and Tibullus sang praises to love of youths. Ovid delved into this pathway of love, and Petronius found it equal to love for women.

Thus from the Romans and the Greeks was received the first heritage of a literature in which the homosexual theme is acceptable and in fact is even dominant. At the same time, the portrait of these cultures shows that the homosexual activity, widely practiced and accepted, justified as having a place in society, neither dominated nor conflicted with the position of the family. The generally inferior social and intellectual status of woman, her relegation to the rôle of housewife and childbearer, encouraged the most passionate friendships among men. The simultaneous homosexual and heterosexual ways of life were possible because they functioned in entirely different directions.

Nevertheless, the voices against homosexuality were beginning to be heard. The population of Rome was diminishing, and a code of morality was required which would tend to increase childbirth. Justinian spoke in strong words, striking fear into the hearts of the people: "It is on account of such crimes that famines and earthquakes take place and also pestilences."

No culture had been more severe in its condemnation than that of the Hebrews—despite their early approval of homosexuality. About six to seven centuries before Christ, a campaign against the homosexual practices was undertaken, on the grounds that they belonged to a foreign people. The Hebrew moral judgments became the inheritance of the Christians. The Judeo-Christian attitude toward sex dominated the prevailing moral code in the centuries to follow, and because disasters outside the realm of man's understanding were blamed upon the homosexuals, they found it increasingly difficult to defend themselves.

During the Middle Ages, homosexuals were likened to sorcerers and linked with heretics. They were burned at the stake. The intellectual and scientific inquiry of mankind during this period was shrouded in darkness. Little was heard in defense of a practice considered both widespread and abominable.

With the revival of learning on the European continent, a new interest in homosexuality was displayed by the men of genius. Leonardo was accused of having had an "abnormal" relationship, and Michaelangelo of having addressed his love sonnets to a male. The spirit of the Renaissance culture was imbued with an undertone of homosexuality, but the social attitude was so severe that the outspoken defense of Roman and Greek times was no longer possible. There were no voices heard against punishment, and accusations were vehemently denied.

There were many trials and death sentences during the years that followed, but seldom a word of protest. The homosexuals feared to defend their practices, yet no severity of punishment sufficed to diminish the desire or inhibit the fulfillment.

The first expression of a changed attitude appeared in the Napoleonic Code, which omitted homosexuality from its list of crimes. Thus for the first time since the ascendancy of the Judeo-Christian concept of morality, it ceased to be illegal to practice homosexuality. However, the hostility of society has diminished little during the past centuries, despite the scientific inquiry into the question during the last fifty years.

To the homosexuals, this hostility is unjust, although it is so taken for granted as a part of the scheme of things that it is difficult to imagine social behavior in other patterns. Yet each person who feels a sense of outrage against man's inhuman treatment of so many fellowmen must ask himself whether he would not share in society's hostility if he did not carry the burden of the outcast. It is indeed like the Negro who sees the injustice of the white man in such sharp and unmistakable focus, unable to conceive that millions of reasonable and reasoning and otherwise fine people can fail to see this gross inhumanity, and yet who must stop to wonder whether he, too, were his ancestry different, might be one of the rabid oppressors.

Why does society condemn? Why is the homosexual an outcast among men? What are the social and psychological reasons for this hostility, its sources, its justifications? Is it necessary for the preservation of our social structure? Is it effective as an instrument for thwarting the growth of homosexual practices? These are a few of the questions that the social psychologist must face. But as a contribution toward an understanding of these problems, let me express what I believe to be the true meaning of hostility. First the sources; then the justifications.

Whenever a minority group is maltreated by society, there is to be found a great sense of satisfaction in many of the majority or dominant group. The inferior status of the minority implies a superior status of the dominant, and each member of that dominant group seeks to identify himself with that superior feeling. Thus mankind in its misery receives some small satisfaction by keeping the Jew in subjection, making it possible for some Christians (followers of the Christian Front, for example) to feel that they are "better people." Poor whites of the South, in their miserable economic dilemma, find some small salve in the feeling that they are better than their equally wretched colored neighbors.

"It is a curious fact," wrote Herman Melville about a century ago, "that the more ignorant and degraded men are, the more contemptuously they look upon those whom they deem their inferiors."*

Faced with constant sexual frustrations and paradoxes, restricted by a sexual morality which is self-imposed but which cannot be enforced, humanity finds some source of joy in the lower position it can assign to the invert. The man-on-the-street, teaching his children continence while practicing infidelity, believing he was a sinner when he masturbated, secretly desiring to cohabit with almost every female passerby while condemning in the harshest terms the victim caught in the flagrant act, protecting the virginity of his daughter yet condoning sexual activity on the part of his son, bored and dismayed by his wife's frigidity and by his own inability to arouse and to satisfy her—this man, not at all atypical, is anxious to believe that there is some poor miserable creature who is sexually more a misfit than himself. He laughs at the eunuch, and his laughter gives him greater faith in his own

---

* Herman Melville, *Omoo: a Narrative of Adventure in the South Seas* (New York: Harper & Bros., 1868) p. 42.

potency. And, finally, the "fairy" becomes the victim of his anguish. He substitutes invective for reason, ridicule for logic. His ego is boosted, and by an unconscious comparison he becomes good, normal, righteous, manly—hence, superior! His is the better way; therefore he is the better person.

Herein can be found the psychology of the superiority feeling which is fundamental to majority-minority group relationships. In a civilization in which insecurity is so widespread, homosexuality is a convenient scapegoat.

Another source of condemnation, and perhaps even more important, is found in the bisexual character of the libido. It was the contention of William James that most men are potential homosexuals; inversion, James wrote, is "a kind of sexual appetite of which very likely most men possess the germinal possibility."* And if, as Freud says, there is some vestige of heterosexual memory in all homosexuals, as becomes evident upon analysis, a thoroughgoing analytical study likewise reveals the homosexual character—latent, repressed, sometimes sublimated and driven into the unconscious—of even the most perfectly adjusted and most "normal" of men.

The eminent sociologist, Westermarck, has pointed out that many philosophers have been puzzled by the extreme condemnation of homosexual practices. He is able to explain the severity of punishment and the extremity of moral judgments only on the basis of the unusually strong disgust which most individuals feel toward these acts. But this explains very little, for it is necessary to understand why there is such a strong feeling of disgust; why people are punished for carrying out acts which disgust other people; why there is such severe punishment among some peoples and not among others. The answer to these questions is found in the bisexual character of man, as testified to by William James, Freud, and many others. "Freud feels justified," writes Adolph Meyer, "in assuming directly a bisexual start in every individual."†

Modern man takes flight from the homosexual (or the heterosexual) drive that he carries within him. The normal man, as he is called,

---

* William James, *The Principles of Psychology* (New York: 1890) II, 439. Just why James spoke of "most men" instead of all men in this passage is difficult to understand.

† *The Commonsense Psychiatry of Dr. Adolf Meyer* (New York: McGraw-Hill, 1948), p. 263.

banishes this strange and troubling desire from his mind, forgetting that he ever harbored such ugly thoughts. He not only rejects the drive toward his own sex for himself, but he transgresses upon the rights of others by rejecting them for his brother or neighbor, as well. *Chacun à son goût* becomes unacceptable as a guiding rule in this sphere of activity, for so tolerant an attitude might release the great force of this drive within the man who requires condemnation, harsh treatment, self-righteous rejection, precisely because these are the very cement of the walls that dam the forbidden emotion.

Mankind finds limitless uses for hypocrisy, not the least of which is the secure feeling it offers to the heterosexual. Nothing convinces the individual of his own normalcy so much as the stern spirit of condemnation.

I have personally known cases that attest to this utilization of hostility as a weapon of repression, and modern literature offers several examples. In my own experience I recall with vividness the advances Gerald made to me when we were children in our early teens. We sat together in the cinema, and his hands wandered, fondled me intimately. Then, a few days later, he asked me to wrestle with him in the gymnasium. Our bodies fought and played together until his own fell away limp, and I knew that he had used the gymnastic exercise for sexual fulfillment. As youths do, we drifted apart soon thereafter, not to meet again until several years later when we were both in college. The intervening years had taught me a good deal about homosexuality, its widespread occurrence, its early manifestations among adolescents. I was prepared to meet in Gerald a gay youth, but this was not the case. He had nothing but disgust for my way of life and stoutly denied that the incidents I have described had taken place in our earlier years.

Fiction provides numerous examples of this severity being displayed by the suppressed homosexual. In Vidal's *The City and the Pillar*, the sexual relationship takes place between two young boys; one becomes, or already is, gay, while the other forgets the incident completely and is revolted when his companion attempts to repeat the act a few years later. The gay college youth in Thomas's *Stranger in the Land* is approached by his roommate during the latter's intoxication, but the next morning, in revolt—and primarily against himself—the would-be-normal man severs the friendship, demanding that one or the other find quarters elsewhere. Along a somewhat different line is Jackson's *The Fall of Valor*, in which an intelligent protagonist, unaware of repressed homosexuality, condemns the sports attire worn by tennis-playing youth, his condemnation being nothing but a defense against the rising emotional surge within him.

The unknown is mysterious, and to it are attributed by many the qualities of witchcraft, sorcery, deviltry, and supernatural evil forces. In primitive society the unfathomable were regarded as being possessed of the devil, and in later years men and women were burned as witches by communities which could not understand them. Homosexuals were, in this manner, associated with religious cults by the Peruvians, and with sorcerers by the Scandinavians. Punishments for homosexuality and for sorcery were identical in many lands, and even the same word was used to denote the practice of homosexuality and of witchcraft.

From the vantage point of the twentieth century, such attitudes are scoffed upon, in the superior way that a cultured people always looks upon the backwardness of times past, assured that superstitions have been abandoned in the progress of history. But in the attitude toward the homosexual the average person, unable to understand, faced with a mysterious repugnance which is intimately related to his own sexual personality, frightened at a concept because fright is protection against attraction, proceeds to behave as did the colonial peoples toward the "witches" of New England. Is it, perhaps, in the baffling character of the unknown that there can be found the origin and significance of the word *queer?*

To condemn is much simpler than to understand. It is not an easy task to look inward, to examine rationally, to understand the reasons and the origins, to determine whether the activities of certain people are harmful to their fellowmen. To that strange realm beyond man's comprehension, the mystic aura of faith or the sharp excommunication of the bedevilled is frequently assigned. These are but two sides of one coin, and indeed have not the homosexuals been the priests in some societies, the pariahs in others, and both at the same time in still others? It is mental laziness—a characteristic of all majority-dominated cultures and all majority-dominant groups—that finds greater facility in passing harsh judgments than in searching for the truth. "Sticks and stones will break my bones . . ." the child learns to retort to the tormentors, but the names do hurt, because they take the place of thought. Call the invert *a queer, a freak, a fairy*, or *a c——r*, and not only is he characterized, but this is a replacement for genuine study of a natural phenomenon.

Condemnation, furthermore, is definitely contagious. Because society condemns with such unassuaged cruelty and unswerving perseverance, it becomes intellectually and socially disreputable not to join in the universal judgment. For an individual who is himself not homosexually inclined to find himself out of sympathy with society's treatment of the invert requires a combination of faculties that is indeed rare—a critical and imaginative mind, a spirit skeptical of socially accepted folkways, a deep insight into an alien group. But having arrived at this sympathetic viewpoint, he finds that his opinion invites the suspicion of friends, family, and associates. Does he partake of the tendencies he defends, they wonder. Inasmuch as such suspicion is disadvantageous, and for the heterosexual unnecessary, it is the easier path to refrain from expressing one's sympathies, and easier yet is the road of failing to develop them. Men and groups, otherwise interested in social injustice in all its manifestations, fail to raise a voice in defense of the invert, not only because of lack of understanding, not only because the invert himself has not defended his position, but also because of the suspicions and disadvantages falling upon those who speak in defense of the homosexual.

Society first condemns, and then penalizes all those who do not join in the chorus of condemnation. It becomes a handicap not only to be a homosexual, but even to be in favor of rights for homosexuals—a condition not prevailing in other minority group relations, except under the extreme situation of being pro-Jewish in Nazy Germany or militantly pro-Negro in the southern part of the United States. What greater assurance of self-perpetuation could be developed by any majority group?

Hostility toward a minority, it is today understood, is something that is taught, inculcated in subtle and overt manners from the time that one is a child. There is nothing to indicate that there is an instinctive aversion or disgust for the homosexual; in fact, the remarkable acceptance of the homosexual by many cultures would indicate that the opposite is the case. But if the joke and the sneer, ridicule and lie, punishment and fear, are utilized to teach people to hate, they will hate. The parallel with other minority-majority relationships is apparent.

A further source of hostility is the stereotype thinking of heterosexuals. A homosexual is arrested for prostitution; therefore homosexuals are prostitutes. A homosexual is murdered by a young man after an affair; therefore homosexuals are sadists, and their lives are filled with violence. A homosexual has shared apartments, and beds, with six different men during the past year, each time swearing that he has discovered the love of his life; therefore homosexuals are promiscuous, fickle, and unstable. A homosexual sits on a park bench and powders his nose; therefore homosexuals are a bunch of goddam fairies, mimicking women and making public exhibitions of themselves.

Most of these instances occur from time to time. Many of them are not at all more typical of homosexual associations or people than of their counterparts in society at large. Like the Negro in America, the homosexual who is arrested on a charge of murder is not arrested merely as a human being, a man charged with a capital crime. He is characterized both as a murderer and as a member of a given minority group, and the two concepts become intermingled in the public mind.

Stereotype thinking is shorn of its respectability and shown to be absurd when it is applied to the majority group. Supposing every murder, burglary, crime of passion, narcotics violation, habitual intoxication, and other felony carried the characterization that the person guilty were a heterosexual. "John Blank, who kidnapped and murdered the pretty little three-year-old daughter of his lifelong friend, was disclosed to be a heterosexual, police authorities and psychiatrists said today." Or the embezzlement story might well read: "Trusted by the bank to whch he had risen to be vice-president, the defendant, a notorious heterosexual, admitted that he had been pilfering funds for a period of twenty years."

The stereotype problem is not quite so simple, however, and in later chapters I shall show that there are certain traits, both of a desirable and an undesirable nature, that are encountered with greater frequency among homosexuals than in the population at large. There is a greater amount of certain types of crimes among homosexuals, and certainly greater instability, restlessness, promiscuity. Although at this moment I wish merely to emphasize that the stereotype is a source of hostility, any intelligent discussion of the stereotype must involve an investigation to determine whether society has not itself made it necessary for minorities to pursue certain ways of life that are socially less acceptable than those demanded by its culture. If homosexuals are arrested under rather sordid circumstances, seeking sexual partners in places forbidden by public law, shall society not stop to ask whether the cause of this action is the banishment of their pursuits from so many of the accepted pathways of life? Even the homosexual who becomes an alcoholic—an extremely rare case, as I shall point out—can frequently lay his defeat in life at the doorstep of his tormentors. Thus there is created another vicious circle: the homosexual is driven to unacceptable pursuits by social condemnation, and then social condemnation finds a source of justification in the unacceptable pursuits!

To analyze the dominating motives of the many neurotic homosexual-baiters is not my aim; it would lead into a myriad of individual case histories that are not sufficiently typical to be important. But I have found certain recurrent features among heterosexuals, and one is that homosexuality in the opposite sex represents a challenge to the ego. Many normal men (and certainly women) wish to believe themselves virtually irresistible. They are Don Juans and Casanovas. It is beyond the imagination of the average man that a woman might choose a female partner in preference to himself. The sexually awakened woman is absolutely insulted by the man who rejects her offers, and is more than jealous of the man who is able to win affections and attentions where she has failed. In *Serenade*, James Cain has depicted the jealousies of such a woman, who finally drives a knife through an invert who is taking her lover from her. The insult of the scorned, the jealousy of the challenged, the anger of the ego-hurt—these are the roots of a frustration that manifests itself as hostility to homosexuality.

Finally, let me suggest that there is, in the condemnatory attitude of the average man, something of envy of the new sexual freedom that has either been adopted by or forced upon the invert. It is well-known that the only moral law respected by homosexuals is one that must be self-imposed. It is a law of mutual free will, modified by such disciplines and loyalties as are found mutually desirable. There are no legal marriages, no double standards, no divorce courts, no unions that have outlived their usefulness and are held together by economic or social exigencies. Two individuals are free to live as they see fit, whether they have known one another for minutes or for years; they are free to form their bonds and to dissolve them upon mutual agreement. The heterosexual society heaps scorn upon those who follow such law (or lack of law), even as it envies the simplicity and the logic of this moral (or amoral) code. Ironically enough, the homosexual society, such as it is, envies the stability of heterosexual morals, even while it heaps scorn upon the double standards, the property status of woman, and other outmoded and indefensible concepts.

It would be impossible for the hostility of society to survive if these sources were recognized. They are therefore vehemently denied, denounced, laughed out of court, and in their place there are justifications. Homosexuality, among other things, is said to be unnatural, contagious, injurious to the human race and to the individual, and a denial of the meaning of God.

How absurd the opposition to homosexual practices can become, how hypocritical may be the self-righteous indignation of society, is illustrated in a statement that appeared in the September 18, 1950 issue of *Life* magazine.* The exploiters of Negro labor in South Africa, according to the writer of that article, do not hesitate to send their slave-like workers into the mines for a mere pittance, force them to toil from morning to night and then sleep in these mines so that they may commence their labor at the first sign of daybreak, and lock up the men at night "in crowded compounds, without women or families, for nine, 12 or 18 months." The publication, however, expresses alarm because this is a "system that breeds homosexuality." Here are men who came as invaders to a foreign land and seized nature's resources; who extract for their greed the sweat of the brow of the workers; who offer them a few crumbs and a system of ungodly race hatred; who never show the slightest vestige of interest in the nutrition, health, welfare, or happiness of their subjects save when profits are affected— these men grow indignant lest their own imposed working conditions breed homosexual practices. The mask is torn from the niceties of justifications. Only by deep psychological need among these exploiters can their interest in this one phase of the welfare and morals of black Africa be explained.

But this utilization of justifications—and the latter may or may not be based upon accurate appraisal of the facts and a system of logical

* "Black Africa and Its Problem: In a Black Land White Rule and Human Liberty are Clashing," *Life*, September 18, 1950.

argumentation—to replace the true sources of the folkways, is well-known in majority-minority relationships. The anti-Negro sentiment in America plays a psychological and economic role in the South: it keeps satisfied the miserable poor whites, divides them from the Negroes, permits economc exploitation. But these motives are not known to the followers or even to the leaders of the Ku Klux Klan, who have been inculcated with stereotype thinking, lies about race purity and other genetic factors, and fears of their own very insecure position.

It is only in the light of such an analogy that this use of justification (or rationalization) can be understood as a concealment of the true reasons for hostility. But these reasons, denied with vehemence though they may be, are basic: the superiority feeling engendered in the insecure heterosexual; the use of condemnation as a means of suppressing that portion of the libidinous urge directed toward one's own sex; the assignment of deviltry and witchcraft toward the unknown; the difficulties of a searching study to understand; the social advantage gained from joining the chorus of condemnation; the ease of stereotype thinking by the dominant group; the challenge of homosexuality to the sexual ego; and the use of condemnation as a means of suppressing the envy for the attainment of a certain degree of sexual freedom found in the homosexual way of life.

And now, what are the rationalizations offered to justify the suppression of homosexuality, and what arguments can be presented to refute these rationalizations?

Chapter 3

Hostility: Its Justifications

A drive as powerful as homosexuality could not be suppressed without the creation of an elaborate and seemingly convincing system of thought that supports, sponsors, and rationalizes that suppression. One cannot pass laws, create outcasts of otherwise acceptable people, banish to within the walls of prison and to the confines of ignominy, without justificatory argument. This is quite aside from the motive for condemnation, often hidden and usually unknown to those who are most voluble in its expression. Modern society contends that homosexuality must be condemned as wrong and immoral, and discouraged as harmful. These contentions are not self-evident, and in order to impart to them the force of law and of universal acceptance, an intricate system of precepts in their support is established.

To examine the anti-homosexual argument, it is essential to turn aside from name-calling and invective, and drop those words which make an assumption of condemnation (as *degenerate* and *pervert*), before such an assumption is proved.

Basic to the rationalization of hostility is the statement, actually codified into law, that this form of sexual activity is unnatural. Although seldom used in psychological literature, the characterization of homosexuality as unnatural is to be found in penal codes, and is widely accepted by laymen.

It is argued, in support of this contention, that the sexual instinct was intended by nature to bring together a man and a woman, in the usual form of coitus, for the purpose of procreation, and that such a sexual act is necessary for the survival of the human race. Any other sexual activity, it is stated, is therefore a perversion of nature's intentions in endowing the animal—human and other—with a powerful neural impulse that is seeking pleasure, release, and fulfillment.

This is a rather complex series of arguments. Actually, this charge that the practices are unnatural requires analytical study along each of the following lines:

1. Are the homosexual practices unnatural?
2. Are the usual and accepted heterosexual practices less unnatural?
3. If one were to concede the unnatural character of homosexuality (or of sodomy, fellatio, etc.), would this constitute an argument against these practices and a justification for their being outlawed by our society?

First, are these practices unnatural? Two human beings of sound mind and mature age decide to seek and succeed in obtaining pleasure from various types of contacts between their bodies. Let us assume that neither employs the force of strength, the persuasion of maturity with a child, the enticement of financial gain, the concealment of disease. Their action is not only voluntary, but it is the natural calling of their temperaments, as these temperaments have evolved and developed as a result of various environmental conditions. In fact, no other course of action would be natural to them. Nothing would be so unnatural as to thwart and deny themselves.

The charge that there is something unnatural is understood only in the light of an individual who, because these practices are contrary to *his* nature, therefore decides that, *ipso facto*, they must be contrary to everyone's nature. That is not only an egocentric but a woefully unimaginative viewpoint. I contend this, and this alone: that homosexuality is perfectly natural for most of those who practice it.

However, is it not, many will ask, contrary to nature? It would require a supernatural force to state what nature intended. Nature's intentions, if such can be said to exist, should certainly be individualized for each person having a sexual drive. For some of those people it is contrary to nature's intentions to cohabit with the opposite sex, and for others the reverse is true. Nature, it is conceded, may very likely have intended that the majority of males and females find their enjoyment with the opposite sex. This merely means that it would be contrary to nature for homosexuality to replace heterosexuality as the main source of sexual enjoyment for humanity. But it definitely does not indicate that it is unnatural for it to be a secondary source of enjoyment for humanity at large, or a primary one for a minority of people.

If mankind were able to return to the primordial instincts, it is possible that it might be discovered that nature intended the animal to obtain pleasure in both types of sexual enjoyment, and perhaps—as Gide has suggested in *Corydon**—the widespread homosexuality among males, not only in human beings but in other forms of animal life, might be nature's manner of providing an outlet for the sexual impulse which is usually stronger in the male. Based on that assumption, exclusively heterosexual or homosexual pursuits would be unnatural products of this civilization; both would be neurotic symptoms; and only the true bisexual would be pursuing a natural mode of living.

Whether or not this be a tenable theory, this fact remains: that homosexuality is perfectly natural for homosexuals; the suppression of homosexuality is most unnatural for those who desire its fulfillment.

But how shall the heterosexual practices be characterized? If we start from a premise that only a drive which unites man and woman for procreative purposes is natural, what can be said of other types of sexual indulgence? Society must condemn, in equally harsh terms, as indeed the laws do, these so-called "unnatural practices" between men and women, even though they be wedded to each other. Masturbation becomes unnatural, for it is certainly not designed to utilize sexual energy for procreation. But nothing demonstrates the absurdity of the charge of unnaturalness so much as its application to birth control. What could be more man-made, man-contrived, more of a deliberate thwarting of the aims of nature, than the use of a receptacle to prevent the sperm from fertilizing the egg? If nature had intended that man and woman, during the course of love-making, should have a choice as to whether they wished to have offspring, might she not, in her majestic imagination and with her infinite capacity for variation, have created two vaginal orifices for sexual use? Some method of birth control is in almost universal use by men and women, who are little troubled that it is unnatural, which it most certainly is. Could any impartial person find it less obviating of the intentions of nature than love-making between two men or two women?

It has been stated that only the Catholic Church is completely consistent, recognizing the unnatural character of various sexual practices from sodomy to birth control, but the Church is teaching another

* André Gide, *Corydon* (New York: Farrar, Straus, 1950), second dialogue.

manner of thwarting the will of nature. This consists of the practice of preventing conception by the rhythm method. Is there any evidence that nature intended the animal to feel a stronger sexual urge when the egg is not fertilizable? Anyone who has studied zoology, or even watched a dog in heat, knows that sexual attraction and passion are heightened when fertilization can take place. The rhythm method is most unnatural. It is contrary to the laws of nature to choose the times for sexual pleasure when there is least likelihood of procreating —after the contention is made that the aim of the sexual drive is exclusively for the purpose of procreation!

The heterosexual society is enmeshed in its own contradictions when it contends that homosexuality is unnatural, for it not only fails to prove this charge, but by the force of its own argument demonstrates how completely unnatural are the heterosexual activities of most people.

But what if the charge were true: namely, sodomy and fellatio are unnatural, and heterosexual coitus perfectly natural. Why should this be an argument, in and of itself, against homosexual practices? Is it not a fact that civilization is itself a negation of nature? The wearing of clothing, the covering of certain parts of our bodies even when the weather is not inclement—these are surely unnatural acts. Homes, machines, television sets, telephones, synthetic therapeutic agents—all are unnatural. All are contrary to the wishes and intentions of nature. Human beings were endowed with voices that could produce sounds, and ears that could perceive them within a radius of no more than a few hundred yards, but we create an unnatural system of talking to other humans hundreds or thousands of miles away. If certain sexual behavior must be banned because it is unnatural, why not ban the telephone as an instrument of unnatural living? And what shall be said of the unnatural release of the energy imprisoned by nature in the atom?

The charge that it is unnatural for a man to make love to another man is not only false and inconsistent, but is actually meaningless. It is an effort to employ an evil-sounding word to describe an experience, in the hope that the connotation of evil will be placed, not only upon the word, but upon the experience.

In commenting upon this question following the trials of Oscar Wilde, Lord Alfred Douglas wrote: "To call a thing unnatural is not only not necessarily to condemn it but is even to a certain extent to commend it. Everything that diverges from the normal may to a certain extent be called unnatural, genius and beauty among them."

Let the birds in the trees and the wild animals of the forests decide that certain practices are contrary to the laws of nature, for they live by these laws, and their conclusions would be consistent with their ways of life. Do they ban homosexuality? Is there a single instance of their inflicting punishment on one of their members who practices it?

But enough of the unnatural! Condemnation, it is argued, is necessary, and punishment as well, because without it homosexuality might spread, threatening the welfare of mankind, corrupting our youth. Here, again, there are many arguments, and they require analysis.

What insecurity, what inferiority feeling, the heterosexual displays when he states his fear that only social ostracism is effective in stopping the spread of homosexuality. Is the gay way of life so attractive, are its pleasures so remarkable, that the straight people believe that converts will be won over in greater and greater numbers? How can people, in one breath, condemn a force as being unnatural, and then state that a permissive attitude would produce unlimited converts? This is, in effect, a concession that the homosexual instinct must be very strong—though often latent, suppressed, or sublimated—in all humanity. In other words, if the fear of conversion has any validity, it is a concession that, far from being unnatural, homosexuality must be one of nature's primitive instinctual forces. Or, perhaps, is it contended that it is both?

Actually, of course, punishment is no deterrent. It may make some homosexuals angry, others bitter, others ashamed, but it has never made a straight person out of a gay one. It has, at times—for better or worse—succeeded in preventing the fulfillment of a homosexual desire, but it has never displaced that desire. And even the thwarting of the fulfillment is rare. The fact is that millions of people the world over are carrying out acts, or seeking to carry them out, which acts would, if discovered, bring down upon them disgrace, unemployment, financial ruin, and imprisonment—sometimes for life. And yet these people are undeterred.

Condemnation, in fact, does not deter, nor would assuagement have the contrary influence. The laws against homosexuality have not stopped homosexuals, and it is certainly difficult to argue that the existence of such legislation has been the factor that has kept heterosexuals from straying to the forbidden path. The lifting of condemnatory attitudes would encourage discussion, enhance man's efforts in search for truth, enable a free intermingling of the dominant and the suppressed groups, but it would not encourage homosexual practices except among those already so inclined. The very real problem of sexual acts conducted by an adult with an adolescent or child, and the possibility of such acts having a permanent influence on the life of the younger person, affects the homosexual and the heterosexual, one not more than the other. But it is a problem entirely unrelated to society's attitude toward the voluntary relationship entered into by two adults of the same sex.

Any psychologist can testify that if one were to question the majority of people who have not had any homosexual experiences in their lives, and were to inquire as to the reason for this lack, the most remote response would be the fear of disgrace, ruin, or punishment. The heterosexuals claim that they have no desire for the so-called unnatural; that they are repelled and disgusted by the thought. Why, then, the fear of converts?

This entire argument that condemnation is necessary in order to discourage is predicated upon the assumption that such discouragment is necessary for a well-balanced society. Thus, whether or not homosexualism is unnatural is quite irrelevant in judging its social worthiness. It may be quite natural for man to kill, but murder does not therefore become less anti-social. An act is not criminally punishable, whether by law or by social pressure, unless it is contrary to the aims of the social organism.

Now, to condemn merely to discourage is only the end-point of a philosophical aim that has no beginning. One must first demonstrate that discouragement is not only effectively carried out by condemnation, but that discouragement is beneficial and necessary to society.

Thus, a third argument is encountered at this point, and one which seeks to establish a social justification of discouragement. Homosexuality, it is contended, is race suicide. It is bad because it is sterile; it fails to reproduce the human species.

This statement is likewise complex in its implications. First, many contend that mankind has reached a stage in development where, in several lands at least, the problem is to control the further growth of the human race. Certainly China has no need, nor has Japan, of maintaining or increasing their birth rates. In fact, a decrease in population might be helpful. And if a large group of human beings can live their natural and full sex lives without reproducing, so much the better.

If society were consistent in its attitude and sincere in its alarm over the effect of homosexuality on procreation, why does it take such a severe attitude toward illegitimate births, of which certainly, despite social pressures, there are a great many each year? Why is there not a consistent attitude of condemnation toward birth control, instead of the hypocrisy which condones the practice while denouncing the teaching of it? All of the homosexuality in the world could not possibly curtail the population growth of this planet as effectively as could a single manufacturer of contraceptives.

Finally, it is contended that homosexuality is lecherous, sordid, promiscuous, and devoid of the tenderness characteristic of love, and that homosexuals themselves are alcoholics and dope-fiends. The legitimacy of this argument I shall have occasion to examine at another point in this book. But is this an excuse for taking discriminatory action of a social and legal nature against those who do not fit such description? Is there any reason to cast shame upon the activities and inclinations of those who are living socially useful and well-regulated lives, merely because—if this contention be true—others live harmful and wasteful lives?

The argument is furthermore self-contradictory in another sense. Much of the sordid character of the lives of some homosexuals is due to the social attitudes of which they are the victims. Thus society does its utmost to defeat people, to force them into reprehensible pathways of life, to close the doors to better possibilities—and then cites the roads of ruin upon which they have been forced as justification for man's hostility.

Society has attempted many times in the past to utilize the inferior morality, community organization, or public and private health habits of a group as proof of its being inferior and undeserving of better treatment, although society itself (or, to be exact, its dominant section) had forced these conditions upon the less fortunate group. "The lower classes are ignorant, and could learn nothing at Oxford and

Cambridge," the landed aristocracy of Britain used to proclaim. "Therefore it is wasteful and useless to give them a good education." The conditions created by the lack of education and culture, imposed by the upper class, were thus used as the justification for continuing to deny broader educational opportunities. "The American Indian is wild, uncontrollable, and will not hesitate to attack and kill," our historians used to teach us. "Therefore he must be suppressed and confined to a few reservations." The conditions created by our treatment of these Indians were thus used as the excuse to continue to deny them rights, and the denial of such rights laid the basis for continuing the justification of the treatment.

In this fashion the dominant group creates a vicious circle, in which inequality is forced upon a minority, and the conditions resulting from inequality are then cited as justification of the unequal status. That this illogical method of argumentation has pervaded human thinking, even in the era of the Greek philosophers, can readily be established. It has been used against slaves, colonial peoples, against both Protestants and Catholics by their opponents, and against revolutionists, Jews, Asiatics, Negroes, Indians, and many others. It should become apparent that it is fundamental to the social thinking about homosexuals.

If homosexuals seek out one another under admittedly sordid conditions—which they sometimes do, although this is not typical or universal; if they resort to alcoholism or even to narcotics—which they seldom do; if their lives are promiscuous and their loves unstable —which they often are—then is it not socially responsible behavior first to investigate the source of such a state of affairs before condemning the group to a continuation of these conditions?

But homosexuality, it will be argued, is surely hostile to society in that it is contrary to the family organization and to the religious principles of modern culture. This is, to a certain extent, true. The family unit is based primarily upon the union of man and woman. Where do two men or two women fit into this scheme of things? The truth of the matter is that the homosexual creates his own type of family unit, but the fundamental question is that he is not interfering with the family as it exists in modern society. To say that the homosexual does not fit into the family unit is not to prove that he is destructive of it. Surely his activities do not interfere with the majority of people marrying, having children, and (in very great number) becoming divorced.

Similarly, homosexuality is not an anti-religious force, although religion is anti-homosexual. Although some religions have a definite place for the celibate and the spinster, the latter are supposed to be continent, and it is hardly likely that homosexuals in any great number will abide by such religious regulations. But as a justification for hostility this argument would be specious, even if one were to concede its basic premise. For the dominant group creates a system of social superstructures in which no place is left for the homosexual; then denies to the invert access to these institutions; and ends up by denouncing inversion because it does not fit into the very institutions from which it has been banned. If homosexuality were a force destructive of our family institution, it would be because the family has been built in such manner as to exclude the homosexual from its rank. The church denounces the homosexual, banishes him from the folds of religion, and then justifies its denunciation by asserting that homosexuals are anti-religious and anti-church.

Finally, an argument encountered quite frequently can be summarized in a conversation in which I participated: "I have nothing against two guys doing anything they want with each other," a friend, and a straight one, said to me, "but I want them to leave me alone." This statement is neither an accurate reflection of prevalent opinion nor a justification of oppressive attitudes. The problem is certainly not to force homosexuals to "leave others alone." There is no oppression being practiced by the gay group. The problem is to have the dominant society "leave alone"—or lift its suppressive measures—against the gay people. If society really had "nothing against" two individuals who voluntarily follow a homosexual way of life, then why have strict laws and severe social pressure against them? Why restrict their rights of employment and education? Why force them to slink and to hide, under pain of almost universal excommunication?

One frequently hears another argument, and it is a curious one. "If only they would not make a public display of themselves," Johnnie said to me during a very frank discussion. "At college we have about half a dozen, and they carry on in the classrooms and corridors like mad, screeching like women at the tops of their lungs. Their antics are repulsive to me. Why don't they keep this swishing and screaming to themselves, instead of placing themselves on exhibition like museum pieces or circus freaks?"

"But, Johnnie," I said, "they represent only a few. Perhaps their need for manifest exhibition is as great as my need to have a man, or yours to have a woman. But most of us make no display at all of our tendencies. Will you punish the many for the few?"

"Don," he replied, "my knowledge of your group comes mainly from the few—except for yourself. After all, how can I know who the many are, if you deny and hide so effectively? You're mainly a group of cowards and hypocrites." And then he hesitated, and added apologetically, "You know how fond I am of you, Don, but I'm talking about queers on the whole."

I laughed. "Johnnie, that last statement I've heard before. Some of my best friends are Jews, they say—the surest sign of the anti-Semite. But you find the majority of us cowards and hypocrites, while the few are exhibitionists. If we hide our tendencies and reveal ourselves only within our own group, we are hypocrites. And if we expose ourselves, we are exhibitionists. It's damned if you do, and damned if you don't."

Thus do individuals express the main arguments used in justification of society's attitude toward homosexuality, and thus do some people offer defense against such arguments. As I hope to demonstrate, homosexuality can be a potent force, not a destructive one, both for the individual and for society. But the shallowness of the rationalizations of the social codemnation, and the failure to find either scientific or intellectual defense of society's attitudes, merely serve to strengthen a conviction that the logic employed is a façade behind which are hidden the sources previously revealed.

Chapter 4

Civil Liberty and Human Rights

A unique letter appeared some years ago in *The Saturday Review of Literature*.* It might have been written by any of a million people, but it would have been almost impossible to find the individual willing to sign his name and place an address upon such a letter intended for publication. "Since I am a homosexual . . ." were the opening words of the communication, which then continued by offering some comments on the subject by a man personally affected.

The response to this letter, as judged by the published communications, was varied. Several other homosexuals, all anonymous, addressed words of praise and thanks. But one of them issued a warning: "I hope (he) has private income for he must know that he will never be given another job."†

It is rare to find the economic discriminations against a minority taking on the form of legal sanctions, but much more common to find that customs, folkways, and accepted practices make it difficult for certain groups to advance on the economic front in conformity with their abilities. The victims of discrimination, together with their allies, will rebel, utilizing public opinion, pressure, and legal and cultural arguments to obtain redress. These channels are not open for the homosexual minority.

It was for a long time common knowledge that homosexuals could not obtain employment, except in a few lines of endeavor, unless they succeeded in hiding their sexual tendencies from their employers. Many professional groups, given the right to pass upon the character of the individual before granting him a license to permit the practice

* *Saturday Review of Literature,* July 9, 1949, p. 25.
† *Ibid.,* Aug. 13, 1949, p. 24.

of the profession of his training, would consider sexual inversion as a proper reason for exclusion. "You would not want a fairy to be your boy's teacher," the apologist for an educator might say, and then would continue by extending the line of reasoning to lawyers, doctors, dentists, and others.

The private employer, in the domain in which he is sovereign, was seldom more permissive. It was not that he had any well-planned and preconceived line of argument against homosexuals in his employ—he was just against them and would not have them. Thus it became extremely difficult to find employment, and sometimes even more so to continue at work, inasmuch as employers would not hesitate summarily to dismiss a very competent person who became suspect after many years of honest work.

They never fight back! That, more than anything else, is characteristic of the discrimination against homosexuals. They accept, quietly and willingly, only too happy that they have been spared the humiliation of exposure. They accept, with head bowed—angry, hurt, and helpless—and often with some sense that perhaps their lot is not entirely without justification. For the homosexual is not quite sure that it is wrong to practice discrimination against him, and his half-hearted acceptance of the contempt in which he is held is not unique among minorities. "The worst effect of slavery was to make Negroes doubt themselves and share in the general contempt for black folk," writes the eminent Negro sociologist, W. E. B. DuBois. Similarly the worst effect of discrimination has been to make the homosexuals doubt themselves and share in the general contempt for sexual inverts.

Herbert L. is an example. He had been clerk in an office for about two years—a personable, honest, and diligent bachelor of thirty. He was a veteran and this was his first job after receiving the honorable discharge from the Army. At the home which he shared with a friend he kept a purple heart, among other mementoes of a five-year stretch.

The personnel manager was kind when Herbert was dismissed two weeks before Christmas. "We're retrenching—and we don't feel that your job is quite working out."

In the vice-president's office, Herbert was told the truth, told it kindly, by a friend and confidant. "They suspected and they had private detectives trail you. Found out all about your roommate, saw you in certain bars . . ."

"But I did my job well. What difference does it make?"

"That's the way they feel about this thing, Herbert."

"And you? They say the whole industry knows about you?"

"At the top it's tolerated. One's enough in the office—provided they need him that badly."

Herbert and his kind cannot go to the courts, cannot find champions among the defenders of civil liberties, cannot take their case before a union committee. They must accept and then make an effort to hide their homosexuality even more carefully in the future than in the past.

In 1950 a crusade against homosexuals in government service was undertaken as part of a political campaign by a United States senator.* Started as an attack upon the Truman administration, and particularly its State Department and foreign service, it soon extended to all government offices. The homosexual, described by the senator as a sex pervert, became the scapegoat in an internecine battle which was not of his making. Ninety-one sex perverts, it was reported, were dismissed from the State Department, all loyal employees, many able experts in their field—dismissed solely because it was charged that they were homosexuals. And not one appealed. The anonymity of the dismissals or resignations alone was sufficient to prevent an appeal.

A campaign of this sort would ordinarily require little justification. Who would dare to question the fact that homosexuals were unworthy of employment by this great government? It was all well and good to make a national hero of Whitman and teach his poetry to children at school, to honor Tchaikowsky with special concerts, to give the Nobel Prize for Literature to Gide, but a government job in the State Department must not be offered to "a pervert." And ninety-one of them! Why, to the public it must have seemed that the foreign service was overflowing with debauchery, for who stopped to compare the ninety-one with the figures in the Kinsey studies, and who realized that these people constituted less than one-half of one per cent of the 23,000 employees of the State Department?

Nevertheless a few voices were raised in the darkness. Here and there, someone questioned whether these people were not entitled to

* For a remarkable study of this campaign, see Max Lerner's series, *New York Post*, July 10-23, 1950, " 'Scandal' in the State Dept."

pursue their professional activities, earn their living, and contribute to the welfare of their country, just as do their fellow-citizens.

In reply, it was contended that the homosexuals constitute security risks for the government because they are so easily subject to blackmail. Their homosexual inclinations eventually become known to a few, are gossiped about, learned of by the enemy; and then under pain of revelation there is a demand for secret documents and for cooperation. To substantiate this charge, the government found it necessary to cite an Austrian homosexual who fell victim to the blackmail threats of the Russians.

There have been homosexuals in American diplomatic service—at the very highest posts, including ambassadorships—and none has ever been disloyal. Most of these people have nothing to hide. Precisely because their tendencies are well-known, they could never be blackmailed.

There are others whose homosexuality is concealed; but there are few men whose lives could stand a thoroughgoing investigation, who do not harbor secrets that are unknown to family and close associates. The fact is that disloyalty was not charged against a single one of the State Department homosexuals, nor was there ever a spy scandal involving ambassadors, consular officers, or other homosexuals in the service of the American government; and the sole homosexual in the history of this country who has been charged with corruption was accused of accepting bribes—not of giving them.

The entire charge regarding security risk is nothing but a confession of the bankruptcy of the anti-homosexual drive, and this was definitely demonstrated by subsequent events. For of the ninety-one men discharged from the State Department, a few sought and obtained government employment in other branches of the civil service; yet these men were later dismissed, despite the fact that no function of security was involved in the new jobs.

Consider, however, the vicious circle in which the dominant group places the minority. First, it sponsors a moral attitude of hostility which it claims will terrorize the minority into committing acts of disloyalty, and then it seizes upon this potential disloyalty to justify the attitude which created it.

Many unprejudiced attorneys believe that there is sufficient breadth of power in the wording of the laws to permit exclusion of homosexuals from government jobs. The rules governing employment by the Civil Service Commission state that "immoral conduct" is a reason for disqualification from a job, and "immoral conduct" is defined in the *Manual of Regulations* of the Civil Service Commission as "action not within the sphere of conformity with the generally accepted standards" of the community. Inasmuch as the dominant society excludes the minority from its generally accepted standards and makes it impossible for anyone to come forward to challenge such exclusion, the government policy can be legally justified.

Soon after the campaign in the United States Senate had gotten under way, the Senate appointed a subcommittee of the Committee on Expenditures in the Executive Departments to make an "investigation into the employment by the Government of homosexuals and other sex perverts." Did this official body set out to determine whether homosexuals make desirable employees? Let the report speak for itself:

> The primary objective of the subcommittee in this inquiry was to determine the extent of the employment of homosexuals and other sex perverts in Government; *to consider why their employment by the Government is undesirable;* and to examine into the efficacy of the methods used in dealing with this problem.* (*My emphasis*–D. W. C.)

It goes without saying that a body which sets out to consider why the employment of a group of people in government is undesirable can come up with some good reasons, but an investigation of this type can hardly fall within the purview of impartiality. The report of the subcommittee reiterated the charge that homosexuals are poor security risks, but also found that they should not be employed in jobs where there is no question of security. Their behavior is criminal and immoral; it is "so contrary to the normal accepted standards of social behavior that persons who engage in such activity are looked upon as outcasts by society generally". . . . the homosexuals conceal their activities because of the social stigma . . . these people lack emotional stability . . . their moral fiber is weakened . . . they have "a corrosive influence" on other employees . . . they can pollute an entire office . . . and they gather other homosexuals around themselves.

These arguments could be answered seriatim, and many of them I have dealt with elsewhere. But if they are valid as reasons for

* *See* Appendix A, Document No. 2.

exclusion from government employment, then why not private employment? And if homosexuals are to be barred from both public and private employment, then where are they to turn?

Other minorities that are excluded from the mainstream of the economic life of a country have recourse to public opinion and to the courts, but such is not the good fortune of the homosexual. Others develop their own economic life, form their own businesses, thrive in their own communities, but the gay people are only occasionally able to accomplish this. They do find a greater degree of acceptance in some fields of endeavor, and in America these are precisely the same fields that have been readiest to grant opportunities to other minorities: entertainment and publishing, to name two.

One of the most disheartening aspects of the economic discrimination is the frequency with which it is practiced by homosexuals against each other. Because of the veil of secrecy behind which he functions and the ever-present fear of exposure, the homosexual is most reluctant to give a job to a friend or to hire a stranger whom he suspects. If it were to become known that the new employee is gay, suspicion must inevitably fall on the person who gave him employment. Self-protection demands that a homosexual completely isolate his business from his social life, and this in turn means that he joins the discriminating group, albeit with misgivings.

How severe is the denial of civil liberties can be seen by the fact that the homosexual is the only veteran, except those given dishonorable discharge, who does not obtain the benefit of the so-called G. I. Bill of Rights. Most servicemen who were homosexual or partially inclined in that direction had no difficulties with the authorities during their terms of service. They might have escaped service had they so desired by revealing themselves to the medical officers. Few chose this path. The homosexuals included privates and high officers. Many were cited for unusual bravery; others were wounded, killed, and honored with the most coveted medals conferred upon soldiers and sailors. Most of my friends are veterans, and they were never accused of a sexual offense while in the service. A few, however, were known to be homosexuals and were given discharges when this became necessary, but they were usually discharged under some other provision, inasmuch as the commanding officers, aware of the stigma attached to a record that showed sexual abnormality, were anxious to protect those who had to be discharged. The few who could not remain in service throughout the war were given an honorable or a medical discharge, and the regulations calling for special handling of homosexual cases were deliberately ignored in the majority of cases.

The special handling, however, was on occasion enforced, and it provided for a so-called "blue discharge"—which was neither honorable nor dishonorable, but was undesirable. It was given to many servicemen, for a variety of reasons. And the armed forces kept, in confidential files, the record of the veteran, which disclosed the reasons for the discharge.

Medical officers specifically assured these men of two things: one, that the reason for the discharge would be confidential; and, two, that they would be given all the rights and privileges of anyone else obtaining a similar type of discharge from the services. These soldiers and sailors were told that they were being treated like sick people, and not criminals. They had committed no wrong, but were ill, and if other ill soldiers were allowed benefits after the war, these men would receive the same.

Such promises were later brushed aside when, by executive order of a Veterans Administrator—curiously enough, one of the last orders of a retiring Administrator—anyone having a blue discharge for homosexuality was barred from receiving any and all government benefits under the G. I. Bill of Rights, except those specifically granted by Act of Congress. Thus no government-subsidized education, no business or home loans, no bonus. Once again, only broken promises. But the important fact here is that no other medically discharged men, including those disassociated from the army as psychoneurotics under Section Eight of the Medical Discharge regulations, were barred from such benefits. Only the sexual invert!

Now, what did Congress state in its original law? Only this—that benefits should be accorded those servicemen who were discharged under "other than dishonorable conditions." And it remained for the Veterans Administrator, acting with sovereign authority, to rule that homosexuality is a dishonorable condition. If it had been the intention of Congress to bar from the benefits of the law all those having undesirable as well as dishonorable discharges, it could certainly have expressed this in clear terms. It remained for a Veterans Administrator not only to set himself up as psychiatrist and sociologist, and declare that homosexuality is a dishonorable condition, but as lawmaker and jurist, and declare that a discharge under dishonorable conditions does not refer to a dishonorable discharge, but to any alienation of service under dishonorable circumstances!

If this administrative decision is allowed to remain, what is to prevent a Veterans Administrator, by executive order, from denying rights and privileges to soldiers accused of miscegenation; or to those who protest against jim-crowism; or to those who are non-conformists in any other respect?

And who raises a voice in protest against such discrimination? No one. Where was the American Civil Liberties Union? Nowhere. Who took the case to court and challenged the right of the Veterans Administrator, under the law and under our Constitution, to take such action? No one. In fact, the Act of Congress which grants the Veterans Administrator the right to make a decision of this type is specifically exempt from court review!

Barred from many avenues of private employment and from government employment, barred from many educational opportunities, barred from serving one's country in the Army and Navy, barred from the ordinary channels of expression of public opinion through newspapers and magazines—this is the extent of civil liberties for the homosexual.

It has been pointed out that the difference between treatment of minorities in the democracies and in totalitarian lands lies essentially in the right of those in the former countries to protest and appeal. The courts are free, and discriminatory action can be fought by legal means. Yet this does not hold true for the homosexual minority. The price for making the struggle is public disgrace and further economic discrimination, a price so great that society in this manner has protected itself against the possibility that its own customs will be challenged.

Only an enlightened public opinion can serve as a weapon in the struggle to maintain civil liberties and human rights, but society immunizes itself against such enlightenment, not only by imposing social disgrace on all those who would speak boldly on the subject, but by a conspiracy of silence. It would be difficult to find an example more striking than the refusal of the *New York Times* to report a single word on the Senatorial hearings in which charges of sexual perversion were made against State Department employees. Despite the significant political aspects of the matter and its deep interest for readers of the newspaper, not one word was published by that paper. It is reliably reported that members of the staff of the *New York Times* were advised that the entire matter must be ignored. Thus was a major political scandal treated by America's foremost newspaper.

There are no laws against homosexuals appealing, protesting, expressing their opinion, but the channels of communication are simply not open for these purposes. Book publishers have issued a considerable amount of fiction and a number of biographies, but have restricted the general literature to esoteric and medical books, and even paid advertisements for novels on this subject are rejected by many leading newspapers. Many publishers have stated orally that they would not dare to touch a manuscript for popular consumption which defended homosexual practices, even if it were interesting, intelligently written, a potential best-seller, and deserving of a large audience. Articles with vague and obscure hints at the true situation have appeared in a few of America's major publications such as *Esquire* and *The Cosmopolitan*, but these articles, sympathetic as they were, skirted the subject. They did not meet the issues squarely. As a rule, however, the breakdown of silence takes place only when a publication (as did *Coronet Magazine* in 1950) opens its pages to a particularly one-sided and scurrilous article, without pretending to allow the other viewpoint to be presented.

The denial of civil rights would ordinarily inspire a vigorous defense, but the conspiracy of silence makes such denial little known outside the circle of victims. To those who hear of such things, it is simply assumed that, by tradition, the discriminatory process is a proper one.

Many are the reasons given for exclusion of the homosexual from private or public employment. "The homo is unstable," it is said (because a single homosexual has proved unstable); thus the hostile society suggests that if stability can be demonstrated, the discrimination would be lifted. But this is not at all the case.

"The homo seeks to seduce others to his ways," it is said, implying that "his ways" are inferior and yet at the same time are so attractive to others that they will fall easily into the trap.

"The obvious homo is a disgrace. The stigma that falls upon him is reflected on his associates and his employer . . ."

And so it goes. Under the circumstances the homosexual can only take refuge behind the mask. He wishes to enter the armed services; therefore he pretends that homosexuality is abhorrent to him. He seeks a government post, and talks to his fellow-employees of his lady friends. He comes before the court, and states that he is shocked at the disgusting charges made against him.

But, most ironical of all, his life of pretense is used as the supreme argument against him. "The homo is a liar," I have heard it said. "He lies to his employer, to the government, to the courts, to his friends, to his family—and probably to himself. His entire life is one lie from beginning to end."

Thus if he dares to show his true inclinations, there is awaiting the road of the outcast—discrimination, social ostracism, economic defeat. And if, in self-protection, he is forced to make a pretense, there comes denunciation for living a life that is a lie!

In this situation the dominant heterosexual group is without an answer. It has nothing to offer the homosexual except denunciation and more denunciation. Economically it approves of barring him from almost any line of endeavor, regards his presence as a disgrace to employer and fellow-employee, but knows that he must live. It denounces those who make known their proclivities, and then ferrets out those who seek to hide them. It banishes the discovered homosexual from the schools but admits that education should not be denied. It openly states that it is not practical, desirable, or justifiable to make prison the end-home of the invert—and most people would rise up in protest at the very thought—but a suggestion that homosexuals be imprisoned is merely a statement that society's laws be enforced. And, if not imprisonment, what is to happen to hundreds of thousands or millions of people?

Society, in a word, finds itself with a group of people who cannot be assimilated, cannot be wiped out, and cannot be recognized. And just as the psychiatrist has no other solution except "let them live" (which means, by implication, let them live and love as they see fit), so the sociologist has no solution except "let them work, let them be educated, let them develop all of their individual talents and social usefulness."

It is my contention that the lifting of social and economic discrimination is the only practical and justifiable program that has been suggested for dealing with the homosexual. That such a program implies a broadening of the democratic structure of America by expanding liberties to a new group and in a new direction should make it more attractive to all Americans. That it is the sole way out for the rectification of a social injustice is its own *raison d'être*. That it will, at the same time, awaken an increasing number of people to the problems of minorities, of all types and characters and origins, should make it more urgent to the men and women of this country. And, finally, that such a program will serve as a protection of the aims of democracy in an era when all democratic thought is threatened will become apparent with the passage of time, and is a contention which I shall attempt to prove in the latter part of this book.

Chapter 5

A World of Law-Abiding Felons

Many people are under the impression that the homosexual is in constant conflict with the law. In a narrow sense they are correct. Although there are few homosexuals who are ever arrested or convicted of crimes, and relatively few who are successfully subjected to blackmail, there is an incessant conflict between the life of the homosexual and the official statutes and penal codes.

The sexual practices indulged in and desired by most homosexuals are illegal in the United States and are punishable in some states in a manner which often recalls the witch-burning of medieval times. Because there is so much confusion as to the status of homosexuality under the law, I shall start by outlining the facts, after which I shall offer some critical comments.

In the United States the laws regarding sex crimes are for the most part under the jurisdiction of the individual states, except where transportation from one state to another is involved. Therefore the laws can be inconsistent with each other in spirit and in content, can have vastly different definitions, interpretations, and penalties, so long as none of them is in violation of the United States Constitution.

There is, first of all, very little agreement on the definitions of the terms under which the homosexual's activities are encompassed. The authoritative legal dictionary defines *buggery* and *sodomy* in practically identical terms, and each is used interchangeably as "a crime against nature."* The typical definition cites sodomy as "a carnal copulation by human beings with each other against nature, or with a beast," which definition would embrace not only homosexuality of any sort, but bestiality, and the so-called unnatural relationships between a man and a woman.

* *Black's Law Dictionary* (3rd ed.; St. Paul: West Publishing Co., 1938).

The common law, which is the basic inheritance upon which American law was built, limited sodomy to anal penetration and, curiously enough, required proof of emission. The act was therefore not confined to two males; it could be performed by man and woman; but could not be committed by two females, and did not include fellatio and cunnilingus. At a later date it was provided that proof of penetration without proof of emission should be sufficient for a conviction of sodomy.

Today there are a few states that continue to define sodomy more or less in terms of the traditional common law and restrict the acts constituting the crime to those treated under the common law. In Mississippi, for example, it was held that the act of cunnilingus could not be considered sodomy inasmuch as penetration had not taken place.*

In several other states, although the crime has been defined in terms of the common law, the state penal codes have been interpreted by the courts to cover sexual practices other than anal penetration, including copulation by the mouth.

Finally, about half of the states have redefined the crime, stating in specific or general terms what acts constitute sodomy. This is sometimes done in general terms, as provided by the Iowa statute, which declares anyone guilty of sodomy who "shall have carnal copulation in any opening of the body except sexual parts, with another human being."† The Maryland statute is both specific and general, and includes heterosexual practices, not merely by inference, but by direct statement: "Every person who shall be convicted of taking into his or her mouth the sexual organ of any other person or animal, or who shall be convicted of placing his or her sexual organ in the mouth of any person or animal, or who shall be convicted of committing any other unnatural or perverted sexual practice with any other person or animal" is declared to have committed sodomy.

Probably the most specific definition of the act encompassed by these laws is given in the Minnesota penal code, in that it includes heterosexual and homosexual, male and female; the active and passive partners, bestiality, and anal and oral penetration: "A person who

---

* All citations are given in Appendix B, where they will be found under the name of the state.

† All statutes and penal codes cited in this chapter are quoted in greater detail in Appendix B.

carnally knows in any manner any animal or bird or carnally knows any male or female person by the anus or by or with the mouth, or voluntarily submits to such carnal knowledge . . . is guilty of sodomy."

It is interesting at this point to emphasize that nowhere do the penal codes specifically treat of this as a homosexual crime, nor is the word homosexual used. The main entries for the so-called homosexual offenses are treated in most of the states under the titles "crime against nature" or "sodomy." A few states use combinations of the two, or such other terms as "sex perversions," "buggery," and "lewd or lascivious acts," and in addition there are many arrests and prosecutions for homosexual behavior under such statutes as "obscenity," "public indecency," "lewdness," "vagrancy," "indecent exposure," or "disorderly conduct." Of the forty-eight states, only two, namely New Hampshire and Vermont, have no specific laws dealing with sodomy or crime against nature, or one of their synonymous terms. However, this does not mean that the acts encompassed by such terms are legal in these states. Homosexual practices are outlawed in these two New England states under the titles of "lewdness" or "lascivious acts."

Unless a homosexual act has been committed by force and violence, the consenting party is considered an accomplice. Now it is a general rule of law that the testimony of an accomplice, without corroboration, cannot be considered sufficient for a conviction. Although this was upheld in the state of Arkansas and elsewhere, in an Illinois case it was held that the uncorroborated testimony of an accomplice is sufficient to convict when the same is competent and sufficient to justify a verdict of guilty, if believed by the jury.* The dangers inherent in such a departure from the common law are quite evident, for it opens wide the gates of blackmail, and it is quite contrary to the basic principle that guilt must be established beyond a reasonable doubt.

If the infractions against the protection usually granted to defendants are few, insofar as uncorroborated testimony of the accomplice is concerned, they are more frequent so far as indictments are concerned. The American legal and judicial system holds that a defendant is entitled to be presented with an indictment which carefully specifies those acts constituting the offense charged against him, so

* Kelly v. People, 192 Ill. 119 (Illinois).

that he may be placed on notice of all of the elements of the proceedings he faces. However, sodomy is one of the few crimes where this rule of law has in several states been relaxed, the courts claiming that the acts are so sordid and so immoral that the specific listing of them would be a source of public embarrassment and an affront to the community. In an Indiana case it was held that so lewd and degrading were the offenses that lack of the specificity of the indictments was justified,* and Maryland has gone so far as to incorporate into the statute an official statement that particular acts need not be specified in sodomy indictments. Texas and Georgia courts have ruled that such indictments are faulty and that notice of the specific acts charged to the defendant must be given to him in the indictment.

Although a sexual relationship between two women is morally regarded as being no less reprehensible than that involving two men, the statutes in a number of states are not as clear nor are the punishments as harsh as when men only are concerned. In Ohio it was specifically held by the courts that the statute, although encompassing fellatio, did not include cunnilingus, and in Georgia it was held that, as sodomy is defined in that state, it could not be committed by two women. Only in Arizona is there specific mention of cunnilingus as a punishable felony, although several statutes are so broad in their definitions that they could be interpreted, if the courts so desired, to include this act.

At the present time (1951), twenty-three of the states have laws which either specifically mention fellatio or define sodomy in terms that, in my opinion, or in the opinion of the courts, are sufficiently broad as to encompass this act.

What are the punishments upon conviction? The state of Georgia makes it mandatory that a sentence of life imprisonment shall be meted out to anyone convicted of sodomy, whereas Connecticut has a maximum of thirty years imprisonment, and Minnesota does not send the convict to jail for more than twenty years. A full list of the prison sentences and/or fines provided by statute is given as part of the excerpts from the statutes of the forty-eight states, presented as an appendix to this book. A reader of the list should bear in mind that the Bill of Rights to the United States Constitution, in its Eighth Amendment, states that no person shall be subjected to cruel and unusual punishment.

* Glover v. State, 179 Ind. 459 (Indiana).

Most homosexuals, as mentioned before, are only slightly concerned with these laws. They are on the statute books and represent a reflection of certain moral judgments, but there is a time lag between the change in public attitude and legal attitude. On the statute books these laws are a threat to homosexuals because there is always a possibility that they might be invoked at any time. But a much greater threat comes to the community at large, because the laws involving sodomy, unnatural sexual behavior, and the like transform the majority of our adult population into felons. We have become a nation—and for that matter a world—of law-abiding criminals. If our laws covering sex crimes were to be enforced, we should have to transform entire states into huge concentration camps, and there would hardly be enough people remaining free to act as jailors.

Some shrug their shoulders and insist that a law on the books which is unenforced and unenforceable does no one any harm, but this is a short-sighted view. It imposes the onus of criminality upon all those who, despite their moral uprightness, find themselves forced into conflict with the law. The individual may be a lawyer or even a judge, but by his very nature he has been branded a criminal. The constant awareness that one has committed a punishable felony is always present and takes its psychological toll of the individual. Only the public's colossal ignorance of the sodomy statutes has relieved the heterosexual (including the married man and woman) of the equal burden of guilt-feeling for felonious lawbreaking.

However, the sodomy laws are not only an invitation for a contempt of lawfulness in general. Their invocation from time to time, under special conditions motivated by vengeance or brought about by ill-fortune, has resulted in extreme cruelty for the victim.

The widespread contempt in which these laws are held and the apathy with which they are left unenforced by police officers are indicated by the fewness of the arrests. During the ten-year period from 1930 to 1939, there were in New York City only 1396 arrests for sodomy and only 414 indictments, with an additional 333 indictments for carnal abuse. Even if all of these cases were homosexual, which they were not, it can readily be seen that the police have not apprehended the statutory felon with sufficient frequency to command respect for the law. Three per cent of the adult male population of New York City, let us assume, were homosexuals during this time—a very small percentage, as all studies of incidence indicate.

There were, therefore, about 50,000 homosexuals in the city, and even if they had a relationship only once a month, this would amount to more than a million felonies a year, or ten million in the ten-year period. These figures do not include the large amount of practices indulged in by bisexuals and the almost countless sodomy felonies committed by men and women, particularly when married to each other. The figures therefore indicate how absurd is the enforcement policy toward an unenforceable law. Since that time, New York has reduced sodomy, under most conditions, to a misdemeanor.

It has come to be widely accepted in advanced criminological circles that sex crimes must be divided into two categories: those that are considered "outrageous" to the community at large, that shock the public morals, but that do no harm except possibly to the participants (and that is a matter of personal opinion); and those which involve the use of force, violence, and other harmful practices.

The sadist, the rapist, perhaps even the venereally diseased who resists treatment—these people are a menace to any community, and those who would injure or entice children are likewise criminal. But to place such elements in one general category with homosexuals, calling them sex variants or deviates, and then to extend this category to include men and women, both married and unmarried, who enjoy sexual pleasures in a variety of ways, is to becloud the very real issue of sexual criminality and to injure the possibilities of effective handling of that problem. And when the state of Oregon makes it a felony, punishable by one to fifteen years in the state penitentiary, for any person "to sustain osculatory relations with (in plain English, to kiss) the private parts of any man, woman or child," the absurdity of the statute makes law itself a laughing stock in the eyes of any intelligent person.

The homosexual is, unfortunately, in a position before the law where he cannot effectively fight back. The civil liberties groups show little interest, and their lawyers are loath to engage in such cases. Laws whose unconstitutionality is considered by many to be patent remain unchallenged because no one dares come forward with courage to issue such a challenge and take the consequences thereof.

The homosexual cannot stand up in court and say: "Your laws are behind the times. I cannot be ashamed of what I have done, but

only of those who have pried into my private life and arrested me."
Even if he were successful in his day in court, he would be exposing
himself to the blows that must fall on those who would drop the
mask. So that he goes into court and insists upon his innocence, plays
the hypocritical rôle forced upon him in self-protection, denounces
the "queers" and the "fairies," and brings character witnesses to prove
that he is too fine a person to do such a terrible thing! How degrading
to have to play the comedy of the courts and to pretend to share the
world's contempt for that which one secretly aspires to defend.

Another aspect of homosexuality and the law that has gained wide
discussion, and that is as little understood by the public at large as is
sexual inversion generally, is the matter of blackmail. Most homosexuals live at least a semi-secret life and make some effort to conceal
their sexual leanings from business and personal associates. The public
thinks of these people as prey of the blackmailers, although blackmail
is as rare among homosexuals as is arrest for sodomy. One person of
my acquaintance, frightened lest a person he had met at a pick-up
might make a scene at his office, gave him a dollar on a couple of
occasions and then notified the police. The offender was arrested,
and the accuser was obliged to deny that there had been anything in
the way of "ugly intimacies" between them. The defendant, frightened, was given a suspended sentence, and there the blackmail effort
ended.

Blackmail, when reported to the police, can be effectively curtailed,
and inasmuch as the blackmailer will usually deny his guilt, it is not
difficult for the homosexual at the same time to protect his community position. A much more difficult situation arises, however, when
the blackmailer is a member of the police force. There are such large
numbers of corrupt policemen who victimize homosexuals that some
law-enforcement agencies actually have secret members entrusted
with the task of discovering extortion practiced by the officers of the
law. Usually a district attorney, particularly if approached by a lawyer, can handle the situation of the blackmailer-policeman with both
delicacy and efficiency.

The main area of the dispute between the homosexual and the law
centers around such offenses as are misdemeanors and may be covered
by "disorderly conduct" or some such similar statute. It involves two
people talking to each other on the street, and one inviting the other

to accompany him to his home or to a hotel; or it involves a similar conversation that may take place at a bar or in a park, or even in some semi-public place, such as a washroom. Then a badge is shown, and one of the persons is placed under arrest. Sometimes there is an exchange of five or ten dollars and the entire matter dropped at that point. Or the person is brought into court, perhaps held in jail overnight, and either fined or given a suspended sentence. His record is at that point blemished, and the arrest may become a permanent part of the police files. Obviously the person arrested is no threat to the community, was doing no harm, and, when he invited an adult stranger to share his bed, was transgressing no law necessary for the protection of society or of its component individuals.

In New York City, over a period of three years, 15,000 sex offenders charged with disorderly conduct were referred to a rehabilitation center conducted by the Quakers. Most of the 15,000 defendants were homosexuals, and their crime consisted in proposing a rendezvous to a stranger in a park or a bar, for example.

So long as these arrests take place, not only will there be petty corruption and bribery, but the homosexual will be followed by a constant fear that he may, at any moment, be placing himself in a trap. Thus the difficulties of a free and full life are compounded by the threat that even the marginal pleasures may be invaded by the police authorities, and this may bring about disgrace, disaster, ruin.

The repeal of the antiquated laws against homosexuality, with their frequent denial of civil and constitutional rights, would be a step in the direction of the communal rehabilitation of the homosexual so that he might find his place in modern society. However, it would be little more than one small step. It might aid in awakening the public to the absurdity of its extreme condemnation and thus serve to allay hostility. But the main problem would remain—public opprobrium. The pariah can take but small satisfaction from the fact that he is no longer a lawbreaker. The homosexual's chief concern is neither with civil rights nor with legal rights, important as these are. His is the problem of condemnation, which involves the necessity for concealment, imposes a burden of self-doubt and self-guilt, and creates a condition which inhibits the struggle for amelioration.

Part Two

PSYCHOLOGY

Chapter 6

Looking Inward and Backward

A force that dominates a person's life so much as does the homosexual drive compels one to turn inward to answer the question of why he is what he is. Among some it may be intellectual curiosity; among others it may be in quest of a system of justifications, but all homosexuals feel that they are forced to seek the origins of their sexual temperaments. In most instances I find that it is in the moments of greatest anguish and despondency, when pity for a supposedly difficult lot in life seems to enshroud a person in darkness, that minds are turned to self-analysis. Thus the realities of life, particularly as a result of the relationship of man to society, imposes upon most homosexuals a personality both sharply introspective and essentially introverted.

The question of the origin of the homosexual drive in the individual has in recent years attracted more honest analysis, more forthright examination, than any other aspect of this problem. This is because the matter has been confined in the main to the professional psychiatrist and not to the legislator, moralist, or parent. Whether his postulations have been right or wrong, the psychiatrist has no reason to give other than an objective answer to this question.

By an unforeseen coincidence that was fortunate for science, the findings of psychiatrists were acceptable to society at large, because they seemed to fit into the pattern of social hostility. Society at large seized upon the evidence that sexual inversion is not congenital; the psychiatrists did not encounter popular resistance to their contention, although many other conclusions of the same psychiatrists were ignored when society found it convenient to do so.

Unfortunately, little is being heard from the subjects themselves as to their attitudes toward the various theories of homosexual genesis.

Experiences as related to psychiatrists, and to a lesser extent church-men and other advisers, have of course provided the background material for the building up of a theory or group of theories. How-ever, I should like not only to present my analysis of these theories from the fresh point-of-view of the layman and the homosexual, but at the same time to examine the reasons that have prompted many to accept certain conclusions and have predisposed other people to reject them.

For a long time the idea of inborn or congenital homosexuality was widely accepted both by psychiatrists and sociologists on the one hand and by the practicing members of this sexual minority on the other. As clinical evidence, the allegedly widespread effeminacy among homosexual males and the corresponding masculinity in the Lesbian world were cited. It seemed that some individuals were indeed "mixed in the making"—that they were born, so to speak, as females in a male body or vice versa.

Before the validity of the viewpoint of inborn homosexuality is examined, let it be emphasized that it was tenaciously expounded, despite evidence to the contrary, by homosexuals themselves. This was because, as a theory, it answered certain needs; it was, in short, a conclusion that they wanted to reach, whether supported by the facts or not. First, it was a justification for the attitude of helplessness. If his anomalous condition were inborn, the individual could believe in the impossibility of overcoming it without considering himself a weakling. Thus it closed the door on any effort which some people felt ought to be made to cross over to the path of the other world, for such a passage, if this were a congenital condition, seemed by the very nature of things outside the realm of the scientifically possible. Inas-much as most homosexuals are practically incapable of wishing to be cured, and since the very nature of homosexuality precludes a genuine effort to change, it provided a justification for the attitude of either self-acceptance or resignation.

Second, with the world imposing what for many amounted to an unbearable burden of guilt, the theory of inborn homosexuality served as an exoneration. It placed the entire blame for tabooed activities on some force entirely outside a person's control, and the guilt which many carried for merely harboring desires, no less translating them into action, was easily assuaged under these circumstances. If this is what some people were born to be, then whether it be right or wrong, good or bad, it surely was not their fault—such was the reasoning.

In the third place, the theory of inborn predisposition answered effectively the argument that the pursuit of this forbidden love was unnatural. What could be more natural to an individual, a man would ask himself, than to pursue the life that he was created to live? What, on the contrary, is more unnatural than to try to force a change to a life entirely foreign to one's nature? In this manner a particularly strong epithet hurled against homosexualism—the charge that it was unnatural—could be successfully rebutted, if not ignored.

Finally, a fourth purpose was served by the belief in inbred homosexuality: it served as a prop to the theory, so prevalent at the turn of the century, that inverts constituted a third sex. They were neither males nor females, but an intermediate group having unusual talents, inclinations, and instincts derived from a special position between the sexes. The invert, according to this method of thinking, had a better understanding of women than had normal males; had a superior sense of form and enhanced proclivities for aesthetic appreciation. Certain writers claimed that in many respects he was a superior person, and this gave homosexuality a place in the scheme of things, a reason for being. Such reasoning, being a response to the group and individual degradation to which people were subject, answered the concept of inferiority with a contention, frequently obscure, of superiority.

In commenting on this belief in inborn homosexuality, Freud pointed out that homosexuals maintain that

> . . . they are men who are forced by organic determinants originating in the germ to find that pleasure in the man which they cannot feel in the woman. As much as one would wish to subscribe to their demands out of humane considerations one must nevertheless exercise reserve regarding their theories which were formulated without regard for the psychic genesis of homosexuality.*

In other words, although Freud found it a useful theory from the viewpoint of humane considerations for the invert, he went to considerable pains, in other works which will be cited presently, to demonstrate that it was scientifically invalid, and therefore untenable.

When, in later years, with the development of modern psycho-

---

* Sigmund Freud, *Leonardo da Vinci, a Psychosexual Study of an Infantile Reminiscence* (London: Kegan Paul, Trench, Trubner, 1932), p. 63.

analytic techniques, the psychiatrist began to look upon homosexuality as a manifestation of a neurotic condition, or as a case of arrested emotional development, the first reaction of the homosexual world was to reject this approach because it seemed to run counter to certain fundamental interests. We homosexuals did not want to look upon ourselves as being emotionally ill, unbalanced, immature, or as having adolescent fixations.

Thus the early approach of the homosexual to the problem of the origin of his condition was one of emotional involvement. There was a search for truth, but dominating this was the difficulty of achieving objectivity under the prevailing social and psychological conditions. Certain vested interests seemed to be served by arriving at a conclusion of inborn homosexuality, and they therefore were a deterrent to objective analysis.

However, the homosexuals were not alone in allowing personal interests to influence logic and reasoning, for the heterosexual world was no less guilty of this lack of objectivity. The out-group seized upon every shred of evidence, and suppressed and vilified any other, to show that homosexuality was a developed depravity found in adventurous individuals seeking new and pleasurable sins, in oversexed persons tired of the usual pleasures or denied them because of confinement, or in young people victimized by seduction before they had had an opportunity to mature. But the heterosexual who painted this portrait of homosexual origins was at a loss to explain the effeminate character of many inverts whose physical traits made them easily recognizable. To account for this phenomenon without endangering the theories of degeneracy that were required as part of the arsenal of argument against the minority way of life, some authorities asserted that there were two different types of homosexuals. There were, they conceded, the inborn, to whom some writers assigned the word *invert;* they were the intermediate sex, and they frequently, it was stated, displayed the physical traits and mannerisms of the opposite sex. The second type was the *pervert,* the man who could help himself but who was seeking a special thrill. Many years later, and persisting to this day, a new modification of the inborn homosexual theory appeared, an endocrinological approach, a belief that this entire drive consists of a glandular disturbance.

Thus both homosexuals and heterosexuals developed theories, not in order to seek the truth, but to support a conclusion which they sought to reach. If in some instances they reached the truth, it was only by accident or coincidence.

On the surface the most confusing aspect of this question for many investigators has been the manifestations of effeminacy in the male homosexual and of masculinity in the Lesbian. However, it is my confirmed belief, as well as that of all of the homosexuals with whom I have spoken, that the extremely effeminate homosexual is a rarity even in gay circles. I have been to parties at which forty or fifty persons let down their hair, unrestrained by conventions and inhibitions, and not a person there would have qualified for the appellation of queen, as the effeminate male is called. In the bar the effeminate man is rarely seen, and if he comes to mind immediately when the straight person thinks of the homosexual, it is because he is easily recognized and serves as a particularly convenient stereotype.

In place of the very effeminate, there is an abundance of homosexuals who show some slight signs that display a failure to identify themselves completely with their own sex. In my opinion, based upon close observation, the majority of homosexuals have some slight characteristic that will betray their inclinations to an astute and experienced observer: an unusual inflection of the voice, a movement of the hands or shoulders, a characteristic walk. The very small minority is the queen group, and another and perhaps larger minority displays no sign of homosexuality even to the most careful observer.

Between the queen and the slightly effeminate, there is a qualitative differentiation with many gradations and with no clear line of demarcation. And yet as I sit back at a party and watch the most obvious queen that I have seen in months, or as I observe another at the bar, I am struck by the lack of evidence of inborn homosexual traits.

To me, it is significant that there is a male's normal growth of hair on the face, no development of the breasts, no smallness of hands and feet. In short, the physical characteristics which would be difficult to influence through any emotional disturbance, or in response to any need of the individual, are unaffected.

Instead, there is the extremely effeminate voice, a conscious cultivation or an unconscious development. The gait, the movement of the shoulders, the methods of holding a cigarette or waving the hand, the comb of the hair, the shaping of the eyebrows—these are the signs of effeminacy, but each can be developed by anyone who finds it psychologically necessary to do so. As the queen talks, gesticulates, moves his limbs, he displays an effeminacy exaggerated beyond recognition. He is not a woman, but a caricature of a woman. He is more "swish" than any girl would ever be, and this is because his retreat from masculinity, his effort to identify himself with the opposite sex, is so strong that it has driven him in desperation to extreme methods. Because he cannot be a woman in breast and genital development, in the distribution of hair growth, he must prove with all the greater ardor that he is a woman in those respects not beyond control.

A prominent psychiatrist has come to this same conclusion, through a more systematic investigation. Allen writes:

> *We can state with confidence that there is no discernible difference between the physique of the homosexual and heterosexual by any tests, microscopical, macroscopical, biochemical, or endocrine of which we are aware at present.* As far as we can discover, it appears that the view of Wortis, which is that the homosexual appears effeminate because he wishes to look feminine, is the correct one and that there is no physical differentiation present in the average case.* (*Emphasis in original*)

Although the substance of his observations is correct, Allen exaggerates slightly when he contends that "there is no discernible difference between the physique of the homosexual and heterosexual." He refers only to the majority of homosexuals. There is a minority of males who were predisposed to physical effeminacy, and this predisposition was the important psychic factor in the genesis of homosexuality in these men. These cases are probably few in number; they represent the only exceptions I can imagine to the statement of Allen.

The small percentage of the extremely effeminate homosexuals, and the fact that their effeminacy affects only those bodily expressions and movements that are most easily influenced by emotional development, would indicate that this type provides no substantial proof of inbred homosexuality. As a matter of fact, not only are most homosexuals not effeminate, but many effeminate men are not homosexuals. Extreme effeminacy, often leading to transvestism, and sometimes linked with glandular disturbances, sometimes with homosexuality, in the opinion of many psychiatrists constitutes a separate neurosis, not

* Clifford Allen, *The Sexual Perversions and Abnormalities, a Study in the Psychology of Paraphilia* (2nd ed.; London and New York, Oxford University Press, 1949), p. 119.

to be confused with the drive for sexual gratification with one's own sex.

On the other hand, the widespread trend toward adolescent homosexual interests, frequently taking the form of somewhat innocent crushes, and perhaps resulting in some form of physical contact and excitation, has led to a theory of fixation. All humans, it is contended, travel through various stages of development, and during certain adolescent years tend to lose interest in the opposite sex, look upon intersexual friendships with some degree of abashment and shame, and draw closer to schoolmates, campmates, and others. The emotional development may be arrested during these years, it is said, and the homosexual stage "fixed" at the point through which a person is passing. A feeling of inferiority in relations with girls, a repugnance at the entire idea of sexuality for procreation as a result of the glorification of woman as a symbol of purity, a strong bond resulting in a satisfactory sexual union with a friend—these are but a few of many diverse influences which are reputed to result in this fixation.

The fixation theory, as I see it, likewise explains very little, and few individuals could search their own past, even with the aid of the psychiatrist as a guide, and be satisfied that fixation alone has offered a key to their lives. If fixation had any validity as a theory for the explanation of the origins of homosexuality, it would mean that gay people constitute a group of emotionally retarded and immature men and women. How can the many talents, the brilliant minds, the mature personalities be explained? Perhaps, the advocates of fixation reply, these individuals may be immature in certain respects, and fully adult in others. Such generalizations are rather meaningless, because it would be difficult to find the individual who would qualify for the characterization of true and complete maturity. Where is the yardstick by which maturation is measured? Temper is considered by some a roadsign of immaturity, but no one can argue that homosexuals as a group are more hot-tempered than those who are sexual conformists. Daydreaming and living in the clouds are said by some to be adolescent manifestations, but they can be characteristics of a poet or an inventor, and of people of all sexual temperaments.

There is not only little experimental evidence to substantiate fixation as a cause of homosexuality, but there is good reason to reject it. If the sexual temperament were arrested at one stage of its development, then not only the sex of the love-object, but its age, and appearance, should remain unchanged through the years. It is true that some homosexuals (like some heterosexuals) continue to be attracted to a young person long after they themselves have matured, but this is not only uncommon, but it is very likely due to the greater physical perfection of the youngster. The man of forty or fifty who imagines erotic delight with a girl but half his age cannot be said to have a fixation.

If the homosexual who finds delights with a young person is suffering from a fixation, then how can we account for his partner, who responds to a man many years his senior?

Most homosexuals I have known, however, are little interested and hardly aroused in the presence of immature boys. They were attracted to adolescents when they were in their teens, and the love-objects that seemed elderly when they were young appeared very attractive when they were somewhat older.

If psychiatrists were able to mingle with homosexuals socially, rather than clinically, they would, in my opinion, find it necessary to relinquish the theory of fixation!

The crucial question is to determine what experiences predispose certain individuals and not others to follow the unorthodox path of sexual desires. Whatever these experiences were, they must certainly have been of amazing strength, to have counteracted the cumulative influences of history, school, literature, poetry, cinema, home life, and the countless other cultural forces that suggest and in fact insist upon the heterosexual life. Anyone who pretends that induction of a youth into the pleasures of homosexualism at an early age can, in and of itself, result in his becoming gay, has very weak evidence to substantiate that viewpoint. Why did he become gay, although half a dozen of his friends who participated in similar adolescent play did not have similar sexual development thereafter? But, more significant, why should the one act make a homosexual out of a person after thirteen or fourteen years of suggestion and cultural influence have failed to make a heterosexual out of him?

What are these predisposing influences? In all my discussions with homosexuals—including those who are attracted exclusively or predominantly to the same sex—one observation has been almost universal, and that is the lack of a well-balanced home, where the mother and father displayed affection for each other and for the child. Broken homes, divorces, early deaths, frigid parents, unequal love—one pattern or another can be found in almost every instance.

And yet, with one-third of all American marriages said to end in divorce and with a certain number of deaths of one parent or the other at an early age, how is it that homosexuality is not almost as common as the heterosexual drive? How is it that in the same family, and even among twins subjected to extremely similar conditions of upbringing, there will be the most dissimilar developments? Doubtless the answer lies in the fact that the omnipresent drive toward the culturally acceptable life is so strong that it becomes dominant in most children, overcoming the individual family influences and personal relationships that lead to the homosexual path.

As far as I can gather from observation and study, the homosexual desire seems in most cases to be implanted in those who develop an unusually strong attachment for one parent, or a complete identification with one parent, or a feeling of replacing a parent who is either absent or inadequate. On occasion, an older brother or sister can be substituted for the parent in this situation, but in any event the affection, identification, or replacement leads to an unconscious and tabooed physical desire, resulting in a block against heterosexualism. Incest— and its repression—would be the key to homosexual origins. The strong taboo not only against incest but particularly against the desire for incest, and the conflict surrounding the Oedipus complex, impose upon the child a need for the strongest possible repression of the sexual drive toward the forbidden person. And in the realm of the hidden self, this is accomplished with the greatest effectiveness by a flight from all persons of the forbidden sex.

Numerous personal histories could be related to illustrate the mechanism of this process. Joseph's mother was an austere woman, a club-going career type who found the ordinary humdrum activities in the home too dull for her active mind. A few moments a day was all she could devote to her son, who had the benefit of governesses, nursemaids, and nurseries well stocked with toys. Joseph looked to his father with affection, and when he began to perceive that his idol had turned his attention away from the home and toward other women, Joseph sought in his childish fantasies to recapture him. He would be for his father what his mother had failed to become. In his immature and groping mind, and in the innermost depths of his troubled childhood, he wished to be a woman, so that his father could find completeness in the home and so that his mother's failures would be compensated. Above all, Joseph, yearning for the warmth that his mother could not offer, would ingratiate himself all the more into his father's heart by being his only love. The one person who could offer him the affection he desired would thus belong exclusively to him.

The physical attraction of a man for a woman meant frigidity, unresponsiveness, rejection. Only by taking a man for a lover could Joseph ever find the meaning of love. And in this union he would become, from an emotional viewpoint, the woman.

Joseph developed effeminate traits as a child, shunned athletics and competitive sports, felt that he could not be like other boys. He feared to compete with boys, withdrew from them because they called him "sissy." Perhaps, he thought, he was like a girl.

Yes, I know Joseph. He is reticent, though not bitter, and I have had to piece together his story from many sources. He speaks in soft tones, makes one suspect without being sure, and lives happily with a man a few years his senior. They share their lives, their funds, and their fun; call each other, somewhat in jest, husband and wife; and invite me every Christmas to their anniversary party. But, greatest irony of all, Joseph was seeking his father, and in choosing the path which he unconsciously felt would lead thereto, he lost forever the one thing which he most cherished.

Today Joseph finds men attractive and exciting; in the depths of his unconsciousness they may be symbols of his father. Women leave him cold; they are all his mother. He is little concerned, however, that this was because his mother was frigid and that his present indifference is a protective coating to prevent his ever being hurt as a lover the way he once was as a son. At Christmas time, as I see him put his arm around his mate's shoulder and watch their warm caress, I do not stop to consider that he is really loving a father-substitute. Save to an analyst, this is of no account. New pleasurable pursuits become an end in themselves—not the means toward the end.

Perhaps more typical than Joseph's experience was that of Harvey. The only child of divorced parents, Harvey found his mother's warmth the sole happy consolation of a desolate childhood. She lavished upon him kisses and affection, cared dotingly for his every need. In his fifth and sixth years he complained of nightmares—perhaps imagined—in order that he might sleep with her for the night. Then, his face hidden in her warm bosom, his sobbings would die down as she pressed him closer and he drifted off to sleep. When he was seven years of age, Harvey's mother remarried, and although in later life he could speak of his stepfather as having been kind, intelligent, and sincere, at the time he felt a fundamental resentment. An intruder had entered the home in which he had lived alone with mother, and deeply within himself the little boy who was then Harvey felt that this man had taken his place. Now there could be no sleeping with mother, and affection would have to be shared with a stranger.

In the aloneness of the divorcee's home, Harvey had sought to be husband and lover, not merely son. Within the workings of his little mind, women were already mother to him; to love a woman was to love, desire, covet one's own mother. In the first sexual awakenings, the idea of heterosexuality had a deep repugnance for him; it was vile and dirty; it represented the tabooed love of mother on the one hand and the stepfather intruding into that love on the other.

The sexual drive, blocked from the woman's path, sought its only natural outlet, and Harvey, a strong and athletic boy without any trace of girlishness in him, was aroused by other young men. With them he preferred to play the male rôle, although in the caresses and affections he would become excited toward greater mutuality and more active participation in all forms of lovemaking.

Yes, I know Harvey very well; he talks of his problem and analyzes himself; he could tell you the story I have just related, and he would even add: "How ironic that I should have become a man-lover because within me I harbored so strong and overpowering an early sexual desire for a woman!"

Harvey has had many lovers, boasts of his conquests, and seeks new loves after he has finished with the old. "Do I want the unattainable," he asked me one day, "or am I running away from a specter that pursues me?"

It seems to me that the most significant thing about the stories of Harvey, Joseph, and many more, is their substantiation of the contention of William James, Freud, and others, that the human animal is born with a sexual drive that is directed toward excitement, gratification, and release, toward warmth and love and security, toward the pleasures and excitation of carnal contact. Out of childhood influences, loves, and failures, out of the impact of history and culture, most people find one major sexual path partially or entirely blocked, and the other becomes the main or sole one to travel. Under the influence of home, church, school, and society at large, most adult individuals are able to be directed exclusively toward the opposite sex. An overwhelming repugnance consumes them when they are confronted with the idea of sexual union with their own sex, and the repugnance is an indication that they have repressed and are running away from the homosexual side of their characters.

This bisexuality of the human animal, which is important for an understanding of the incidence of homosexuality and for an evaluation of the hostility of society, was recognized even in the pre-Freudian era. William James, in his classic work on psychology, found that most people have the germ of bisexuality. Basically, instinctually, and naturally—the psychoanalysts have shown—men and women are all bisexual, but most people have fled from one pathway or the other. Under the influence of intoxication the suppressed side of a person's nature frequently comes forward. In my own experience I have seen it come out through a very strong affection for one individual. The natural bisexuality of all people makes explicable the fact that childhood influences can bring out homosexual traits, for the latter could not have developed were they not present in a germinal form. This bisexual start explains why so many adults have had homosexual experiences as adolescents; why such a large percentage of heterosexuals have homosexual experiences in the armed forces, in prisons, and in other places where women are absent, rather than resort to continence, masturbation, or some other form of sexual outlet. Natural and instinctive bisexuality to a large extent explains the repugnance rather than the indifference which the normal person feels about one man making love to another—although other factors are involved in the development of this repugnance. Finally, the natural bisexuality is one method of accounting for the vestige of heterosexual desires usually manifest in gay men and women—although it actually proves only that these people are repressed or latent bisexuals.

The endocrinological approach, which is predicated upon a glandular disorder, seems to be on very shoddy foundation. By the very law of averages, if homosexuality is as widespread as contended, then a certain percentage of those who suffer from gland trouble or hormone deficiencies should be gay. Elementary observation would indicate that such cases are rare. Not only are most "glandular cases" not homosexual, but extremely few homosexuals have glandular disturbances. If an individual whose glandular disorder caused him to be effeminate should, during the course of his development, prove to be homosexual, this rare occurrence would not prove that the glandular condition caused the sexual one. It might possibly be coincidental, but more likely the effeminate traits produced a psychologcial condition in which homosexuality thrived. There is no evidence in the medical literature, to my knowledge, that hormone injections, surgery, or other therapeutic measures involving the glands have ever made a straight person out of a gay one.

This was emphasized in Dr. Clifford Allen's recent erudite study on sexual behavior:

> Kinsey has demolished the assumptions of the endocrinologists . . . We are reluctantly driven to the conclusion that there is, so far, no evidence upon which any reliance can be placed that there is any endocrine difference between "normal" and homosexual. This is in accordance with the clinical finding that castration does not cause a man to be homosexual, nor does it even, in all cases, cause cessation of heterosexual intercourse. Moreover, injection of female hormones fails to make a man behave homosexually if he has previously been normal.*

Now and then one runs across a statement that homosexuality may be hereditary. In 1950 a letter from a physician appeared in the *Journal of the American Medical Association*. The doctor was baffled by a case of homosexuality; he had known the young man's parents and grandparents and had seen no history that would indicate that homosexuality runs in this family. Such a physician is naïve, and his remarks can only serve to indicate the poverty-stricken status of the knowledge of this subject among men of the medical profession. The *Journal*, rightly and categorically, commented that this condition is not hereditary.†

Inasmuch as there is a lesser percentage of marriage and of offspring among homosexuals than among others in the population, an hereditary trait, by the laws of natural selection and evolution, would die

---

* Clifford Allen, *op. cit.*, p. 118.
† *Journal of the American Medical Association*, December 23, 1950, p. 1536.

out in due course. Or it would become more and more rare as time goes on.

Once in a while a case of several homosexuals in a single family is cited. Peter Ilyich Tchaikowsky, his brother, and his nephew were all homosexuals. Among my own acquaintances I know identical twins who, in fact, look so much alike that a person who has been extremely intimate with one is likely to greet the other on the street. I have been told of brothers who were separated in childhood and met again years later, only to discover that they were both gay.

These cases, in the first place, are extremely rare. Most inverts of whom I have knowledge come from families in which they are the only ones so constituted. By the law of averages, even on the basis of coincidence, there would be two or even three in a given family in one case out of several hundred, if this sexual inclination is as common as is now believed. But in all likelihood there is more than coincidence in these stories. The identical twins were brought up under exactly the same conditions, as were Tchaikowsky and his brother; and the brothers separated in their childhood were both subjected to an abnormal family situation by reason of such separation. It is likely that none of these cases would, if analyzed, give evidence of either a congenital or an hereditary predisposition.

The causes of homosexualism seem to be complex, and often several factors influence the same individual. One cause may aggravate another. Difficult though it be to make generalizations, I nevertheless feel that there are some patterns that are to be seen, with individual modifications, in numerous cases. And these I shall enumerate, giving priority where I find greater importance, either because of the strength of influence on the individual or the relative frequency in the group:

1. Unbalanced love of a boy for his mother, reaching heights of physical desire from which there is a subsequent flight.

2. Effort of a boy to replace his father because of the latter's absence, death, or inadequacy, with all heterosexual love representing the love for his mother.

3. Identification of a boy with his mother, resulting in an effort to be like her in every respect.

4. Lack of love from the mother, or loss of mother, with the boy seeking to play the rôle of wife and lover in the psychic relationship with the father.

5. Faulty sexual education, with horrors of sex painted in lurid colors, and the entire thought of sex unable to be linked with love between man and woman.

6. The idolization of woman as something clean, immaculate, pure, to remain untouched and unsullied by a desire that is a vice.

7. Predisposition to effeminacy or to physical weaknesses, with subsequent withdrawal from competition with males; fear of competition with other boys on a physical basis, translated in later years to fear of competition for women.

8. Identification of the boy with girls because of effeminate characteristics which may have been inborn or developed as a result of one of the aforementioned causes.

9. Introduction to successful homosexual pursuits during adolescent years.

Many of these factors can be changed to be related to Lesbians, with other causes entering as well: rebellion against the position of woman in society, the search for power and domination, the fear of pregnancy.

The observations made here constitute a modification, but not a rejection, of the traditional concept of Freud, who wrote:

> In all the cases examined we have ascertained that the later inverts go through in their childhood a phase of very intense but short-lived fixation on the woman (usually on the mother) and after overcoming it they identify themselves with the woman and take themselves as the sexual object; that is, proceeding on a narcissistic basis, they look for young men resembling themselves in persons whom they wish to love as their mother loved them.*

In commenting on the above quotation, Dr. G. V. Hamilton stated:

> To this observation I would add that such fixations are almost without exception demonstrably due to the eroticism of "the woman" in her treatment of the future invert. The incestuous aggressiveness of this kind of mother love leaves her male child no alternative to homosexuality but incest. He must either go on surrendering to his mother as love object or defensively direct his sexual impulses away from femaleness in general.†

In my own observations, I have encountered several cases of homo-

---

* Sigmund Freud, *Three Contributions to the Theory of Sex* (4th ed.; New York: Nervous and Mental Disease Monographs, 1948), p. 10.
† G. V. Hamilton: "Homosexuality as a Defense Against Incest." *Encyclopaedia Sexualis*, edited by Victor Robinson (New York: Dingwall-Rock, Ltd., 1936), p. 334.

sexuality in a family where there was extreme frigidity in the mother and a strong father-son love. While the viewpoint espoused by Freud and Hamilton would seem to be the most common in the study of case histories, the opposite cannot be excluded, and the simultaneous influence of other factors should likewise be considered.

This is confirmed by Professor Allen, who points out that males who are hostile to the mother also develop homosexuality. "The type who has persistent hatred, sometimes for good reasons, for the mother finds it difficult to approach women."*

In fact Allen seems to have come closest to briefly summarizing a psychoanalyst's professional observations in a manner that coincides with my own observations as layman and homosexual. Stating his belief that homosexuality can be caused in one of several ways, Allen lists these as follows:

1. Hostility to the mother.
2. Excessive affection for the mother.⎫
3. Hostility to the father.   ⎬ Oedipus complex
                                        ⎭
4. Affection for the father when the father himself does not show sufficient heterosexual traits; introjection of an abnormal father.†

Nevertheless Allen oversimplifies the dynamics of a father-son relationship leading to inversion, particularly in his fourth point. Allen's contribution is that he recognizes a multiplicity of factors causing homosexuality, but his reduction to four points, of which the last is quite unimportant, and the first three quite general, leaves much to be desired. Finally, he fails, like others, to grasp the plurality of causes in a single individual.

To return to Freud before concluding: the father of psychoanalysis did not exclude father-love as a cause of male homosexuality, but probably interpreted it in terms of craving for an absent mother-affection:

> It may be assumed that in the man the infantile memories of the mother's tenderness, as well as other females who cared for him as a child, energetically assist in directing his (sexual) selection to the woman . . . the frequency of inversion in the present-day nobility is probably explained by their employment of male servants, and by the scant care that mothers of that class give to their children.‡

* Allen, *op. cit.*, p. 128.
† *Ibid.*, p. 127.
‡ Freud, *op. cit.*, p. 86.

This passage would seem to be in contradiction to the previous quotation from Freud, but the two are understandable either as relating to two different types of homosexual development, or Freud may have intended to convey the thought that the children of mothers who give "scant care" to their offspring, in their craving for the maternal love denied them, find their desires for the denied mother love reaching the tabooed incestuous heights.

In the earlier passage, Freud mentioned narcissism, or self-love. Many find in the myth of Narcissus the key to sexual inversion. That all human beings have a great deal of love for self is quite evident and perhaps may be a clue to the behavior of the human being toward children. There is little indication, however, that homosexuals are more narcissistic than other people. If homosexuals look "for young men resembling themselves in persons they want to love," then how can we account for the infatuations between men of various races and colors; men separated by twenty or thirty years of age; men of effeminate characteristics attracted to the very masculine types, and vice versa? All of these situations are extremely common among homosexuals. In fact it would be difficult to find a group of people who search less than do homosexuals "for young men resembling themselves in persons they want to love."

Chapter 7

Is Our Number Legion?

An estimate of the extent of homosexualism in the American community is interesting, although difficult to obtain for several reasons. It is a number important to jurists, legislators, psychologists, educators, and, as we shall presently demonstrate, it is a number which is vital to the homosexual himself.

The obvious reason for the difficulty of arriving at a reasonable estimate of the extent of homosexualism is to be found in the nature of the customs which inflict upon the homosexual a sense of shame and make it advantageous for him to refrain from disclosing his identity as a member of the group. In fact, so strong is the pressure to hide one's predilections that, even in the presence of a self-avowed homosexual, another will continue the pretense, either from habit or for fear of the results of disclosure.

Occasionally one hears a rough estimate given by an educator, a physician, or perhaps a priest, who may believe that an unusual position offers a vantage point from which confidential information is obtainable without reluctance. This is, of course, not the case. Most homosexuals of my acquaintance would not, for example, confide in a physician, despite the promise of secrecy surrounding the profession. The fear of being considered in a despised position, of belonging to an outcast group, is overwhelmng, and the invert prefers either to ignore the matter or deliberately to mislead the would-be confidant.

Inasmuch as the Selective Service System, whereby every young American regardless of physical condition was examined for military service, charted a very large section of the male population, it was thought that a clue to the percentage of homosexualism might be obtained therefrom. The fear of physical danger or violent death, and

the generally advantageous position of the civilian over the soldier
or sailor, made literally millions of young men prefer to remain out
of the armed forces; and homosexual inclinations provided an easy
method of avoiding service to those who sought to remain in civilian
life. Stories that reached the ears of the homosexual civilian, telling
of courts-martial and prison inflicted on friends who were convicted
of sex crimes, served to frighten others from joining the service. This
reluctance to become a soldier or sailor, which was rather widespread
during World War II, and the keen eye of the psychiatrist who interviewed each man, would combine, many thought, to provide a percentage figure disclosing the amount of sexual inversion in the population. But just the opposite was the case.

In the first place, many homosexuals wanted to enter the armed
services and did so—some for the same reasons as did the heterosexual
youths, because they were Americans who wanted to join the struggle
against a grave threat to civilization; others, because they feared the
loneliness of the civilian and the stigma of being civilian when so many
others were wearing uniforms; still others wished to reorientate themselves in a new milieu and looked to the services as a means of plunging
into such a program; a few, perhaps, found in the armed forces a
justification of their own full manhood which they had been forced
to doubt; and some thought of the armed services as being the gateway
to a new gay life.

Most homosexuals therefore deliberately refrained from disclosing
their tendencies when interviewed, and it need hardly be reiterated
that the psychiatrists were capable of detecting only a very few of
the so-called obvious types. Men who had been successfully practicing
concealment from families, employers, friends, and others for many
years did not find it difficult to continue the deception even before the
eyes of a more discerning psychiatrist for a period of five or ten
minutes. Furthermore, a certain percentage of homosexuals—probably
in proportion to their total number—were disqualified for other
reasons such as physical ailments, essential war work, or such, and
therefore there is no record of their sexually inverted temperaments.
Then, too, many of the psychiatrists had sufficient understanding of
the problems of the homosexual in society to wish to avoid mentioning
any such tendencies in a permanent record. I am personally familiar
with several instances in which another cause for rejection was

recorded as the official one, although homosexualism was the actual reason.

The records of the armed forces are, therefore, of little value and can only be misleading. It would be very simple for me to point out, in a few large cities, a considerable number of avowed homosexual youths who were at one time in uniform and who received honorable discharges, as well as several others who were rejected for reasons other than sex. As a matter of fact, a group of homosexual veterans formed a national organization, with branches functioning in at least three cities, under the guise of a veterans' fraternal or benevolent association.

But the advantages to be found in the pretense and the ease with which the pretense is maintained are not the only factors that make almost insurmountable a census report on homosexuality. The basic difficulty is in defining the word. If I were to take a group of twenty-five of my friends, and even if I were completely aware of all phases of their lives and all facets of their desires, I should not find it simple to place them in hard and fast categories of homosexuals, bisexuals (a group at one time almost completely ignored), and heterosexuals.

What is a homosexual? It would seem elementary and almost beyond discussion that without such a definition, a quantitative estimate of the homosexual group in the total population could not be obtained. To cite an analogy, in order to determine that there are some fifteen million American Negroes, or some five million American Jews, these terms must be defined. For example, the word "American" for these purposes refers to the continental U.S.A., the word "Negro" includes all those of known or visible Negro ancestry, no matter how slight, and the word "Jew" includes all those of at least one-half Jewish parentage, regardless of belief. Thus "Negro" includes mulatto, "Jew" includes Jewish atheist. These terms provide boundaries against which individuals can be counted and estimates made for margin of error, for exaggeration, or for omission.

Can the homosexual be defined? It is important to remember that Kinsey and his collaborators defined, not the individual, but his activity. Many people have utilized the extent of activity as an index of the extent of the individuals, although it was never the intention of Kinsey to confuse the two. The married man who feels the strongest urge for sexual gratification with another male, but who,

either because of self-imposed choice, prudence, or lack of opportunity, has his total gratification with his wife, would be classified
by Kinsey, at this period of the man's life, as a heterosexual. But this
word describes only his activity; it does not penetrate into the man
himself. A prisoner, on the other hand, who is capable of some
elementary fulfillment (or perhaps, more correctly, release) with a
male companion, but who nevertheless craves a woman, finds himself
classified with the completely homosexual group at this stage of his
life.

Both of these cases may be extreme, but they merely emphasize by
exaggeration a very general condition: namely, that the degree of
desire and the amount of gratification may not be at all in direct
ratio to each other. Marriage, companionship, prison, naval or army
life, financial or other considerations, and religious scruples may
result in greater frequency of outlet in one direction despite greater
desire in the other. In fact the frequency of outlet may be almost
exclusively in a single direction and the burning needs in the other.
Such cases are by no means rare.

In any critique of the first volume of the Kinsey study, it should
be stressed that he and his colleagues were compiling data on the
sexual *activities*, and not sexual *inclinations*, of the white American
male, and that the interpreters of Kinsey have tended to becloud the
very real differences between these two factors, although their inter-
relationship is undeniable.

Previous to the disclosure of the Kinsey report, there had been
several efforts, based on rather haphazard and unsystematic work, to
estimate the extent of the homosexual temperament in the total population, both of America and other countries. The general feeling
among the mass of people was that the homosexual was a rarity; that
he was, perhaps, one in a thousand, if not even less. The error of
such estimates was three-fold in derivation. It came about from the
advantage of the pretense, the almost complete ignorance of bisexuality, and finally from the ease of recognition of the obvious invert, who
became the stereotype concept and, although a rare individual, gave
the world at large the idea that he was typical.

If the heterosexual was in complete ignorance concerning the
widespread nature of activities and tendencies which were, by and
large, repugnant to him, and if he harbored an illusion, to which he

was very pleased to cling, that "the queer" was a rare bird, the homosexual himself was quite aware of the commonness of his inclinations. The rapidity with which homosexuals recognize one another could only be contrasted with their success in remaining unrecognized by those outside the group. The diverse ramifications of the group life, the important places in culture, industry, society, sports, literature, arts, and wherever one would turn, in which homosexuals were found, gave the homosexuals a growing awareness of the size of their circles. And, finally, those who entered the armed services returned with reports of homosexual tendencies and bisexual activities so widespread that only their absence in any representative group could be considered phenomenal.

"Everybody on my ship was at least a little gay, and most of them more than a little," an ensign on a cruiser whose normal complement was not at all small told me.

"Everybody?" I asked rather incredulously.

He laughed. "Well, Don, at least half," he answered, and then quickly added, "and I ought to know."

Traveling within a small group, walking into those bars where the minority congregates, always keeping our eyes on the lookout for signs of recognition, remembering so carefully every little news story, every suggestion in the newspaper, every word of gossip, it would naturally seem to us inverts that our numbers are enormous. And, fully aware of how large are the numbers who hide, how successful is their effort to conceal, how virile and masculine they appear to the outsider, we understand the source of the errors that have been made in the past in estimating the incidence of sexual inversion.

It has been noted by Kinsey that many homosexuals report that literally all men are, to a certain extent at least, of sexually inverted tendency, and he contends that this obviously fallacious concept arises from the advances of promiscuous individuals who find ready reception wherever they attempt to utilize their wiles and charms. These people, however, Kinsey correctly points out, make their advances only among those most likely to give them a favorable reception. Moreover, the homosexual is impressed by the prevalence of tendencies similar to his own that he finds where others fail to discover it; furthermore, he can with great ease overlook or dismiss the individuals whose affinity to his nature he cannot discover. He has had several experiences in which people demonstrated the gay side of their nature to him either at a period of adolescence, or in a state of semi-intoxication, and then completely forgot it, denied it, banished it to the untouchable recesses of the unconscious (as illustrated in *Stranger in the Land* and *The City and the Pillar*). These various factors, plus the desire on the part of the homosexual to find his type wherever he turns, the comfort he takes in the feeling that his numbers are large, convince him that some degree of homosexuality is present in practically all human beings.

Strangely enough, the invert who is so convinced seldom draws the obvious conclusion: that some degree of heterosexuality must also be present in all individuals. On the contrary, with great indignation he will frequently deny that there is any element of heterosexuality in his make-up.

Can the homosexual be accurately defined, in the sense of a limiting definition which will on the one side include all those properly encompassed by the term, yet exclude the remainder of the population? For purposes of understanding this problem, I would call any person a homosexual who feels a most urgent sexual desire which is in the main directed toward gratification with the same sex. There are several important factors in such a definition. It deals with those who harbor the desire, and not necessarily with those who obtain gratification. Therein lies the great difference between such a point of measurement and that of Kinsey. The Kinsey measurements, of inestimable value as they are, concern only the amount of fulfillment, and although most people seek to fulfill their needs to the extent that their desires impel them toward one sex or the other, many extraneous factors of a social, legal, or other nature are involved. It was never Kinsey's intention to confuse the degree of gratification with the degree of desire.

It will be noted that, like Kinsey, I regard the physiological nature of the sexual companion as the determining factor, and not the character of the relationship. It is absurd to speak of a man and wife as having "homosexual" or even "homo-type" relationships, although latent homosexuality or substitution for such may well be a propelling force in determining that these acts take place. And in the same way, it is impossible, from the viewpoint of psychologist or sociologist, not to say legislator or educator, to view the man who is playing a so-called "male-type" rôle as participating in a heterosexual relationship, when he has a male partner. The only interest such a characterization has for the psychologist is that it throws light on the specific peculiarities of the mind of the individual who is attracted to a relationship but is forced to create an entire superstructure of unrealities to delude himself about its true nature.

In this definition, finally, the main desire, and not the exclusive one is stressed, and therein lies an area of agreement with Kinsey and other workers. No measurement of homosexuality can be made without finding some method of characterizing the so-called bisexuals, and particularly those whose primary interests lie in the homosexual direction.

The widespread nature of bisexual activity and its preponderance even among those who are essentially homosexual were not the discoveries of Kinsey. They had been commented on many times, were part of written history and of both medical and popular literature, and constituted the most common yet least understood phenomena of the entire homosexual question. European authorities often estimated that the population contained twice as many partial homosexuals as complete homosexuals.

It remained for Kinsey to break these facts down into a system which shall be summarized here—a system which, despite its statistical value, has in my opinion limited validity for the purpose of measurement of homosexuals as such. In the Kinsey work, an arbitrary division of the population was made, whereby all individuals were grouped according to the amount of homosexual activity in their lives. The groups were numbered from 0 to 6. At the poles, 0 and 6, were found those whose activities were exclusively heterosexual or homosexual, respectively. Group 1 contained these overwhelmingly heterosexual in outlet, but with a small amount of the homosexual; group 2, more heterosexual than homosexual; group 3, equally divided in activity; group 4, activity more with the same than with the opposite sex; group 5, predominantly but not exclusively with the same sex; and, finally, group 6, the exclusive homosexuals.*

It is clear that there are no rules enabling sharp lines of demarcation to be drawn between such groups. Whereas previous estimates of

* Alfred C. Kinsey, Wardell B. Pomeroy, and Clyde E. Martin, *Sexual Behavior in the Human Male* (Philadelphia: W. B. Saunders Co., 1948), Chapter 21, "Homosexual Outlets," pp. 610 *et seq.*

homosexuality had ranged from about 5 to 10 per cent of the male population, Kinsey shocked America and, as he states, shocked himself with a revelation that more than a third of the total male population had had some homosexual experience, leading to orgasm, after the onset of adolescence. About 50 per cent of the men who remain single until they are thirty-five years of age have had some such experience, and approximately one-third of all males go through a three-year period at some time after the onset of adolescence during which they have "at least incidental homosexual experience or reactions." Approximately one out of every four males has "more than incidental homosexual experience or reactions" for a similar three-year period of time. About 10 per cent of the male population are "more or less exclusively homosexual" for at least a three-year period; 8 per cent exclusively homosexual for such a period; and 4 per cent exclusively so for their entire lives.

I should like to emphasize that Kinsey did not fail to grasp the differences between desire and activity. He is keenly aware of such differences, but his statistical findings which are so frequently quoted refer only to activity. He observed

> . . . that the rating which an individual receives has a dual basis. It takes into account the overt sexual experience and/or the psychosexual reactions. In the majority of instances the two aspects of the history parallel, but sometimes they are not in accord. In the latter case, the rating of an individual must be based upon an evaluation of the relative importance of the overt and the psychic in his history.*

Placing individuals on the 0 to 6 rating scale, he came to the conclusions that, at the age of thirty, the total United States white population, including single, married, and post-marital histories, would indicate that 83.1 per cent of the males rate 0, which would indicate no overt or psychological homosexual activities. Continuing on the scale, 4.0 per cent rate 1; 3.4 per cent are in group 2; 2.1 per cent, group 3; 3.0 per cent, group 4; 1.3 per cent, group 5; and 2.6 per cent, group 6. This would indicate that about 6.9 per cent of the male population at the age of thirty is primarily homosexual (groups 4 to 6). If we reduce the age to twenty, the figure rises to 11.2 per cent.†

* Kinsey *et al., op. cit.,* p. 647.
† *Ibid.,* p. 651.

The Kinsey report was a bombshell to the American populace. There was an immediate effort to disprove the validity of the findings because these findings were distasteful to a large number of people.

"It is characteristic of human nature," Sigmund Freud had written sometime before, "to be inclined to regard anything which is disagreeable as untrue, and then without much difficulty to find arguments against it."* The prejudices of the American public were brought into play, and the people sought desperately to believe that these figures were absurd, ridiculous, and fallacious. Thus an army of statisticians, psychologists, and sociologists came down upon the Kinsey report, seeking to find error therein rather than to evaluate it with objectivity.

A barrage of criticism, directed particularly at his findings on homosexuality, greeted Kinsey, but there was very little in his statistical work to challenge. The method was above reproach. It took into account memory failures, deliberate lying, exaggerative bravado, fear, shame, self-protection. Furthermore, an entire group of checks, both on individuals and on percentage results, was made to determine whether the former were accurate and the latter typical.

Despite the remarkable cross-checking of Kinsey, and despite the advantages that the homosexual group can obtain from his disclosures, some minor reservations should be made. It would seem that in any community, school, or other group, where a voluntary partial sample of the population was taken, those few who volunteered for the Kinsey interview would by their very nature be non-typical. They would include more than an average share of people having sex problems which they wished to discuss, whether they be the proud or the ashamed or the exhibitionistic-minded. Whereas such an interview might bring forth the homosexual in a classroom more quickly than his schoolmate, it would also inhibit a certain number of inverts who always fear discussions and disclosures, no matter how intimate or confidential. These two factors, in my opinion, would probably not balance each other out. It is my experience that the homosexuals are more anxious, not less so, to volunteer for such discussions.

The large amount of activity on the part of individuals who have at least one, and usually more than one, sexual experience with both

---

* *A General Introduction to Psychoanalysis* (Garden City, N. Y.: Garden City Pub. Co., 1938), p. 368.

sexes, calls for further clarification of the bisexual phenomenon. It should be emphasized that many of those who have had a certain amount of experience in both directions are not at all bisexual. *"Even I* once had an affair with a woman," said B., who in these words expressed the absurdity of considering this a manifestation of bisexuality.

Despite Kinsey's seven groups (the 0 to 6 system), many people still persist in perpetuating the rather meaningless oversimplification of individuals into three categories: namely hetero-, homo-, and bisexual. Some writers have preferred to consider that all those capable of homosexual experiences are either "neurotic" or "normal" homosexuals. The former consists of people who have had a psychological background which produced either a block against the heterosexual way of life, or a flight from it; the latter would encompass individuals capable of homosexual gratification, but not to the exclusion of other forms of sexual pleasure. The very terminology is unfortunate, for it remains to be proved that there is anything neurotic about the preference for one's own sex, and the word itself has an unpleasant connotation implying a disease or a disorder. Without excluding such a possibility, it should not become a part of a definition and hence prejudice any investigator in this field.

The concept of neurotic and normal homosexuality, further, makes the bisexual study quite difficult. It offers no key to the degree of preference for each sex by the "normal homosexual," nor to the successful completion of heterosexual relations over long periods of time by the neurotic. In other words, does the normal actually desire his own sex, or is he merely capable of obtaining pleasure from it? Does he desire both sexes? As for the neurotic, are all heterosexual relationships impossible for him? These are but a few questions unanswered by the proposed terminology.

From both a psychological and a sociological viewpoint, a more useful classification would consider all individuals participating in activities of this type, or desiring to do so, as either compulsive or facultative homosexuals. The former find an urgent drive, or a compulsion, for this type of gratification. The latter are capable of enjoying it, but do not find it absolutely essential to the pursuit of their lives. To confuse the two groups is disastrous; the mere fact, for example, that a facultative homosexual relinquishes his male sex partners with ease does not offer any evidence that the same can or should be done by all of those partners. I am primarily concerned in this book and in my studies of the subject with the compulsive homosexual and the problems of his relationships with himself, with society, and with his friends, family, and lovers. In certain instances, his problems are similar to those of the facultative homosexual, but for the most part they are of a widely divergent nature. As a matter of fact, the facultative homosexual may be a contradiction in terms, for if a person has a faculty for accepting or rejecting these relationships, he should probably not be termed a homosexual of any kind or type.

Of great interest in the past has been the division of homosexuals into the "passive" and "active" types. Here, again, the division is artificial and the language misleading. The choice of the two words in question is poor, because the partner playing a "female-type" rôle in a physical act is at the same time the "active" person from a homosexual viewpoint but the "passive" partner in the sexual act; and the opposite is likewise true. If this confusing area is put aside, and it is agreed that the words refer only to the "homosexually active" (who may be, and often is, "sexually passive"), then only one objection has been answered. A few homosexuals must, out of a compulsion, an inhibition, or a preference of some other nature, always be the passive, others always the active, but most cross the border at will. In fact, the line of demarcation is nonexistent. It is a figment of the imagination. Two people in sensual interplay enjoy activities of all types, flowing from active to passive with ease, being the former at one moment, the latter at another, and then both simultaneously; or playing an active rôle one night, a passive another; or active with one partner, less so with a second, passive with a third.

I am not at this moment concerned to any great extent with the prevalence of Lesbianism. Many homosexuals have noted, however, that their female counterparts are fewer in number, and I have pondered over this observation. Whether it will be borne out in the future works of Kinsey and his associates, I do not know; at the moment, the relative scarcity of female homosexuals can be accounted for in several ways, some of which center around the contention that the observation is itself an illusion. Women, it is said, dance together in public, go arm in arm to the theater, do not hesitate to kiss each other—so that these socially acceptable conventions are used to hide Lesbian activities. Women go into the armed services, bob their hair like men, wear tailored clothes and even slacks without arousing the suspicions of the community.

The assertion is made by others that the homosexually-inclined women make less "display" of themselves, do not gather with frequency at the bars or even at gay parties, and therefore are little seen except by those who are part of their intimate group.

This would not account for the fact that there are few such women even within the intimate group, and that such women's groups are themselves relatively small and confined.

If Lesbianism is less prevalent than male homosexuality, an explanation may be found in *Corydon*, in which Gide maintained that homosexuality was nature's outlet for the excess of sexual drive in the male animal. If this excess actually exists, as seems to be the case, then it would manifest itself in the infant, and since a highly developed infant sexuality is in many cases a prerequisite for the homosexual impulse in later life, then it would be developed mainly in the males, among whom are found the most intense sexual drives during infancy. Incidentally, the most severe objection made by Dr. Beach to the entire thesis of Gide is that it failed to account for the widespread nature of female homosexuality; but since Lesbianism is relatively rare, rather than relatively frequent (as compared to inversion among males), Beach's objection is quite invalid.

If, furthermore, homosexuality is considered, as the Freudians contend, a development of a strong over-attachment or fondness toward the parent of the opposite sex, then it can readily be seen that this would be a more frequent phenomenon in modern society between mother and son than father and daughter. The mother is the constant companion, nurse, caretaker, from the moment of birth; for several years the child is seldom out of her sight, and if there is an enforced absence, there has been built up an intense longing to come together again. The father, in a society which is economically patriarchal but socially matriarchal, goes to work, fondles the child for a few minutes on his return, and repeats the pattern the following day. Though there may be an equality of affection toward the child from both parents, there is a greater and deeper display of it from the mother.

Because of the relatively weaker sexual urge in women, the female who is repelled by the heterosexual relationship can, and frequently does, take refuge in an outlet that is largely denied to the male, namely frigidity. The imperious nature of the male's sexual drive excludes this pathway as an alternative choice.

In summary, there can thus be three concurrent forces that have an additive effect in producing greater male homosexuality: the stronger infantile sexuality, the nature of the parental relationships, and the female's retreat into frigidity. Lesbianism may, of course, be caused by other factors: the search for power, the expression of dominance, the fear of pregnancy; but male homosexuality can likewise arise from a variety of causes.

I am personally convinced, based exclusively on my own observations and experiences, and without any statistical studies or research to substantiate me, that the homosexual males (counted by my definition of main and compulsive desires) outnumber the Lesbians by about three or four to one. I am aware that this runs directly counter to the observations made by a number of outstanding scientists and clinical observers. I can only report that their theories have no relationship to the facts, and that their subjects for observation have been pathetically atypical.

Some of my homosexual friends assert that the males outnumber the females by as much as ten to one, and I believe that the source of their error lies in the relative infrequency of promiscuity in the female circles, a question to which I shall return in another part of this book. If a group of people are frequently "on the make," if they are seeking partners (and different partners) night after night, then they will be in apparent or visible circulation, and it will seem that they are more numerous than is actually the case. The Lesbians do not fit this picture as much as do the gay men, and therefore they appear to be even less numerous than they actually are.

It is frequently stated that homosexuality is on the increase. Why are statements of this type made, without any basis in scientific inquiry? Are people who contend that inversion is spreading actually seeking a justification for a new wave of repression on the basis that leniency has created fertile ground for the germination of this impulse? Or are they fulminating against the morals and mores of modern society in all its manifestations, against modernism in philosophy, art, literature—and sex? Or are they on a crusade against atheism, heresy, communism, or democracy—whatever may be the opposition—and seeking to link the spread of disapproved sexual mores with an opposing philosophy?

"I tell myself that people have always lied when customs have forced people to lie, and, nothing authorizing me to believe Sodom more populated today than it was yesterday, I become somewhat suspicious in regard to some of our ancient authors," comments André Gide.*

A brief history of the rôle of the homosexual in former eras will convince a reader that this form of life has not been indigenous to one country nor particularly prevalent at one time. It was widely known and practiced at all times and in all lands, but commented on more frequently and practiced with less secrecy at certain times.

"Male homosexuality has certainly been prevalent in this country (England) since the time of the Norman Conquest," writes an English barrister in commenting upon the trials of Oscar Wilde. ". . . In spite of the severe penalties to which those practising it were liable, homosexuality continued to flourish in the eighteenth century."†

As a matter of fact the self-same comments, often expressed with indignation, about the current spread of homosexual practices were made by observers in almost every previous era. The prediction was made by a fictional character created by Smollett in the mid-years of the eighteenth century that in all probability "homosexuality . . . will become in a short time a more fashionable device than simple fornication." Today, two centuries later, the prediction has not yet proved true, yet it is still being repeated. If such observations had been accurate, then we homosexuals would no longer be a numerical minority.

The conclusion seems indisputable that people are today more aware of the existence of homosexuality because of a growing revolt against the oppressive taboos and against the conspiracy of silence. There is every reason to believe, based on a study of history, that in former times the impulse toward and, in all likelihood, the gratification of homosexual love were as prevalent as today. This conclusion is

* André Gide. *The Journals* (New York: Alfred A. Knopf, 1949), III, 86.
† H. Montgomery Hyde, editor, *The Trials of Oscar Wilde* (London: William Hodge, 1948) pp. 375 and 379.

verified by the findings of Kinsey to the effect that the frequencies of homosexual gratification of twenty years ago were not unlike those of our day.

Considering the differences between the counting of homosexual activities and of homosexuals; the extreme difficulties of defining a homosexual; the inhibitions and fears that prevent a true count— we must be satisfied with the vague and rather approximate figures of scientists who have offered estimates. These range from 1 or 2 per cent of the population (for the exclusively inverted, males only) up to 8 or 10 per cent. The estimates will seem conservative rather than large to those of us who are "in the life."

Actually, the exact figure on prevalence of homosexuality is only of academic interest. The significant factor is that such a figure is amazingly large. Two per cent of the male population past the age of sixteen, for instance, would, in the United States alone, mean one million men, to which a large number of women must be added! But the 2 per cent is extremely low; if the still conservative estimate of 5 per cent is taken, then the three million mark is reached!

What is the significance of these figures? First, some people have called for a revision of our sex laws exclusively because of the number of people who are "criminals" under the wording of such laws. Yet prevalence, in and of itself, is not a socially desirable reason for recognition of a mode of action. Race hatred is extremely prevalent in many parts of the world, including the United States; that does not make it good, moral, righteous, or legally recognizable. And if murder were practiced by increasing numbers of people who espouse a lawless way of life, that would hardly be reason for judicial recognition. The practice of homosexuality is prevalent; but less so than the practice of anti-homosexual discrimination. If numerical occurrence alone is to be the justification for institutionalizing an action into the customs and laws of the country, then this would be an even stronger argument against the homosexual than for him.

The social and legal attitudes, which I have described, are to be justified, explained, or condemned apart from the irrelevant factor of the number of people involved. Those who say that if the laws against homosexuality were enforced, there would not be prisons enough to hold all those who should be arrested, are hardly giving a rational argument against those laws. If the same were true of robbery, would these people call for the legalization of the act of stealing?

Is there, then, no significance at all to be found in the tremendous number of homosexuals? On the contrary, the imposing figures present to dominant society, and to every heterosexual in that group, a frightening prospect. One out of five, or ten, or even twenty! Every thinking person must realize that his brother, his child or unborn grandchild may be one of this large group who is being cast out. Everyone who expresses condemnation must feel uneasy that there may be homosexuals among the closest friends, in the home, or in the family. I have heard people say in the presence of several of my gay friends that they do not know a single homosexual, so rare is the species! This is typical of the innocent ignorance of a great many persons.

The large number of homosexuals has another impact, perhaps more important than the first. It offers to every gay person a sense of relief in the knowledge that he harbors impulses shared by millions of his fellowmen. In the depths of his depression, this sense of potential solidarity with a large segment of humankind is a source of strength. He may have known many others like himself, but he had not thought in terms of millions. For if he is base and vile and his practices are unnatural, then these terms must be applied to an amazingly large minority of the human race. In short, to think in terms of millions is to relieve the burden of believing oneself to be a "freak of nature."

Finally, a minority involving millions of people in the United States presents problems which must be answered. Millions cannot be excluded from government and private employment, from participation in the armed forces, from educational opportunities, without creating a social problem of major dimensions. If there were a thousand homosexuals in America, it would not be more justifiable to exclude them from the privilege of becoming government employees, but there would be no major economic repercussions of such exclusion. If three million people are unassimilable into the economic life of the country, then that is a matter of deep concern for every American.

In the millions who are silent and submerged, I see a potential, a reservoir of protest, a hope for a portion of mankind. And in my knowledge that our number is legion, I raise my head high and proclaim that we, the voiceless millions, are human beings, entitled to breathe the fresh air and enjoy, with all humanity, the pleasures of life and love on God's green earth.

Chapter 8

Individuals and Stereotypes

Each group in a society is made up of individuals who in most respects are as different from each other as they are from other human beings. When similarities are found, whether of a physical or psychological nature, they may be due to the very nature of the situation which established a number of people as a group; or may be brought about by the impact of a relationship with other and usually dominant forces; or they may be imagined by others as a group trait, a creation either of ignorance or of thinking in terms of stereotypes.

Homosexuals constitute a group in which the variation from one individual to the next is as great as in the world at large. There are certain mental characteristics, emotional traits, and ways of life that may, however, be found more frequently among inverts than others, whereas there are some manners and mannerisms generally attributed to homosexuals, yet encountered no more frequently among them than in the entire populace.

A few examples come to mind. The male homosexual is effeminate: the picture of the "fairy" and the female impersonator, the transvestist at the drag. It is my belief, as expressed in the section of this book devoted to the genesis and incidence of inversion, that this effeminacy is psychologically induced and that it is found to a marked extent only in a small proportion of homosexuals. Actually the effeminate invert usually forms a subgroup within the group, for he is *persona non grata* among the more virile. "I am no better than they are," a homosexual of the virile type will say, "but I just couldn't afford to be seen in their company." If a homosexual must wear the mask, he cannot associate with those who have discarded it. For the "ambisextrous" men, the effeminate people, on the fringe of a fringe of society, as it were, play a rôle which is neither recognized nor appreciated. The lack of suspicion surrounding most homosexuals in their daily lives, which makes it so easy for them to carry their masks and conceal their activities, can be attributed to man's common illusion that all male homosexuals are recognizable at first glance.

Another concept common to the general population, yet having only the slightest relationship to reality, is that all homosexuals are alcoholics. In recent years the general realization that parts of the homosexual society choose to gather at gay bars has strengthened in the public's mind the association of alcoholism with homosexuality. Actually only a small proportion of gay people are seen at these bars, and then they like to take one or two slow beers over a couple of hours while they talk, make new acquaintances, look around with desiring curiosity, and listen to the latest popular music.

Now and then, one will encounter a homosexual who is an habitual drunkard, but he is rare, and there is not one whom I know who is so fond of his liquor that he is incompetent to shoulder his responsibilities. The gay individual who takes to the bottle is one of those few who become hopelessly defeated and seek an outlet in which sorrows can be forgotten. He is running away, constantly fleeing from a specter that pursues him, and he fears the life he must face in his sober moments. He is more frequently the repressed than the overt homosexual, and in the efforts to bolster his repression he takes refuge in alcohol. Intoxication is his flight from a feared reality. This is, in our estimation, the only meaning of the portrait of Don Birnam made by Charles Jackson in *The Lost Weekend*.

Why is homosexuality so frequently associated in the public mind with intoxication, if there is no foundation for this relationship in fact? First, because the public likes to seize upon any hostile trait, no matter how far-fetched, and believes it to be characteristic of an entire group to which it is hostile. The public at large perpetuates, by the concept of ugly racial stereotypes, the lies about races: the Negro is dirty, the Jew is a usurer, the Irishman is a drunkard, the Scotsman is stingy, the Italian is addicted to crimes of passion, and on and on *ad nauseum*. Having known, heard about, or read about a

single homosexual alcoholic, people are willing and anxious to believe
that all homosexuals are drunkards.

To separate the fact from the fiction, it is almost unnecessary to
reiterate that most homosexuals are not alcoholics. However, it is not
quite so easy to state that most alcoholics are not homosexuals. Alcoholism seems, in many people, to lower the barriers of convention,
to bring out the repressed, to find crude expression for the sublimated.
Under such circumstances, many people, with little or no conscious
tendency toward the invert's way of life or mode of love, will find
themselves not only assenting to seductive advances, but even seeking
outlets for a male-directed impulse.

How shall we account for the fact that physicians, psychiatrists,
social workers, sociologists, penologists, jurists, and others have so
frequently reported that homosexuals are alcoholics? Only by
virtue of the fact that they have little or no contact with the "normal
homosexual." Their contact is with the individual who has become
mentally or emotionally ill, or who is in distress. They do not know,
or cannot realize, that for each such person, there are a hundred
or a thousand others who will never find need for a psychiatrist, and
who will never be brought before the judge or fall into the hands
of the penologist.

The extreme ignorance of the viewpoint of those who have
gathered their information from a restricted group of atypical people
is illustrated by Samuel Kahn, who compiled his data as a prison
official, and who wrote: "Most homosexuals are drug addicts, but
most drug addicts are not homosexuals. As a rule the male and
female homosexuals begin their addiction either at twenty years
of age or before."*

Another fiction: the homosexual is a depressed, dejected person,
frequently on the brink of suicide, or actually ending his hopeless
life after many years of despondent struggle. This portrait is
probably further from the truth than any other, and to some extent
its wide acceptance may be attributed to the novelists who have
ended so many books on this subject in a mood of despair, violence,
and even suicide. *The City and the Pillar, The Fall of Valor, The
Sling and the Arrow, The Invisible Glass, Stranger in the Land,*

---

* Samuel Kahn, *Mentality and Homosexuality* (Boston: Meador Publishing Co.,
1937), p. 52.

Special Friendships, Twilight Men, and *Finistère*—among many others —all end with hopelessness for the invert. Several of these books bring the invert to self-destruction; the others leave him no other path to follow.

Few suicides are homosexuals, and few homesexuals commit suicide. Perhaps homosexuals are so accustomed to the slings and the arrows of a life in which they have been buffeted from one difficulty to another that they find it easy to accept a philosophical approach to the torments of human existence. Never having a day or a moment completely free from the burdens of life, they become immune to its most dreadful moments and do not succumb to the lure of self-imposed finality.

Those who cannot conceive of homosexuality except in terms of human tragedy should read the opening lines of the autobiography of Hans Christian Andersen:

> My life is a lovely story, happy and full of incident. If, when I was a boy, a good fairy had met me and said, "Choose now thy own course through life, and the objective for which thou wilt strive, and then, according to the development of thy mind, and as reason requires, I will guide and defend thee to its attainment," my fate could not, even then, have been directed more happily, more prudently, or better. The history of my life will say to the world what it says to me—There is a loving God, who directs all things for the best.*

One would have to search diligently in order to find a more cheerful summation of life in the entire literature of autobiography than was given by this great Danish homosexual writer.

So much for the fiction about homosexuals. What of the facts? Is there a psychology of the homosexual group, a red thread of continuity flowing through the entire group, characteristic of most of its adherents yet unlike that of the outer world? I believe that there is, in the sense that all of the cultural values of the invert are conditioned by his sexuality and its relationship to society; but the nature of these values, their forms and the responses thereto, may differ as much among homosexuals as in any other section of the population. This may appear paradoxical, but it is quite explicable.

Let us take, for example, the psychology of homosexuals in their

---

* Hans Christian Andersen, *The True Story of My Life* (New York: The American-Scandinavian Foundation, 1926), p. 1.

attitude toward religion. It would be impossible to say that homosexuals, as a group, are pious or irreligious, orthodox or reformist.
These people are found in every religious group, among the most and
least orthodox, in families of preachers and of non-believers. There
is no religious group—unless its entire culture is different from that
of the modern Judeo-Christianity—that has fewer homosexuals in
proportion to the total number of adherents, and therefore none that
has more. Upon maturity, when many men and women decide the
extent of piety and faith which they choose to practice, there are
many inverts—just as there are many people generally—who become
devout in the religion of their birth or of their choice, while others
turn their backs upon religion and become militant atheists or indifferent skeptics. These roads are diametrically divergent. What makes
the homosexual different from the man who does not share his problems is that these irreconcilable paths owe their origin to a common
factor: the individual's sexual temperament.

For some homosexuals, faith in God is the last refuge and the only
home. "The Lord made me, and He alone can understand me," a
prominent actor said to me. "Where else can I turn in my bleak
moments except to God and to His Son? Where can I find the strength
to continue my struggle, and the belief in myself that I need so
desperately when I have sinned, except in my church?"

This man is not alone in turning to religion. I have known at least
two preachers who were homosexuals and who found great consolation in their prayers and meditations, and it is claimed by Moll and
others that several popes were inverts. Homosexuality is said to have
flourished in monasteries for centuries, according to many writers,
and the attraction of two male youths for each other, in an atmosphere
of religious devotion, has been beautifully depicted by Roger Peyrefitte in *Special Friendships*, and by Hermann Hesse in *Narzisse und
Goldmund*. There are convincing passages in *The Well of Loneliness* that depict the religious faith of the invert.

There are two men in their thirties with whom I have been friendly
for several years. When Ernest was in the hospital, Michael went to
church each day to pray for his lover's recovery. He prayed to the
Lord Who, he said, would surely hear his voice, and he prayed in a
church which frowned upon the very love which he sought, through
prayer, to be able to continue. I sat at Ernest's bedside, and Michael

said, "I prayed that I might have you home with me soon, and that is why you are getting along so well." And Ernest smiled and said, "I find something beautiful about your calling on God for help to accomplish something that His emissaries consider a sin."

For many inverts, religion, despite its organized resistance to their way of life, offers the answer to the problem of conscience. "God would not have made me what I am if it were wrong," they say, and therefore the religious belief is necessary to their happy state of mind. But other inverts rebel against all organized religion. They have been thrown out of the Temples of the Lord, and they denounce the Temples. They see religion as their historic enemy, the leader of the taboo, the organizer of suppression, the creator of hypocritical standards of morality in which they can find no place and no peace. They embrace the cause of the anti-religionists. There is nothing for them, they say, in God's scheme of things, and hence they not only reject His scheme, but denounce it as a man-made myth. "You make love all Saturday night and then go to church bleary-eyed Sunday morning!" they scoff.

These people associate with each other, live together, love together —pious, agnostic, and atheist. How can one say that there is a unity among them on the religious issue? Only in this sense, that their homosexuality is the chief factor in fashioning their attitudes toward this aspect of our culture. And the same could be said of their attitudes toward literature, law, politics, and other phases of life.

If there is any characteristic of homosexual life that has been instrumental in the development of homogenous group traits, it is probably the pretense and the mask. Millions of people could not possibly live through each day of the year, concealing, pretending, deliberately lying, without reacting in similar manner.

For one thing, most homosexuals have a highly developed cunning, an ability to grapple with difficult situations in a sly manner, to improvise, think quickly, react on the spur of the moment. At any time, they may be called upon to cover up, deny, retrace footsteps; and alert minds have been forced to accept a training for this exercise. The homosexual must become an actor, playing a rôle that he does not live, reciting not only lines that have been well learned, but lines which the actor has actually written.

All of this develops in many—and I exempt those who openly

proclaim their sexual natures—a facility for the utilization of false-hood. The use of the lie is literally forced upon the pretending homo-sexual, and as a result he often develops a contempt for the truth, an inability to distinguish between fact and fiction, between reality and pretense, a predilection for extending the lie to other phases of his life, a justification of falsehood as a tool in the struggle of living.

Another disconcerting aspect of the impact of homosexuality on the behavior of the individual is found in the widespread instability that characterizes gay life. It is not only that many go from love to love, but seem to flounder hopelessly in a search for direction in education, in preparation for a career, in holding a job, in organizing a sound financial and social life. Under these circumstances it is all the more amazing that so many outstanding men of science, art, industry, and public life should have made their mark in society.

More, perhaps, than those of his brother, the interests of the invert are short-lived. His cultural loves are likely to be as fickle as his physical ones. His entire life seems motivated by restlessness and characterized by rootlessness.

In school, many of the gay graduate with the highest honors—when they graduate. Their educational mortality rates are abnor-mally high, despite excellent scholarship and unquestioned ability. Between the ages of twenty and thirty, a disproportionately high per-centage are traveling from job to job, from school to school, or from school to job, dissatisfied, untrained yet able, knowing not what they seek, but constantly seeking. They lack guidance, even more so than do other youths. The parent, the older brother, or the teacher, because they would look with horror upon a revelation of the youths' sexual lives, cannot gain their confidence even in matters far removed from sexuality.

But, more than that, there ceaselessly permeates through the entire personality of these youthful inverts a restless urge to find a more satisfactory solution for the problems of life. Wherever they may turn, whatever they may start to study or learn, life seems to be short of its promise and meaning. Somewhere else, in another land, another school, another city, on another job, in another career, perhaps greener grass will grow. Perfection in love-mates, in career, or in any other phase of life, always is just out of reach, almost within the grasp. A little movement, a mere change of course or twist of fate, ever so slight, should bring it within striking distance, they reason. On and on they search, drift, change, seldom stopping to sink roots or to build a lasting edifice on a durable foundation.

In most respects the inhabitants of the world of Sodom are not more like each other than they are like those in the other or hostile world. Some are calm and some are hot-tempered; many are selfish and avaricious; others are sacrificing and selfless. In their pursuits of interests, in their idiosyncracies, each is an individual unto himself. Generalizations about them are usually wrong.

Nevertheless, all live a life that has certain features in common. They face the same humiliations and rebuffs, have similar qualms and self-doubts, wonder in like manner as to the origins of their personality traits. So great an experience in common has brought forward similarity of reaction. From the hearts and minds of many people, there have come determination to struggle, sympathy for the lot of others unjustly vilified, compassion for fellowmen in all plights and circumstances.

Out of great handicaps come great sources of strength. How this mechanism operates in the homosexual personality and how it manifests itself for personal and social benefit form the subject of another section of this book.

Part Three

PATTERNS

Chapter 9

Take My Word For It

The special language created by a minority group may have several purposes. It can be aimed at making unintelligible to others that which is perfectly understandable to a few; it may have a more or less euphemistic aim, softening the blows carried by certain words, although expressing their meanings; and it may seek to be descriptive in a colorful manner.

The language of homosexual life has in it an element of cant—the keeping in secrecy from the out-group that which is clear to the in-group; it has the argot that is characteristic of any trade or profession; the slang that is on the fringe of our language just as the homosexuals are on the fringe of society; the euphemisms and their counterpart from which they grew, the hostile words and expressions. It is a language similar in some respects to that of the underworld; in others, to that of the theater; and finally, it is suggestive of the language of a professional minority, such as the physicians. Actually the two phases of the special language of homosexuality—the words and phrases used by the world at large, and those employed by the inner circle—are almost unrelated to each other.

There are two broad characteristics of what I should like to call the homosexual "cantargot": first, that it has failed to develop in the natural way because of the conspiracy of silence in which the subject is enshrouded; secondly, that in the connotations, pro and con, that are implied by special words, the cantargot is remarkably suggestive of that of the racial, religious, and national minorities of the United States.

How widespread is the silence and how far-reaching its effects are indicated by the fact that even the scientific terminology is frequently absent from otherwise complete and authoritative dictionaries; and that even the authorities cannot agree on the meanings that should be assigned to such words as *homosexual, invert, pederast,* and *sodomist.*

As for the connotations of special words, the homosexual is sensitively aware of the stigma attached not only to his practices and desires, but to terms associated therewith, and he seeks to create or to utilize synonyms with a more agreeable connotation. Sometimes the outside world is hardly cognizant of the origin of a term it is employing, nor of the aura of ill-feeling that it will engender. The majority will use words like *wop, chink,* or *boogie* with no conscious malice, believing them to be nothing but descriptive, and ignorant of their deep and hurtful meanings. Even more subtle are the reasons that certain terms become unacceptable. For example, *Negress* and *Jewess* are no longer respectable words, although no one would object to the terms *Negro* or *Jew.*

The homosexual in America has been described by people in society at large by various words and phrases, each of which usually carried a sneering connotation. Best known among these words are *fairy, pansy, nancy* or *nance, Mary, sissy* or *sis* (sometimes *sister*), *fag* or *faggot, queen* (an important variation being *fish-queen*), *queer, homo, c——r, freak, fruit* (he is *a fruit* or he is *fruity*), *man-lover* or *boy-lover,* and on occasion a *Wildeman.* In England, and in legal and some other circles in the United States, *bugger* has been in frequent usage, and the practice called *buggery.* My English friends tell me that in England the word *bugger* has an extremely hostile connotation, comparable to the worst terms used in the United States.

The female homosexual has been called, almost universally and with considerable acceptance, a *Lesbian,* sometimes (although rarely) a *Sapphist.* Sometimes *lady-lover* or *woman-lover* is heard. In the inner circles, the cantargot includes such terms for the Lesbian as *dike* (or *dyke*), *stud,* and *bull* (more frequently *bull-dagger*).

The homosexual feels that the many terms used for male inverts are all inadequate. First, they describe a stereotype, the effeminate male: *fairy, queen, sister, nance.* Secondly, those that did not originate as description of an effeminate person became that through the evolution of language and through association; an example is *pansy.* *Queer* is obviously unsuited, because of its typing of an individual's personality.

Many homosexuals are, in the totality of their lives, not queer people at all, and many heterosexuals are extremely queer. The word *queer*, in every other sense, leaving aside its colloquialism, has a tainted characterization about it that is unattractive, and therefore is to be shunned. The word *fag* is particularly humiliating. The evil that it carries can only be compared, as I see it, to some of the worst terms that America's dominant culture has used to humiliate and suppress racial groups. And, finally, the making of a slang synonym for almost anything or anyone nefarious, with no regard to his sexual inclination, of the term *c——r*, is comparable only to the hatred expressed by our society against out-of-wedlock children, who in addition to being characterized as illegitimate, are called *bastards*. Like *c——r*, the word *bastard* is used to describe anyone on whom contempt is heaped. In this way, an insulting connotation is implied in a word which, in its literal meaning, should merely describe the status or activity of a person.

It is a curiosity worth noting that in many lands the description of homosexuality has been associated with things foreign. The English word in common favor, *buggery*, is derived from *bougre*, which means *Bulgar*. A French book of the nineteenth century, whose title may perhaps have been inspired by the traditional Franco-German rivalries, was called, *Homosexualité, l'amour allemand*. Homosexuality, the German love! Indeed, at a time when France was becoming increasingly aware of the widespread nature of sexual inversion within her own confines. Certain of the forms of homosexual practices, and for that matter of heterosexual indulgences, namely fellatio and cunnilingus, are called in America *French love*, with the verb *to French* frequently used. *He Frenches* or *she likes to French* will be said, and almost any adult knows the meaning of these expressions. A homosexual is sometimes called *a Greek*, or more often *a Greek lover*, and homosexual friendship called *Greek love*. One of the many underworld synonyms for an active pederast is *turk*.

In conjuring up the Bulgar, the Frenchman, the German, the Greek, or the Turk (and, no doubt, there are other examples), the dominant heterosexual society has often sought to characterize homosexuality as foreign; seeks to associate it with immigrants and sometimes with enemies; and would therefore give the impression that it is not indigenous but rather un-American. It is ironical, but understandable, that the name of one nation that has been a traditional friend should have been employed; and of another whose civilization people are taught to admire and to emulate!

A minority group frequently reacts to the name-calling by similar activity against the majority. The homosexual, in inner-group language, is likely to call a heterosexual girl *a fish*, and a man who is attracted only to women is *butch*, but neither of these words is considered derogatory by those who use them.

For many years, homosexuals found a burning need for a language that would not have unpleasant connotations. The words must be free of the stereotype concepts, free likewise of hostility, and less cumbersome and heavy than such a word as *homosexual* itself. The language must be utilizable to describe all those sexually directed in their passions toward their own sex, regardless of virility or lack of it, regardless of the type or age of the person coveted, or of the character of the physical relationship entered into. It was in this spirit that Ulrichs, a German writer and civil servant, proposed that homosexuality be called *Uranism*, and the individual a *Uranian* or *urning*. Ulrichs found inspiration for his etymology in the planet Uranus, which, of all the planets visible to the naked eye, is furthest from the sun and therefore nearest to heaven; love for one's own sex was likewise the most heavenly of physical passions, he contended. The derivation, with its glorification, might have been overlooked, but the word had a particularly foreign flavor and never seems to have become popular in our tongue, despite rather widespread employment by Edward Carpenter and other glorifiers of homosexuality around the turn of the century.

Carpenter himself used other euphemisms. He liked to call homosexuals *the third sex* or *the intermediate sex*, but in these words, heavy and long, were scientific connotations unacceptable to the Freudians. Another writer, André Tellier, called his subjects *twilight men*, whereas Radclyffe Hall referred to inversion as the *no-man's land of sex*.

In the meantime the scientific terminology was rather obscure. Somehow the word *invert*, although quite acceptable, never became widely used within the group. Suffice it to say that its meaning is known, but it is seldom heard in conversation. Entirely unacceptable, on the other hand, is *pervert*, which brings forth the ugly picture of an elderly man accosting a child (the latter may be male or female, but the criminal inclination of the older man is described as a perversion). I have opened library books in which the homosexual is referred to as *pervert*, and in the margins are vehement notations: *No, invert—not pervert!* Many of my friends have expressed similar distaste for the word *deviate*, for they resent the repulsive grouping of homosexuals with all sexual nonconformists: the sadist, the child-molester, and others.

In most of the English-language literature, *invert* is used interchangeably with *homosexual*. It is Gide's contention*—and his opinion is shared by many—that *an invert* is an effeminate homosexual; he is the woman of the love-match seeking a man; his personality and sexuality, and some of his characteristics, are inverted, so to speak. The *pederast*, Gide maintains, is the lover of youth, the older man of the Greek man-boy relationship. The *sodomist* (or shall we say *sodomite?*) is the lover of the older man, the boy seeking maturity. Such lines of demarcation and absolute classifications are difficult to make and the arbitrary definitions are disputed both in the scientific and in the legal literature. In such writings, sodomy is usually not confined to homosexuality, and pederasty only to a certain type of physical relationship, which is usually of a homosexual character. At any rate scientific and popular, not to mention legal, confusions, and the removal of these words from the everyday language, combine to exclude them from serious consideration.

Needed for years was an ordinary, everyday, matter-of-fact word, that could express the concept of homosexuality without glorification or condemnation. It must have no odium of the effeminate stereotype about it. Such a word has long been in existence, and in recent years has grown in popularity. The word is *gay*.

How, when, and where this word originated, I am unable to say. I have been told by experts that it came from the French, and that in France as early as the sixteenth century the homosexual was called *gaie;* significantly enough, the feminine form was used to describe the male. The word made its way to England and America, and was used in print in some of the more pornographic literature soon after the First World War. Psychoanalysts have informed me that their homosexual patients were calling themselves *gay* in the nineteen-twenties, and certainly by the nineteen-thirties it was the most common word in use among homosexuals themselves. It was not until after Pearl

* André Gide: *The Journals* (New York: Alfred A. Knopf, 1948), II, 246.

Harbor that it became a magic by-word in practically every corner of the United States where homosexuals might gather, and in the decade following America's entry into the Second World War I find that it was used with increasing frequency not only by novelists, magazine writers, and gossip columnists, but even by radio announcers. And yet, even to this day, despite its decades (if not centuries) of use, it is practically unknown outside of homosexual circles, except for police officers, theatrical groups, and a few others. Mencken, in his studies of the American language, shows no indication of familiarity with the word, despite his going to some pains to mention several synonyms of secondary importance.

Gay . . . gay . . . gay! Life is gay, the party is gay, the bar is gay, the book is gay, the young man is gay—very gay—or, alas! he is not gay! "Look up my friend—he's gay" . . . "youth, gay and witty, seeks correspondent" . . . "did we have a gay weekend!"

Gay! The word serves many purposes. It is like the Z. of Tchaikowsky's diaries and letters, a secret code that will always be understood by some, never by others. "There was much Z.," Tchaikowsky wrote in his diary about a party he attended on April 23, 1884,* and the diarist of today would express it in almost the same words: "The party was so very gay!" Not only is correspondence quite safe from being understood in the event of interception, but even conversation can be held in which the homosexuals in a room use a language which they alone understand, but, unlike the situation prevailing were a foreign tongue being spoken, the others present are unaware of their ignorance.

Gay is simple and easy to say and free from the usual stigmas. Its usage has thus grown with great rapidity. A few homosexuals object to it, but for lack of a better term they, too, employ it. One of the most desirable purposes it serves is that it facilitates discarding the mask by offering a language free of odium. Thus, among homosexuals, the euphemism brings franker and fuller discussion. One seldom would hear it said: "At the age of thirteen, I realized that I was a *fairy*," nor would this be said substituting the word *queer*. One version might be: ". . . that I was a homosexual," but most frequently the word *gay* would be used.

The word serves as a signal, a sign of recognition. In a conversation

* The Diaries of Tchaikovsky (New York: W. W. Norton & Co., 1945), p. 27.

there is an exploration, a search to know whether the other is likewise hiding behind a mask. And then one person uses the word and awaits a response. The cue cannot be misunderstood.

The secretive and fraternity-like language has its dangers. The homosexual world is not completely isolated. The man who is planning to lure the homosexual in order to victimize him, to assault and to rob him, or to set a trap for blackmail, frequently employs the language of the group in order to allay fears. And the probation officer or detective, interrogating a suspect, uses the inner-group language likewise to trap:

"This man who you were out with tonight—you know he's gay?"

A denial brings a torrent of new questions: what do you understand by the question?—did you understand it to refer to his being queer? —how do you know that's what the word means?

Within homosexual circles, the use of the word is almost universal, but its acceptance is often with reluctance. Some object to its ambiguous meaning, which is precisely what the group has found most advantageous about it. An advertisement for a roommate can actually ask for a gay youth, but could not possibly call for a homosexual. Even *Lesbian* would be an impossible word to use in this connection, and hence the female inverts are beginning to use the word *gay*, although less frequently than the males. Those who contend that it is a distortion of the language, because many homosexuals are not gay in the traditional meaning of the word, whereas many heterosexuals certainly may be, are actually consistent, for they protested with equal indignation against the appellation *queer*. But a word like *gay* is manifold in its uses and is not so easily discarded.

Some of the usefulness of *gay* diminishes as its meaning becomes more widely understood. New and wider circles are constantly becoming familiar with the word, although the public at large, except for theatrical and artistic people, literary groups, bohemians, underworld characters, and police officers, are unaware of its slang meaning. However, as it becomes better known, its secret character, and the advantages derived therefrom, are to a certain extent vitiated.

Gay requires an antonym, and the antonym is *straight*. This, too, is widely known and used among homosexuals, and has thus become a magic password. The conversation at the bar between two strangers:

"I've been in this town for a week, and it's dull as hell."

"What's the matter—everybody you meet straight?"

The word in one sense is even more valuable than *gay*, in that its confinement to homosexuals has been so carefully guarded. There is hardly a homosexual in certain parts of the United States who does not know and use it, just as he knows and uses *gay*, but it is extremely rare to find it known among those people whom it is meant to describe.

But, in another sense, it has always been considered an unfortunate word, because it characterizes the heterosexual and, therefore, by implication, the homosexual. The former is straight; therefore the latter is not straight, he is crooked. *Straight* is the slang word for legal and moral correctness: *to go straight*. Hence the homosexual is not straight, does not go straight. This is euphemism in reverse. Instead of finding a mild and delicate word for something disagreeable, the homosexuals have found a manner of expression which, by implication, is harsh and indelicate for something which, to them, is quite agreeable.

Although *gay* is used throughout the United States and Canada, *straight* is hardly known on the West coast, except among those who have migrated from the East. In San Francisco, for example, the gay circles refer to other people as *jam:* "She's gay, but her husband's jam," a person will say. *Jam* is used in the East, but would hardly be considered an everyday word.

In fact, the geographical variations in the homosexual language are probably more severe than are to be found in most of the analogous slang, because of the lack of any volume of printed literature. The words cannot be used on the radio, and are seldom found in print. Visitors travelling from one part of the country to another find it impossible to introduce the slang of their native region, and soon begin to use the terms that are understood in their new surroundings.

It is characteristic of the special nature of the semantics of gay life that the peculiar usage of words in a given context is readily understandable even to those who have never before encountered them. A well-known novelist to whom I was introduced was exchanging questions and answers with me about my experiences. After I told him that I was married, he asked, "Does your wife know the facts of life?" I had never heard this cliché used in this particular connotation, but sensed immediately that *to know the facts of life* meant, for him, and for many others, as I was to discover, *to be aware of the homosexual stream of life.* A few weeks later I posed the same question to a friend who had asked me to look up a companion of his on my vacation. "Does he know the facts of life?" I queried, and he immediately replied as if my expression were an everyday one to him, although he later confessed that he had never before heard the words used in that particular sense. In similar manner, many other expressions might be cited which would be incomprehensible to the straight person, but immediately understood, on first usage, by the gay world.

Because there is no organized society of gay life, no recognized source of authority, no book of rules, no lexicons and lawmakers, no public press that gives permanent form to the language, there is considerable fluidity in the use of special expressions. Even spellings can differ. More than once I have received correspondence concerning *gae life*, although this struck me as an affectation until I realized that it was close to the French, *gaie*. But the expression *in the life* is used to mean, on the one hand, "being gay," or on the other, "living a gay life." If employed in the first sense, it would include the suppressed married person, but in its second sense only those who, in one form or another, give expression to their homosexuality. An everyday word in the gay life is *trade;* it is common for a person to refer to another as *trade*. "Out looking for trade tonight?" someone will jokingly ask; or, "There goes the best trade in town." To me, the word originally meant a young person who accepted money in return for sex. My friends are quite vehement in insisting, however, that *trade* is the person indulging only in certain types of physical homosexual relations—the meaning which seems to be prevalent at this time in the larger cities of the United States. And on inquiry I found one person who rejected both of these definitions. "If you and I should shack up for a one-night stand," he said, "then I would just be trade for you, and you would be trade for me."

One should not overlook the many expressions of a regional or national character, in addition to the sharp geographical differences on which I have already commented; and also the words used by hoboes, underworld men, and police, all of whom have special terms for homosexuals. Their expressions are seldom known and never used by the gay world itself. I learned from a book, for instance, that the British hoboes call the homosexual *a pouf*, but I have never heard this word in America. *The Dictionary of Underworld Lingo* makes a strong distinction between the active and passive pederast; for the former, such words as *daddy*, *joker*, and *wolf* are used, among others. The passive is defined by no less than sixty-eight different words or phrases, from *apple pie* to *works*. Most of these are unknown in homosexual circles (unless they may be known to homosexual criminals, a matter on which I am not competent to offer comment). Some of the words are most colorful: the passive pederast, caught in the act, has his *jeans at half mast*. In *The American Dictionary of Slang* I counted 174 synonyms for *homosexual*. Among these were some repetitions and some variations that consisted of slight changes in spelling. Most of the words were of infrequent usage: *agfay*, *lavender boy*, *mason*, *nola*, *queervert*. Although this book contains a supplement dated 1947, and although the underworld lingo book cited earlier was published in 1950, neither of them mentions the word *gay*, which for years has been the most common synonym for *homosexual* used by the homosexual.

Other words are of passing fancy, taking themselves from a song hit, a movie, or perhaps even a book of popular interest, or from the humorous allusions to sex that gay and straight people encounter in life. One evening I was invited to a gay bar that had been nicknamed *the snake pit;* while there, a companion to whom I was talking excused himself, saying that he had to go to *the advertising club*.

"In our particular theater of war," a veteran related to me, when we were discussing the terms used by and for gay people, "they were called *night-fighters*. It all started by their being called *night-cruisers*, but this became a little too obvious, and so it was changed to *night-prowlers*, and finally to *night-fighters*." Most veterans insist that they did not encounter this word in the service.

All in all, the homosexual groups do not create an entire and self-sufficient argot of their own, in the manner of the underworld, the jazz followers, and others. Their terms are few in number and are mainly confined to descriptions of their own activities. The bisexual companion is *ambisextrous*, the gay group is *the circle*, the masquerade ball is *a drag*, the transvestist is *dressed in drag*, to behave effeminately is *to camp*, the person who is effeminate is called *a camp*, his opposite number is *rough trade*, the obvious crotch is *the basket*, or sometimes *the canasta*, to look for a temporary love-mate is *to cruise*, and a partner whom one meets and never sees again is a *one-night stand*, while the middle-aged man still seeking a young lover is *an auntie*. A few of these terms, as one can see, are used in a similar sense by hetero-sexuals: *to cruise* and *a one-night stand*, for example. Some words have synonyms: *a camp* is also *a bitch;* but change the vowel, and one has the antonym, *a butch.*

Much of the resentment against individual words is due to the con-ditions under which they are spoken. In the mouth of a friend or a sympathizer, or particularly a member of the circle, the words lose much of the hostile tinge given to them by the world at large. "What is that guy you had lunch with—a queer?" is a question that carries with it all of the semantic implications of a similar sentence in which a racial epithet is used. But the homosexual can use the word *queer,* and many other words, with comfort, because inherently lacking is con-demnation. There is no air of superiority, no slur nor sneer. The word is no more than a communication of a thought. "I want you to meet a friend of mine," a gay person will say to me. "He's a grand guy—and as queer as a three-dollar bill."

The homosexual society requires a word like *gay* so that conversa-tion can be free and unhampered; the fetters of conventional con-demnation have not yet relegated this word to the realm of the out-lawed nor associated it with a stereotype. The group, and its individual members, can only profit by every device that makes possible the act of unmasking. Any semantic effort that facilitates free conversation is desirable. The secret and code-like character of *the gay* and *the straight,* so reminiscent of words and signs of fraternal orders, will be needed so long as there is a submerged and semi-legal society of homosexuals, and new words to meet new exigencies will have to be found.

In the meanwhile, the world at large, comprising those of all sexual temperaments, lacks an acceptable term that is the male counterpart of *Lesbian.* Like *Lesbian,* such a word might logically come from the great civilization where homosexuality flourished as an accepted part of the mores and where it was an inspiration to philosophy and art—the culture of ancient Greece. A word like *Dorian,* for instance, might be valuable as a part of our language. It would, like *fairy,* be synony-mous with the male homosexual, but without the implication of effeminacy and without the hostile sneer associated with *fairy.* Like *Lesbian,* the word *Dorian* could encompass a relationship, a thought, a philosophy, an individual, without regard to the sexual fulfillment of the desire.

Chapter 10

On the Gayest Street in Town

A minority retreats unto itself, forms a world within the world, forced on the one hand by rejection from the populace at large, and encouraged on the other by the myriad of interests and activities common to the group. Wherever one travels, up and down this land, there is apparent an in-group magnetism, not only along racial, religious, national-origin lines, but of professionals among themselves, or among the deaf-mutes and the blind, or those who adhere to a single political tenet. The members of the groups, and the groups as a whole, cross paths outside their narrow confines, some frequently and others at rarer moments, some fearfully and others boldly, some with great pleasure, others with extreme anxiety.

No group is so little known, yet few groups are numerically so large as that composed of homosexuals. No group has so little recognition and acceptance, is so apparent in its lack of organization, yet exercises so strong an influence and contains so many people who have gained wide public acceptance as individuals. The existence of this minority grouping is acknowledged by many, tolerated by some, threatened by others. It is not a new phenomenon; it is a group that has struggled in practically all lands for many centuries. One writer describes it as *a submerged world*, while another speaks of *a society on the fringe of society*. Both are correct, accurate, yet incomplete, for there is not one submerged world, one society on the fringe of society, but several, almost countless, different and disparate and dissimilar and almost disconnected, yet all having some relationship to one another, sometimes through an individual or two who travel in several of these submerged-island societies at once, or related on the other hand merely by the similarity of pursuits and personalities, or perhaps related primarily by the association that exists only in the imagination of the hostile world.

There is not one group life, but many, just as no one pattern of existence could describe the lives of all the deaf-mutes in this country, or all the Communists, or the second-generation Armenians. Some living patterns will reassert themselves in all these islands, character-istic of the entire minority. But others depend on the individuals—their personal, professional, and intellectual predilections.

Some sections of the gay society are filled with a keen and lusty interest in the common bond that brings the individuals together. They read, wonder, discuss, question. But others ignore the bond, or accept it, pursuing their interests, seldom conversing or reading about their special characteristics, and even failing to appreciate the preoccu-pation of certain people with the homosexual problem.

Or a group may be brought together, driven by the sensual impulse, seeking new forms and new partners for the love of the flesh, hoping to find the excitement and satisfaction that is always within the grasp, yet somehow is so elusive, seldom brought to fruition without some pang of disappointment. While another group may find its social and cultural interests far from the field of the search for sexual outlet, and there one encounters sharp words of warning and a shunning that approaches a social ostracism against the more adventurous, the more promiscuous, the more indelicate. "Don't bring that groper around again," will be the admonition, and it will be followed, under pain of the extension of the excommunication to the friend of the guilty transgressor.

Living in a gay world! What gay world, and where, and which one? The world of the street corner, or of a special and well-known path in the park, or the lonely and dark street on the breezy lake front, or the banks of a river in one of America's largest cities? Here they come, attracted by the burning desires, seeking release perhaps more than satisfaction, wondering with a driving curiosity what adventures are awaiting, fearful of the many dangers—medical, legal, extra-legal —yet coming with bravado, asserting to themselves that the dangers are quite fictitious and exaggerated.

Here is a particular street in a rather big city. It is well-known, being passed each day by literally thousands who are unaware of the adventure and romance and personal tragedies of wrecked lives that are drawn by the magnet. From the hours of broad daylight they gather, some seeking financial gain, others unmindful of the financial loss, the majority quite unwilling to be a partner in any monetary transaction, whether to pay or to be paid. And a few seeking to exploit, planning to rob, even if it must come to violence—these few usually themselves not homosexual, in fact frequently not bisexual, and creating justification in their minds by thinking in contemptuous terms of their potential victims as "goddam fairies who only get what's coming to them!" Thieves not only in the night but even in the day, protected by a law that is indifferent to the fate of the outcast, but doubly protected by the stigma that attaches to the activity that may be the prelude to violence, a stigma that will hold in silence the tongue of the victim.

The gay walk along the street, and to the initiate they are apparent. No obvious traits are needed to characterize them. No special mannerisms need be displayed to brand them. Here and there a tweezed eyebrow, or two youths walking hand in hand. But seldom are the obvious seen. Virility, freedom from the betraying gait and voice—these are the more common traits, here as elsewhere in the group life.

Some come back to the same street frequently; they know each other, give a nod of recognition, then talk, form a community. But for the most part they are strangers to each other, youths and mature men who return only on occasion, not by plan or appointment or design, but when the convenience of proximity is added to the strength of the desire. It is the amalgam of closeness and qualitative content that brings the steel to the magnet. And, once within its range, resistance becomes difficult, then hopeless . . . so why resist? How much greater is the joy of wholehearted participation!

Some stand idly at a store front, pretending to windowshop, often with hands in pockets. Others walk slowly, turning, looking, staring, walking by, then turning again.

Let us follow, as it were, two gay youths cruising on a gay street. They are walking in opposite directions as their eyes meet and hold each other's for a split second. The eyes themselves loiter, and the two people approach. Sometimes their common ground is established with rapidity. More often a circumlocutious pathway is followed.

"Say, fellow, do you have the time?"

"It must be about eleven. There's a clock over there. It's ten forty-five."

"Oh, yes. Still rather early."

The first approach has come to an end. The abortive efforts at conversation become burdensome. But one of the two takes up the threads again.

"Do you have a cigarette?"

"I think so."

There is an offer of a cigarette, and the faces come close as the flicker of a burning match is held between two cupped hands.

"My favorite brand."

"Really? I smoke almost anything as long as it's a cigarette."

"No cigars?"

"Good heavens, no!"

In the exchange of words, each is seeking a clue. Neither desires effeminacy, yet each needs just a suggestion of it, in a softness of tone, an overenunciation of word sounds, an affectation in the movement of the hands or in the method of holding the cigarette. Each requires this mere iota of the mannerisms of the opposite sex, or to be more exact the mannerisms of the outcast group, in order to reassure himself that this is no trap, no folly that will lead to frustration or even worse.

The weather may be the next resort in the search to keep alive the ebbing conversation.

"A little chilly tonight, isn't it?"

"Not too bad. I've been rather hot myself."

A ripple of forced laughter, not in appreciation of humor, but part of the effort to establish a common bond through the double entendre and the laughter of recognition that follows. The two have broken through the façade of pretense and have made their first attempts toward penetrating each other's secret.

"Take a walk?"

"I don't mind. Got the night to kill."

"I have no plans myself."

"Live near here?"

"I'm from out of town. Massachusetts. I'm stopping at a place near here."

"Whereabouts?"

"Just down the street and around the corner."

"I wouldn't know. I don't get around to those spots very much."

"You should. It's quite a gay place."

The word has been uttered, and the rapport has now been established. From that moment on, there is no doubt as to the direction of the evening. They stop at a bar for a glass of beer, and there we shall leave them. Back to the street we go, while they make their way to an evening of adventure. Adventure? Pleasure? Happiness? It would not be at all unusual if, many hours later, one of these youths might fall asleep in the stranger's bed, happy as he thinks of the partner at his side, and contented with the release from the tension that had gripped him. He has enjoyed the moments after sex as much as the moments during the heights of passion; and in sleep he finds a restful satisfaction. But it would be not at all unusual, at the same time, if the partner were to rise, cleanse himself with care and shake his head as he sees his image in the mirror. He would lock his watch and wallet in a desk drawer, hide the key, and creep into bed, burdened by a guilt that, within him, always follows sex. Only the hospitality demanded of the host, only the wish not to hurt the other as he himself had often been hurt, might restrain him from awakening his companion and asking him to leave.

What goes on in the minds of two people, strangers to each other save for this one encounter, at such a moment? One is asking himself how this youth, hardly known to him, had so aroused him only a few minutes before, so that all reason was obliterated. The truth was incredible. And, in the truth, he saw a mirror of himself: weakness . . . weakness and futility. The pursuit of a love he could never find was a futile road, a dead-end. He was at the same corner as he had been a year before, and it was a blind alley. Where could it lead him? What could be gained toward meaning, accomplishment, and achievement in life by all this struggle to find new love-partners? What waste of talent and time and energy in the search for adventure, when a single partner might give him greater satisfaction, and love-making would not be commingled with fears and remorse. All of this in one mind, while in the other is a blissful peace.

The hour is late, and if we were to return to the street where they had met, we would find fewer people. But two pairs of eyes would in all likelihood be meeting at that moment, holding each other in a dancing, lingering look.

"Say, fellow, do you have the time?"

"It must be about one. There's a clock over there. It's twelve forty-five."

And on and on!

These are the one-night stands. The partners exchange telephone numbers. Sometimes they call each other again; more often they do not. "Ships that pass in the night," a friend of mine calls them, and then changes the subject, preferring to speak of other aspects of gay life.

Do the pick-ups and the one-night stands engender a sense of shame, an overwhelming guilt, that prevents each of the individuals from facing the other on a second occasion? Or are the participants in these fly-by-night arrangements fearful lest their gay friends discover this phase of their activities? Or are these particular homosexuals so promiscuous, so adventurous, so unable to combine sex with fidelity, that only the unknown, the untasted, the uncharted are attractive to them? Or, finally, are they so anxious to separate the love and the sex concepts in their lives, so anxious to flee from affection, that they choose to pursue an aspect of gay life that to themselves is most sordid, least likely to lead to permanent relationship? Is this, perhaps, their method of punishing themselves for being gay? And do they feel "clean" and "guiltless" because they condemn their own activities, and is it easier to effect this condemnation when such activities originate on a street-corner, in a public washroom, at the Turkish baths, or in the SRO section of the opera house?

How complex may be the motives. Perhaps in all of these questions may be found an element of a contributory factor.

The street, the corner—and many another like it in almost all the big cities of the United States—is one manifestation of gay life. It is one of the meeting-places and gathering-places. But it is not typical and, although important, involves few people. Most gay folk, in fact, are little concerned with the events on the street. For the minority of the homosexuals who go to such places, the majority feels anger, scorn, and contempt, but not without a great deal of curiosity and envy.

Chapter 11

Drop Another Nickel In

The main drive toward participating in a group life, and the main shunning of such life, come essentially from one source: identification. In its positive form it is a manifestation of the need for acceptance; in its negative form it is a fear of consequences. One wanders into the bar in the hope of finding the convivial spirit that comes from being with one's own; but, in the same way, the bar is the frightening specter of a mirror that holds up the image of oneself, which is a true image.

From the gay street to the gay bar may be but a few steps, or several miles, but an aura of respectability is to be found at the latter that is lacking at the former. One need not hide one's head as an acquaintance walks by; one does not deny encounters, but on the contrary makes appointments, utilizes the meeting-place for social convenience. But, in the final analysis, it may be that the bar provides a superstructure behind which the libidinous impulses can hide, whereas on the street the passions are denuded, deprived of an aura of romance and culture. In one place it is fun; in the other it is lust. On the street one is behaving like a whore, whether or not one pays or is paid. But the drinks, the music, the atmosphere of friendliness give a far less outlawed aspect to sex, and in fact push the primordial desires from the visible foreground. What does an hour on the street leave a person still without a partner but fatigue and frustration? But in the bar there is little search for partner, seldom a pick-up, and an hour or two spent there provides some light entertainment which requires nothing further to satisfy.

What are these bars? In the bigger cities of the United States they are to be found in abundance, some so gay that to be seen entering or leaving is to invite a "brand"; others somewhat less stigmatized, but nevertheless primarily a meeting-place for the homosexually inclined. Here and there one spots a man, usually middle-aged, offering to buy drinks for almost any accepting young person. He is willing to buy "love," and he may find a young man in need of the money or perhaps merely tempted by it, anxious to sell, happy to have a commodity in demand. Often the older man will be rejected, but not with any great indignation. His kind is not easily insulted.

There is, in fact, little exchange of money, nor for that matter is sexual satisfaction an important drawing factor. Mostly these people come to meet friends and friends' friends, to see who among their vast circle can be found in the familiar hangout that evening, to renew acquaintanceships and to cement friendships. They come to let down their hair, to have a slow beer among those whom they know and who know of them; a slow drink as they talk, joke, gossip, and gesticulate. They come to hear the latest jokes that are making the rounds of the submerged world and to participate in the atmosphere without fear that they are attracting the attention of a hostile society. They come to lay aside their masks, as many cannot do in their own homes, and to take relief as they are laid aside.

Gay bars! In a sense the description is fitting, for here is a gaiety, a vivacity, that is seldom seen in the other comparable taverns, night-clubs, bars, and inns. There is no craning of necks as a bored audience watches a wrestling match on a television screen. Instead, music comes forth unceasing, usually from a nickelodeon. The audience talks to the rhythm, drinks to the rhythm, hums and breathes the air of the music, and looks around as the door opens to see who has just entered.

A new face, and alone. The young man stops in the doorway, his eyes traveling rapidly from one end of the room to the other, here pausing, there hesitating. Perhaps he is straight, some think to themselves, a man who has just wandered in by accident, a thirsty soul in search of nothing but a quenching highball? But one can make the error of asking a question of this type only for the briefest moment. There is an immediate suggestion about his manner of dressing, the comb of his hair, the walk, the rolling of the eyes as he looks around, that characterizes him for the initiate; yet in the straight world he would never be suspect. Everyone is satisfied that no error has been made. The newcomer walks to the bar. The eyes return to their partners.

"Play that song over again!"

"Who's got some nickels for the juke box?"

The music starts, and some songs seem to be extremely popular that evening. If one were able to obtain a report on the music at the other gay bars, the similarity of taste would be striking. Everywhere the same song seems to have taken hold. The youths are humming and singing it as if it were the craze. It has been captured by the group and considered its own. So thoroughly is the air filled with a line from a popular song that to hear it on the street is to know that it comes from the mouth of a gay person. Then the song disappears, not as quickly as from general popularity, and its place of preeminence in every gay bar is assumed by another.

From the outside they look like any bars. What makes them gay is the clientele, usually welcomed by bartenders and owners who find that it is good business to run a bar of this type. Here and there—a rarity even in the larger cities but not unknown—is the bar where the Lesbians gather. But most of them are male hangouts where a few women stroll in, usually with male escorts.

Some are in the most fashionable hotels in town. Others are scattered: in the theatrical districts, the bohemian areas, the rather poor or slum sections. But the dividing lines are not at all sharp; from the high-class hotel to the poorest area, one is likely to encounter the same faces.

The most successful of the bars are crowded and smoke-filled, particularly on a Friday or Saturday night. The clientele is divided into little groups and clusters and couplets, but here and there from one group to another an individual waves, then moves over to the other island. But most of the circles know each other only by sight, or by a spirit of binding comradeship.

There is relief in the open character of the conversation, and with the relief there sometimes comes ostentation. It is the revolt against pretense that offers an impetus to the pendulum, so that, in its swing, it does not halt where the proprieties of convention might demand. At any rate, gossip, jealousy, affairs of heart and flesh are discussed with abandon, and they may be intermingled, for example, with critiques of the music at a concert and talk about the rising cost of living. As in other groups, interests vary, with conversation that is light, but not at all confined to the area that binds these many together.

Let us take our place for an evening at one of these bars, watch the faces, eavesdrop on the conversation. We will look up with the others as a new face appears in the doorway, and we will hear a murmur:

"Look what's coming!"

"Isn't it gorgeous!"

This last comment is not in whispered tone. The inflection denotes desire, the volume expresses defiance.

At one end of the bar, having beers, are three young queens; their eyebrows are plucked, their hair quite obviously bleached, and of course very wavy. Seldom seen in these bars, their presence is discouraged not only by the proprietors, but by the gay clientele. They gesticulate with graceful movements that are not so much feminine as caricatures and exaggerations of the feminine. They talk quickly, and their lips move in manner not quite like the movements of either men or women. They can more aptly be compared to actors, seeking to imitate, yet not at all believing that they are play-acting.

"So I told Margie that she'd just have to find herself a new apartment, because I wasn't going to put up with her carryings-on with all my friends that way, and she got insulted and left in a huff."

"She said you raised a stink when she brought a friend home one night."

"She did? So you believe her?"

"I didn't say I believe anyone."

"Well, you can't believe a word she says."

The onlooker or eavesdropper is puzzled, but the initiate is accustomed to the curious change in gender found in the conversations of a few of the homosexual circles. Perhaps no other aspect of their lives is so amusing and, even to many inverts, so revolting. Nothing that these people do stamps them as being apart from the others so much as their conversational use of *she* for *he*, *her* for *him*, in the most matter-of-fact manner. And yet, after a few hours with groups of this sort, there is hardly a homosexual unable to say *Joan* for *Joe*, *Roberta* for *Robert*, although with some trepidation and self-consciousness, perhaps even mocking himself: "She's nice," referring to a male entertainer.

A few gay young men, standing near the gesticulating group, listen to the conversation with amusement and contempt. "My, how those faggots camp!" one remarks in a loud voice. A bleached blond turns and the retort is quickly forthcoming, "Are you jealous, dearie, because nobody wants your trade?"

Some of the bars have dancing, but it is usually confined to male and female or occasionally to two females. Seldom, save at a private party or a masquerade ball, are males permitted to dance together.

As the evening drags into the night and then into the early hours of the morning, and as the curfew approaches, the crowd gathers and thickens. (Don't these people ever go to bed, one might ask.) But even in the crowded atmosphere, a few have only intensified loneliness. They are unable to integrate into the circles, and to go off into the night alone is insufferable defeat. For them, even the new-found partner is only temporary relief. They can neither escape from a life they rebel against, nor can they become a part of it. They come to the bars, sit and drink beers, and then go to their homes dejected and defeated.

But in the full flush of the evening, among the many who come to drink and to linger, no such spirit is apparent. Everything is jovial and laughing. All the world seems gay. People laugh, they drink, they discuss their loves, but they drink with care and moderation, seldom to the point of intoxication, and their love lives do not extend beyond the pale of acceptable conversation.

Some are concerned at every moment with the why of their lives: reading, searching, wondering endlessly. Others take themselves for granted, and they can think only of their latest conquest, or more likely of the one still to be conquered. And sometimes their minds go back to the small town where the home life had to be abandoned because of the stifling atmosphere, the lack of freedom of movement, the constant stream of gossip and suspicion.

"Another beer, Joe."

"You must've gotten a raise. That makes three tonight."

At a table are three young men and a woman, four people that make up two couples. The female is rather rare at this bar. Many eyes wander. All ask: Is she? Is she gay?

No, she is not gay, this very charming woman. She is here with an escort and two very dear friends. She is, in fact, one of the relatively few women (and he one of the few straight men) found in every circle of homosexuals. They are people who have gravitated toward a group of which they become almost a part, attracted by a curiosity, forming a bond through a very deep personal friendship, and becoming in their own eyes self-appointed protectors. These people are like links between two different worlds, teaching the dominant not to fear but to accept, teaching the subdued that the entire world is not hostile.

On occasion an unsuspecting one is brought to the bar by a more sophisticated companion, the latter anxious to note his friend's reaction, using it as a clue to determine the sensual leanings. Or a passerby strolls by and enters, perhaps has his drinks and departs, never noticing the male couples who are so eagerly eyeing one another, unsuspecting the erotic atmosphere pervading the bar. Just thirst and fatigue and perhaps some time to kill have led him to the door, and he sits, sips his drink, and listens to a familiar tune, then to depart. These are the people who think inversion so very uncommon. They do not see it in their own offices or factories, in their families, and all around them at the bar.

The tunes of a few years back are heard, and one recalls the atmosphere at the time. Only one thing has noticeably changed: gone are the men in khaki and gone are the sailors in blue. Once the servicemen came on their passes and furloughs, soldiers and sailors in very large numbers, uniformed men home with service stars and battle scars, or others about to ship out to the theaters of war. They were brave men who might so easily have gone to the medical officers at camp, or might have spoken to the psychiatrists at the induction centers, using their sexual leanings as an excuse for evading service. Instead, they had gone into an Army or Navy where they were in double jeopardy, both at the hands of the enemy of their country, and at the hands of their own psychological make-up. Then, after the war, they returned to the bars, without uniforms but with veterans' pins, the lame ducks that were a sign of their service, until these, too, disappeared.

A new face enters, looks around, and sees a group that is familiar. The greetings are enthusiastic. There is almost a public embrace.

"So the old lady let you out of her clutches tonight?"

"Yeah, her mother's in town, so I just said I was going to the movies."

"It's a long time, stranger, isn't it?"

Then there follows the barrage of questions to the person who had strayed from the path of bachelorhood. He was now one apart from the rest, not quite belonging, though they knew he was as gay as any. They denounced his hypocrisy, yet envied his adjustment.

"I knew I'd find you two together," the newcomer says to two of his erstwhile friends. "Still a couple of crazy lovebirds?"

"Nothing in this world ever changes," one of the lovers philosophically muses.

"Don't forget to invite me to your fifth anniversary."

"You'll be there. It's Jim who might not be at the party. We think it's a case of pregnancy."

They laugh heartily. "That reminds me," says the newly-arrived married man. "Last month I was traveling with one of the kids from the office. Jackie—he's a swell kid—the most beautiful face you ever saw in your life and the campiest thing you ever laid eyes on. So I went into a hotel in Portland to find if they had a room, and he went to park the car. I asked for a double room, and the clerk asked if I would register for myself and my wife, so I says no, myself and my husband."

Again they laughed, although no one believed the story. He was relating to them what he might have liked to say. Humor is release. They tell their gay jokes, some aimed at themselves, others at the hostile world. But even those which ridicule the gay people are acceptable, because they are spoken by their own.

"Did you hear about the professor who moved to Long Island? He wanted to be in the Queens directory."

A man of forty is offering to buy drinks for a youth of half his age. The latter accepts, and they are now in the midst of exciting plans. Another group heatedly debates the value of municipal concerts, while another exchanges idle bits of information about people and things. A movie now making the rounds is under discussion, and the star is mentioned by name.

"He's so handsome, I could just die when I see him!"

"You're mad. I can name a dozen stars who are better looking."

"He may not be handsome, but he's certainly obvious. He's so gay you expect him to come out in drag."

"You say that about everyone."

"No, you can't miss that he's gay. You know who they say he's living with?"

"No, who?"

"That kid who played in the same picture with him, what's his name?"

"Oh, the hell with it. Let's get out of this bar. Come on over to my place."

The word is passed around, a few calls are made. If we were to follow a group of gay people to a Saturday-night party, we would find perhaps two or three dozen gathered at an apartment that cannot easily accommodate more. The lights are turned low, and a few young men dance with each other to the tunes coming from a record-player. There is a general division into couples, on chairs, couches, even in the corners and on the floors. But a few do not participate in the pairing off. They remain alone, perhaps wishing they were able to seek or ask for a partner, or perhaps just tired of this constant partner-seeking and exchanging.

"Tomorrow's church, and I have to get up early," a lad might be saying, while he has one arm around a friend's shoulder, the other hand holding a drink.

"It won't be the first time you'll miss church."

"But I'm not missing tomorrow, even if I have to stay up all night."

Two youths in a corner are kissing, several men are dancing, several others are arguing about the world series possibilities of the Yankees.

"Oh, for the Navy, the good old days in the Navy. Plenty of lovers and you never had to look for a job."

"Why don't you re-enlist if you liked it so much, dearie?"

"Listen darling, if I could get my old captain, I sure would. All you need to get along in the Navy is a pretty face and a captain with hot pants."

"There you go, bragging again. I suppose you had the admiral, too?"

"Let me tell you about me and the admiral."

But the story is interrupted. From another room at that moment comes a lovely young woman, perhaps overdressed, making a grand entrée—or is it a woman? No, it is one of the boys in the party, a law student well liked by all his companions. From head to toe he has dressed in the apparel of the sister of the owner of the apartment. Lipstick and rouge have been applied delicately, and a hat hides the male coiffure.

"Whoo-o-o-psss!"

There are whistles and shouts of glee, and then a young actor arises from his place, walks slowly and deliberately to the center of the room, bows low and takes the hand of the student to his lips. Out of his memory he declaims from Shakespeare, encouraged by the audience that is laughing and shrieking.

"A ham," a lad whispers, and feigns boredom.

"I'll never get to church tomorrow morning."

"Will you stop talking about church?"

"Let's get out of here. This place is dull."

"Where do you want to go?"

Where to go? Always the question—where can one go?

Can one run away from the few who extend a welcoming hand in a camaraderie born of affliction? Can one go amongst the enemy, pretending to be one of them, secretly despising oneself for failure to proclaim what one really is?

Where to go? If we return to the bar, as its curfew hour approaches, we find it so crowded that one can hardly move. For the lonely, it might just as well be abandoned. At a table sits a man of perhaps forty-five, alone, looking furtively around, watching, hoping. A sense of aloneness envelops him like a shroud of despair. He, too, is asking where to go.

Home? To no one.

To the baths? There are always the Turkish baths. At least a moment of release. He takes his hat, leaves a tip, goes toward the door.

"Let's all go over to my place," he hears some young people say, but he knows the remark is not intended for him.

The juke box plays, and a few beer bottles are still to be opened. Somewhere in the vast city lovers embrace, a lonely man makes his way to the baths, a gay bar closes, a youth yawns and asks for another drink, another says, "I'll never get to church on time in the morning," while around him a group sings softly, to the accompaniment of a record, something about being in love with a wonderful guy.

Chapter 12

All That Glitters Is Not Guilt

The street-corner . . . the gay bar . . . and finally the drag. Let us take the reader on a third journey to a homosexual meeting-place.

It is Thanksgiving. In one of the larger cities of the United States, tickets and invitations and word-of-mouth information have been circulating in all of the little islands that make up the homosexual fringes of society. The tickets pass around at the bars, and for weeks they have been brought home to lovers at night, discussed at length at many parties.

"Oh, I just don't know what I'm going to wear to the drag!" a youth shouts in a shrill voice.

"Can I get dressed in your house?"

"My sister has a beautiful gown—black velvet. Only I don't know where I'll get a pair of shoes to fit."

"Those high heels. If there's one reason I hate to go in drag, it's on account of the high heels."

"Why don't you go butch? Everybody'll take you for a girl dressed up as a man."

"You mean until they start dancing with me?"

"Don't brag. There she goes, bragging again!"

"Wouldn't she look sweet, masquerading as rough trade?"

The long-awaited Thursday night rolls around. Festivities and fun and carving turkeys in most American homes, and children dressing up in costume in many others. Before one of the largest halls in the city a crowd of neighborhood children gather, with a sprinkling of their elders. They stand on the sidewalks and form a gantlet, and they tease and taunt and, in shrill and obviously imitative voices, they scream like caricatures of women as the visitors arrive. They are, in fact, caricaturing the caricatures.

The hall itself is usually outside one of the more fashionable districts of the city, for it is safer for people to attend this costume ball in a neighborhood where they are not likely to be recognized.

Taxis pull up before the hall, and out come the masqueraders. Automobiles, driven by a man or woman in conventional dress, allow the passengers to alight before the door, then continue to find a parking place so that the driver may return for the evening of fun.

By ten o'clock the hall is beginning to fill; by eleven it is crowded to capacity. The band plays loudly, men are dancing with men, women with women, and men and women dancing with each other, or perhaps not quite sure of either the sex or the sexual temperament of the partner.

There are beauty and grace and grotesqueness all interwoven, sometimes a little of each in a single person, sometimes only the loveliness of the successful female impersonator, or only the horror of an individual who can never be what he was not made to be.

Are they play-acting, these men and women in masquerade, and their friends who are wearing "civies"? Some hardly take themselves seriously. They laugh, giggle, flirt and are coy, and then become engaged in their big affair of the night. Others have come to watch. They feel they are not quite one with these people, and they would not participate in the masquerade, yet they are participants, despite themselves. They are irresistibly attracted, yet they condemn themselves for all that is degraded around them. They are happy to be there, yet sad that such things be; they regret that they are a part of it, and yet envy those who are able to be more a part of it than themselves.

When I last attended a drag, not very long ago, I watched a sailor dancing with a young man. The sailor was in uniform, his companion in a tweed suit. They both talked loudly and vociferously. Their bodies were in exciting contact, their faces close upon one another's. They had no secrets from the world on this night; even their words must be shared. I could not help but be an eavesdropper.

"Ever come here in drag?" the sailor asked.

"Just once, never again," came the reply. "How about you?"

"What do you call this?"

They laughed and danced, and I passed on to another group. A man and a woman, each about twenty, were gracefully gliding along the floor. A man and a woman . . . they were not the only such pair in the hall. They seemed so contented together. Their intimacy seemed to arise from the closeness of knowledge, not of contact. Are they sweethearts, or man and wife, I asked myself. What are they doing at the hall of the outcasts on this night? Did they arrive by accident, or have they friends or brothers here, or are they among those rare souls who especially enjoy the company of gay folk, although they are not themselves gay? Or, perhaps, are they thrill-seekers and slummers who have merely looked in upon another world?

These are the questions I ask myself. The band stops, and as they walk past my table, I ask them to join me for a drink. They accept and are seated, order drinks as I stare at the man. In this atmosphere the stare has lost its rudeness. Perhaps the face, with its telltale signs of never having been shaven, will betray the true sex, the biological sex, or perhaps the evidence will be found in the figure. Now my stare has trespassed the bounds of good taste even for this hall, but it is greeted only by a mysterious smile from one who is taking a delight in withholding the answer from my probing curiosity. I ask, but I might just as well ask the Sphinx. They leave. I shall never know whether they were . . . but what difference. They look like a happy couple.

Perhaps three-quarters of the people at the drag are males, and perhaps a third are in masquerade. Some can be spotted from afar. They trip over their skirts and their shoes. They are clumsy, gawky, uncomfortable. Others require close scrutiny, and a few can never be identified with certainty.

Everyone seems to be having a good time, even the recreational police, who are present in abundance, particularly in the hallways and the washrooms. No intoxication is tolerated, no exposure, no lewd behavior.

At midnight, the striking of the drum, the flashing of the lights, and the floor is cleared. The parade of the queens will take place. Every male in female attire who so chooses may get in line. The gowns are mainly on the lavish side, with here and there some striking simplicity. But mostly one sees flowing skirts, flamboyant colors, an ostentatious overdressing. Many wear wigs; while others have scarves skillfully tied around their hair. There are no visible crew-cuts among them.

One by one they march to the platform, each stopping to pose like a model. Each turns around, shows form and figure to the judges and the audience, smiles coyly, listens for applause, and then descends. Perhaps the march continues for an hour. After the first few rounds of applause, the audience gives only a cursory clapping, except for an outstanding costume or an extremely effective impersonation.

Now and then the judges halt the march and examine more closely, seeking conviction that this is impersonation and not fraud. No woman may compete with these men who have faced the competition of women all of their lives.

Then the awards, with the queen being crowned, and second and third prizes given, followed by applause and protest, and by more dancing, drinking, flirting, weeping, long into the hours of the night. The time of departure draws near. Some part, alone and lonely, wishing to remain, although anxious to forget the evening. Others make their way out with the friends or lovers with whom they had come. Some leave in the company of new-found friends. For them, the evening of adventure remains to be explored. The night is young and does not end even when the sun comes up in the morning.

"An outrage!" exclaim many citizens when they hear of the drag, and their judgments are reflected by many homosexuals. "These drags are a disgrace. That's the sort of thing that gives the gay life such a bad name," one of my friends is fond of saying to me.

"No one compels you to go," I retort. "But I know a lot of people who get a great kick out of them and who look forward to them from year to year."

When I see these men and women in masquerade, and at numerous other places where large crowds of gay people are gathered, as on a special boat-ride and at very large but informal dances, I cannot help but feel that the wearing of the clothes of the opposite sex (or *transvestism*, as this phenomenon is called) is but a very small part of the appeal of such affairs. The gay folk do not go for the thrill and the adventure, nor are they seeking new friends. I do not believe they are primarily motivated by a need to exhibit themselves. In the main, what attracts them to the drag is the feeling that they will be among many of their own kind. Here they are known, liked, and accepted for what they are. It is a masquerade, ironically enough, where one goes to discard the mask.

The drag—if there is anything in the relationship of the homosexual group to the dominant society that is anomalous, it is the drag. That it is desired by the homosexuals is an indication that they find unsatisfactory so many of the ordinary pursuits of entertainment and relaxation. That it is tolerated by a society which condemns so bitterly is an indication that the condemnation is neither whole-hearted nor sincere. If the people congregating at these affairs were the immoral and lecherous types that are depicted in journalism and literature, then it is downright irresponsible, if not immoral, to permit such gatherings, and to send police and detectives to oversee them. The dominant group tacitly admits, by its attitude toward the drag (just as it does by its failure to enforce its own laws) that it is neither willing nor able to carry out the consequences of its own moral judgments. Is it possible, then, that these moral judgments are built on shaky foundations, and are believed in only to a limited extent even by those who sponsor social hostility with the greatest vigor?

For the homosexual minority, most of whom never attend the drags and are little interested in them, and many of whom are indignant at their very mention, these gatherings play a rôle which is not frequently understood. Anything of a semi-legal nature which aids in breaking down the veils of secrecy and in bringing the homosexual life into the open is desirable. It is necessary to compel recognition of the minority, to insist upon its right of assembly as well as publication and agitation, as a prelude to the struggle for civil rights, judicial rights, and finally for social equality.

But, back to those who have come for the night. For a fleeting moment, this becomes their world. The abnormal is the normal, the straight fellow is a curiosity, and love is synonymous with the attraction of one person to another of the same sex.

I breathe deeply and though the air is stuffy and the hall noisy, it is refreshing and quieting to know that I am where I can feel that I belong. For this brief moment of unreality, many days of sorrow are worth living.

I look around and see the tortured, the grotesque, all of the tragedies of lives not yet lived. In their costumes, and out of them, I am with these people, and I hope that they enjoy this moment of peaceful triumph as much as I do.

It was at one such drag, as I watched a very lovely and graceful person being crowned queen of the night, that a companion muttered to me: "Happy soul for an hour, but what a guilty unhappy person you can be sure she is."

I looked quizzically at my friend: "I am not at all sure," I said. "I have learned one thing in the gay life that people from the outside cannot seem to believe."

"What is that?"

"All that glitters is not guilt."

Chapter 13

Love Is a Wonderful Thing

No phase of gay life, except the impact on the individual of being an outcast of society, is so disconcerting to members of this minority group as the search for a life-mate with one's own sex. Is it possible or desirable for two people of the same sex to be in love with each other, just as a man is in love with a woman; to show the same affection and interest, to offer the same loyalty, to form a union as permanent?

Each human being walks alone through the pathways of life, but if the basic insecurity of this aloneness can be lifted by a companionship in which there is mutuality of interest, the burdens of life are made easier to carry. "Live alone and like it," said an author with a flair for a snappy title, but most people cannot follow this advice. There is a need to share life with another person; a delight in turning the key and, on opening a door, finding the warmth of another waiting in the home; of having a friend with whom to laugh and on whose shoulder to weep; in being a whipping-post for the pent-up angers of the one who is loved, or of having a beloved who willingly and happily plays this rôle.

During a person's early contacts with homosexuality, he notes the freedom of sensual play characteristic of the youthful group. The promiscuity of the gay adolescent is quite apparent, but seems to be not unlike that of the straight young man. Every adolescent and youth seems to be driven by a sexual urge that is non-discriminatory, imperious, and promiscuous, and most of the youths seek women, some seek men, others seek (or accept) both or either.

As he matures, the gay young man, either by reading or personal contact, hears of lifelong attachments that have the permanence, the strength, the fidelity, the jealousy, of marriages between man and woman. In fiction, and occasionally in psychological or sociological literature, such "marriages" are described or even glorified. In *The Well of Loneliness*, Radclyffe Hall depicts these loves as altruistic, selfless, and devoted. Other writers point to the lack of such permanence as characteristic of homosexual life, but many young gay people reject this approach, choosing to believe that their way of life will lead to the discovery of love.

In their late teens and their early twenties many of these young people—although not all, as I shall presently describe—continue to sow wild oats. Their love lives consist of a constant change of partners, of infatuations that last for a day or a week. Out of these experiences come several rationalizations: some arrive at a conclusion that love and homosexuality are mutually exclusive; others believe that sooner or later they will find the road of love; and another group, in their disillusionment, claims that partner-changing is a better way of life, offering wider experience and being more natural to man's instincts. "Don't try to ape the other world," a friend warned me. "We are different. We are meant to sleep with one another, and not to get 'married' to each other." This viewpoint is adopted by a character in *The City and the Pillar*, who not only defends the one-night stands, but finds them preferable; and Gore Vidal, author of that novel, states that the protagonist "fell in love with a few (young men) but, since most of them were just passing through town or were married, nothing ever came of these one-night stands."* One need not belabor the point by showing how little value is ascribed by such a writer to the words "fell in love."

There are, as I see it, several impediments that make difficult the formation of a permanent and marriage-like union between two men, and several forces that act to inhibit the possibilities of a lasting love. However, such a love is, to my mind, not impossible, but merely difficult to achieve, and its achievement is not only rare among the gay, but in the straight world as well. Nevertheless, for certain psychological and social reasons, it is more often encountered in the majority group.

First, the inner resistance that many homosexuals display toward their own tendencies is reflected not only in a resentment and contempt, frequently unconscious, of their partner, but a hatred of him,

---

* Gore Vidal, *The City and the Pillar* (New York: E. P. Dutton, 1948), p. 277.

for without the partner the individual would not, or could not, be indulging the desires he secretly despises. While many Freudians contend that in all love relationships there is such resentment and hatred, probably more of it is to be found in the gay life than in legal marriages, but particularly if the individual has not yet learned fully to accept himself and those like him with understanding and pride.

It is one thing to conceal activity for self-protection against the enemy. It is quite another to harbor a deepgoing shame within oneself. When the latter is present, there will frequently be an abnormally large amount of hatred for the sexual partner. A homosexual harboring such hatred does not wish to combine sex and affection, but to separate them. He wants to sleep with strangers about whom he cares not twopence, and then discard them, only to seek new strangers for the next experience.

If, in the search for companionship and security, a permanent union is established by a homosexual of this type, there is frequently present an unconscious death-wish, a strong hate element, that may result in the flare-up of tempers, attraction to infidelities, and eventually "divorce."

The homosexual who is inclined to fight against himself will resent his partner, and this pent-up feeling will sooner or later manifest itself, either in such obnoxious treatment as to cause the partner to withdraw from the relationship, or in a voluntary withdrawal of the individual himself. He is not likely to forsake the homosexual life, but merely the partner.

A second factor influencing the individual to pursue a constant and relentless search for new partners, or in other words to live promiscuously, is that by his psychological nature the invert is frequently not seeking a man, but is utilizing his ability to obtain sensual pleasure with a man as a means of fortifying a flight from some other and more strongly tabooed attraction. The nature of this taboo, which is usually incestuous, and the manner in which it affects the homosexual drive, are discussed in the chapter "Looking Inward and Backward." If the love-object is not the thing ultimately desired, but is only a substitute for or flight from something else, then the love act may never become so completely satisfactory as to exclude the desire for new and different experiences with other lovers. Promiscuity, in the final analysis, for many such people extends beyond the needs of the human being for variety and may be an expression of frustration. One of the sources of their frustration is the inability of the love-object to fulfill the basic desires and the deep-rooted needs of the individual.

This frustration is furthermore aggravated by another problem, one biological rather than psychological in source, and that is the difficulty many inverts have in finding a partner with whom full physical enjoyment can be mutually obtained. Lovemaking is rarely developed into a fine art with modern man, but the homosexual is confronted by physical barriers that inhibit satisfactory fulfillment. As a result, it is rare to encounter the passions that commence with tenderness, rise with excitement, are prolonged in ecstasy, and find simultaneous release in a moment of mutual love born of harmony and rhythm. "Two men do not fit, physically, biologically," a businessman who is also an invert said to me. "I want a man, but when I have him, I cannot get the pleasures out of him that I am really seeking—and I cannot give him the pleasures he requires." The result is that, instead of desiring the same man again, there is frequently a desire for a second one, followed by the third, the fourth, and the hundredth.

Despite these threefold difficulties which I would describe as being, respectively, of a sociological, psychological, and biological genesis, many homosexuals do discover sooner or later that there is a single individual for whom attraction is combined with affection, sex with friendship, physical love with numerous common interests, and for whom desire not only does not diminish, but continues unabated, actually strengthened by each sexual experience and heightened by the passage of time. The curiosity to seek new forms of pleasure with a variety of partners diminishes and becomes secondary to the wish to preserve the beauty, the sincerity, and the happiness of the special friendship.

Under such conditions a more or less permanent union is sometimes formed. Every submerged homosexual circle knows a few examples of such a union, or it may have several in its midst. If the individuals are unmarried, the bond results in their eventually living together; if married, they may make special vows and unusually tenacious agreements with each other. Some such partnerships approach the heterosexual concept of marriage, and therefore it would clarify matters if a comparison and a contrast with such legal marriages were to be made.

Let us consider, first, the method of selecting the companion. Among most heterosexual groups a clear differentiation is made between the choice of a partner for sexual pleasures and the choice of a life-mate. Sexual attraction is, of course, basic in the latter relationship, but it does not exclude other and usually more important factors—interests pursued in common, intellectual stimulation, understanding and acceptance of modes of life. The period of courtship is rather prolonged, and each gives careful consideration to the matter of marriage, aware that the step is considered well-nigh irrevocable.

Once married, the husband and wife are subjected to legal, biological, social, financial, and ecclesiastical pressures to continue the marriage until it be dissolved by the inevitable coming of death. The granting of a divorce is frowned upon by the church, made costly and sometimes embarrassing by law, and involves the possibilities of alimony arrangements and the difficulties of disposition of offspring as concomitant problems.

A considerable proportion of married people, however, do indulge —with a frequency that is only lately being acknowledged—in extra-legal fornication, sometimes with a single partner over many years, and at others with changing partners. Kinsey stated that "it is probably safe to suggest that about half of all the married males have intercourse with women other than their wives, at some time while they are married."* No doubt many others would like to indulge, but fear the consequences or lack the opportunity.

Despite the care with which the mate is chosen, the public commitment made by the act of wedlock, the frequent issue of offspring, the many pressures on the individuals to continue the marriage undissolved except by act of God, and the accommodation found in widespread adulterous outlets, it is estimated that one-third of all American marriages entered into in recent decades are ending in divorce.

The homosexual, on the other hand, makes his union rather haphazardly. He gives little consideration to the consequences of the "marriage," for there is no binding pressure. Either party can pack his bags and move. Divorce is just as simple as that.

The love-mate is often chosen with little regard for interests in common, but merely out of mutual physical attraction and consider-

* Kinsey *et al., op. cit.,* p. 585.

able erotic satisfaction. These factors are important, and no one can deny the significant influence of sexual frustration on unhappy marriages between otherwise well-mated men and women. But the carnal joys alone can seldom make a union complete or permanent for most people.

Far from a severe social, legal, or ecclesiastical pressure to bind together the homosexual union, the pressures are in the contrary direction. Everything is done to make the union impermanent—lack of understanding by families, ridicule by associates and neighbors, suspicious questions of prying persons, often fortified by legal and quasi-legal actions.

When one adds to the difficulties of achieving sexually adjusted happy alliance the lack of restraint on the formation and rupture of such a union, it can readily be seen that the instability characteristic of many areas of homosexual life is of a complex origin. This problem, and not the effort to cure, suppress, change, vilify, or punish the homosexual, should be the one to which fuller attention is given in the future.

I recall a young lady of my acquaintance, confiding in me during a searching discussion. "At first," she said, talking about her brother, "I pitied him, and felt that the tragedy of his life was his inability to establish a permanent relationship with a woman. Today I have a slightly altered viewpoint. I regard it as the tragedy of his life that he cannot establish a permanent relationship with a man."

This viewpoint is expressed in a work of fiction by Georges Portal, *The Tunic of Nessus.* "What troubled me on your account, my boy," says the uncle to his nephew, "is all these dissolute adventures, these chance meetings, this incessant running from one pleasure to another. Couldn't you choose a friend and keep him a long time?"*

Is the homosexual, considering all of these difficulties, actually more promiscuous than other men? In his actions, yes; in his desires, no. It is not only that there is little restraint on the homosexual's promiscuity, but the fact is that every male who is not woefully undersexed is essentially an undiscriminating satyr. Most men want women. They want many females, and any females. They will whistle after every girl on the street, unless restrained by social convention; they will visit the prostitute without knowing in advance what the partner

* Georges Portal, *The Tunic of Nessus* (Paris: Les Editions Astra, 1939), p. 320.

will look like. There is hardly a man who cannot be "made" by the nymphomaniac—unless the man is a homosexual.

The woman, on the other hand, is restrained. She chooses her partners with care, she is aroused by only a few, or even one. "The human female," writes Kinsey, "is much less interested (than the male) in a variety of partners. This is true in her pre-marital and extra-marital histories and, again, it is strikingly true in her homosexual relations."[*]

The key to the puzzle and problem of homosexual promiscuity is therefore quite simple: the promiscuous (heterosexual) male meets the discriminating (heterosexual) female. She acts as the restraining factor. He cannot indulge indiscriminately without her, but she will not permit him to do so with her. But, the promiscuous (homosexual) male meets the promiscuous (homosexual) male, and the restraints are entirely removed. And the proof of this, if proof were needed, is found in the statement Kinsey has made and which I have quoted above, and one which corresponds to the facts as seen by any astute observer in homosexual circles; namely, that the females do not follow the promiscuous patterns so common among the males.

The importance of this observation is that homosexuals (and others) must realize that there is nothing in the nature of homosexuality that prevents a stable relationship. It is not heterosexuality that contributes stability, but the presence of a female.

Nevertheless, despite the severe difficulties, it is not at all impossible to encounter among males affection whose duration is long-lived and faithful; devotion and sacrifice comparable to that of legal marriages; fidelity such as distinguishes love and marriage from the pursuit of sensual pleasure. Wherever these features are found, a fruitful life has been built around a rewarding relationship.

To describe two such lovers, the nature of their affection, the binding forces that hold them together, the types of lives they lead—such a description might be only misleading, for no typical lovers can possibly be found, any more than a typical husband-wife relationship exists. One might, however, cite as an example Claude and John. Their "marriage" is more than ten years old. In Claude's family, John is accepted not only as the business partner, but even, albeit in a rather jocular fashion, as Claude's lover. In fact, Lena,

[*] Kinsey *et al.*, *op. cit.*, p. 589.

two years Claude's senior and the only other child in the family, has introduced John as her brother-in-law on more than one occasion. The laughter that greets such a remark is not scornful nor is it pitying; it is both friendly and compassionate.

John and Claude have a wide circle of friends, both in and out of the gay world. There are theatrical folk, literary people, men and women they have met while they were students or after they had opened their bookstore. It would have been a simple thing for these men to "pass"—to borrow a word from another minority culture—but they long since determined that such was not for them. Their masculine appearance, their voices and their mannerisms, would betray their nature only to the most thoroughly initiated.

The love of these boys started in college, when they were both lettermen distinguished in athletic activities. Claude had been an outstanding swimmer, swift in the water and with the strength that gave him remarkable stamina and versatility, no matter the stroke or the distance. "Sometimes in the middle of a race, as I fall a stroke behind, I remember like a flash that I am queer—and I know I just have to win," he told John one day before a football match. And John played brilliantly that day.

After graduation they were separated by two different theaters of war, and when they were mustered out, they took advantage of the G. I. loans and established their thriving business.

"We had to have a business of our own—or be doomed to pretend to employers all our lives," John said. "And if there is anyone among our acquaintances who does not know that we are gay, it is only because the subject has never come up."

What happened in this case, and in many others, to make possible a permanency of relationship, was the establishment of bonds of mutual interests. In place of the child in most families, there was a social circle in which they moved. In place of an economic dependence of homemaker on breadwinner, and the responsibilities derived therefrom, there was a business partnership which created for each an economic need for the other. And by openly proclaiming their methods of living, they relieved themselves of the need for hypocrisy and pretense and found themselves without the shame brought about by self-degradation.

Herman and Alex are another couple. Herman is somewhat older, the more intellectual, always taking a kindly interest, aiding, guiding. No doubt, in the far confines of his lover's mind, Herman is the father-image. To the outside world it seems that Alex takes, that Herman gives. But Alex offers youth, beauty, vivacity, charm, and Herman is receiving more than physical satisfaction, important as that is to him. He has found companionship, an object for his affections, a protégé, and he receives moments of deep tenderness which are precious and for which he chooses to ignore the many bursts of temper, the surliness, the periods of silence, the unexplained absences, the mysterious telephone calls, and the indignant and almost violent denials. The suggestion of infidelity is an insult, says Alex. "What do you take me for," he asks his friend, "just a common whore?" And Herman will apologize for doubting, will beg for forgiveness, while Alex, in triumph, goes off to his newest conquest. But he always returns, sometimes ashamed, somewhat defeated in his efforts to remain true, but beneath it all and in his own way, he is deeply in love with Herman. Alex has a favorite line of poetry; he once told me that if homosexuals could only understand and accept this eloquent line, their relationships might be more permanent: "I have been faithful to thee, Cynara, in my fashion."

During the first years of their life together, Herman kept himself in ignorance of his companion's indiscretions. In fact, friendships of long standing were threatened by the hints of those who wished to enlighten Herman. But as time passed, he came to understand, and he struggled desperately to hold on to what he wanted. His jealousy made Alex the more determined, for was it not a struggle against being dominated and possessed, against having another dictate how one should live? So that each changed his attitude somewhat, and they found a *modus vivendi*.

"Alex must require these side affairs, but by now I realize they don't mean a thing in his life unless I make them mean something. They are little momentary events, prompted either by curiosity or by my own inadequacies as a lover, and they always end with his return. If he suppressed these tendencies on account of me, I feel he would resent me altogether. So I dismiss them as meaningless and unimportant. They just have nothing to do with us."

Thus has Alex interpreted Ernest Dowson for Herman.

There are other couples. Many consist of men one or both of

whom are married. Others involve Negro and white, and both men find excellent acceptance in both Negro as well as white gay circles. There are those in which the relationship is studiously kept from business and personal friends, but known to others—an example of a delicate balance characteristic of a problem the invert is constantly called upon to face.

Whatever the pattern, the ages, the races, the nature of the adjustment to the outside world, the degree of sexual fidelity involved, it can be said without equivocation that those who have found a stable relationship or a true love have gone a long way toward solving the problem of the adjustment of the homosexual in a hostile society, although not to a hostile society. That such a love brings with it new problems does not at all mean that it is a poor solution to the old ones. That it is difficult to achieve does not at all mean that it is a fantastic chimera. That it is mutually exclusive with the road of marriage is not at all self-evident, although the balance of a permanent homosexual "marriage" with a legal marriage is unusually difficult; even more so, in fact, in many ways, than the handling of other patterns of behavior by the gay husband. That it does not entirely solve the problem of the sad specter of the aging homosexual does not mean that it makes no contribution toward such a solution; in fact, it may be that the fleeting nature of youth is inherent in the human tragedy.

Part Four

CULTURE

Chapter 14

From Handicap to Strength

There is an almost universal assumption that homosexuality is a personal tragedy. It is synonymous not only with the lonely life of the outcast, but it is destructive, the contention is made, of the socially and personally "good" forces in the individual. A symptom of a neurotic personality development, it manifests itself, some scientists contend, in combination with other sexual or personality maladjustments. The homosexual, whether for reason or not, is bitter against society, the social scientists believe, and his entire outlook is as a result anti-social. Finally, these people say, the homosexual hates his love-object and expends great energy seeking new partners for erotic pleasure, rather than utilizing his energy, time, and personality for individual or social betterment. All of this is meant to account for and perhaps justify the cultural attitude toward homosexuals in current and recent eras.

Some of the above statements bear a slight semblance to truth. Others are no more characteristic of the invert than of his brothers. Still others are clearly made because of the lazy thinking of the stereotype-minded, who note a single trait or group of traits in one or a few individuals and project the observed phenomena to an entire minority, whether it be racial, religious, or sexual.

The contention, however, that homosexuality can do the individual and society no good as a potent, imperious, driving, and ever-present force is contrary to historical truth, is inconsistent with the character and achievements of the homosexually-inclined geniuses, and is finally at complete variance with the subjective (albeit prejudiced) observations made by those who move within the homosexual groups in our society.

What does it mean to belong to the most rejected of all minority groups? Has it been possible to derive from this seemingly great handicap in life some source of strength? In the shaping of characters and personalities, can the homosexuals become "better" people because of the special, the unusual, even the undesirable position that they are in as they face society?

The ability to use adversity as a source of strength, to turn the handicaps of life to advantage, requires an intelligent mind, and the high levels of intelligence frequently encountered among homosexuals have been readily conceded. Adolf Meyer has stated that homosexuality occurs "in normal individuals, even with specially high intellectual and ethical standards."[*] Havelock Ellis elaborates on this theme:

> The fact that homosexuality is especially common among men of exceptional talent was long since noted by Dante. (Ellis here quotes from The Inferno.) It has been noted since and remains a remarkable fact.
>
> There cannot be the slightest doubt that intellectual and artistic abilities of the highest order have frequently been associated with a congenitally inverted sexual temperament.[†]

In another passage, Ellis states that "inversion is as likely to be accompanied by high intellectual ability in a woman as a man."[‡]

A more recent observer, Dr. Maurice Chideckel, has reported his own observations (which refer exclusively to Lesbians): "The homosexuals we have met so far displayed a high degree of intellectuality."[§] And Max Lerner, a very astute observer, not himself a psychiatrist, wrote: "The fact is that the homosexuals often were a good distance ahead of the armed forces in education and rating and intelligence."[||]

Bearing in mind, then, that the invert is likely to have at least average if not higher mental capacities, how can he, and how does he, utilize not only his intelligence and talents, but his sexual inclination and his place in society as an outcast, for social and personal betterment?

[*] The Commonsense Psychiatry of Adolf Meyer (New York, McGraw-Hill, 1948), p. 263.
[†] Havelock Ellis, Studies in the Psychology of Sex (3rd ed.; Philadelphia: F. A. Davis Co., 1928), II, 26.
[‡] Ibid., p. 196.
[§] Maurice Chideckel: Female Sex Perversion (New York: Eugenics Pub. Co., 1938), p. 91.
[||] New York Post, July 20, 1950.

Characteristic of majority-minority group relations is the concept of superiority that the dominant group develops and that it attempts not only to utilize as justification for its terroristic repressions and as scientific foundation for its group attitude, but to impose even upon members of the minority. Thus within certain racial groups it is not uncommon to find at least unconscious acceptance of many of the tenets of the enemies of the particular group.

Throughout his life, from the moment that he awakens for the first time to the impact of the realization not only that he is a homosexual, but as such is part of a despised group of humanity, an individual is exposed to the propaganda that he is "not as good" as other people. He is told or hears that he (or his like, with whom he must identify himself) is "almost a man," is "half a man," and that he is a degenerate, a deviate, a pervert. He is exposed, in learned treatises no less than in the language of the streets, at the hands of the erudite no less than the ignorant, not only to contempt, but to a definite campaign to demonstrate and even convince him that his way of life is inferior.

From the time of my own high school days, I have heard these judgments and words, sometimes spoken by people I love, sometimes by those I despise. But, alas, I have heard the contempt of the world repeated by many of my gay friends. Gay despite themselves as are all those who inhabit this world of outcasts, they reflected, consciously or unconsciously, the propaganda of the dominant majority.

It is difficult to ignore this self-defeating invective. It took many years of experience in life, and some invaluable psychoanalytic therapy, for me to overcome such influences on my own attitudes. But even before I had succeeded in rebutting and then rejecting the hostile viewpoints, I had reacted to them. Since then, I have learned through observation that my reaction was not unusual.

The world considered me low, held in contempt my kind and therefore myself, believed me an inferior and unworthy specimen of mankind. The need for self-acceptance burned within me, and I could only throw off the influence of those who thought me beneath them by always striving, despite hardship and impediment, to excel even beyond my own capacities. My ethical standards must be above reproach, my honesty greater than that of others, my loyalty to friends and ideals firmer than that of other people, precisely because

—knowingly or not—they thought so little of me, and precisely in order that I might think the more of myself.

The very doubts over my judgment of my personality—the very impact of the words: *I am a homosexual, I am a queer, I am a fairy*—forced me at each turn of life and at all moments of the day to convince myself that I was as good as the next person; in fact, better. It was necessary for me to believe in myself, as it must be for all persons. Because mankind made it so difficult for me to preserve my self-esteem, I found it necessary to hold aloft my own activities, to drive on with my own achievements in order that my faith in self could survive the impact of many crushing blows. And those who have studied the personality adjustments of people in other minority groups, whether of a racial or religious character, will recognize my own struggle as following a not uncommon pattern.

In my studies at school, I could not content myself with doing the satisfactory work of which I was capable. I was always striving to excel over others. It would be my answer even to those for whom I wore the mask of anonymity, for they, too, reflected contempt for me, although they did not know that I was the object of their attitude. It would be my method of hurling back at them their smug opinion of their own selves as superior. I was spurred by a belief that if my learning were greater, my thinking deeper, my talents more creative, then the loftier would be the stature which I would assume in my own eyes.

Here is, perhaps, a phase of the laws of compensation. It is a counterpart of the bravado displayed by the cowardly, the overlording shown by the diminutive, the conceit by those who suffer from an inferiority feeling. In other fields, it is called a defense mechanism, or a Napoleonic complex. But it is not the origin that matters. We are concerned with the results, whether beneficial or destructive to society and to the individual. A small person is anti-social when he seeks to compensate, in his own image, for his inferior height by a display of dictatorial traits in which he uses other people as pawns. That his behavior stems from a factor beyond his control, and may be turned to other directions, does not make it the more palatable for society. And what of the homosexual? Many of his achievements may stem from the effort of the individual to excel in order to combat the influence of universal condemnation on his self-esteem. This is a beneficial consequence, even though it may (or may not) arise from an unfortunate source.

The homosexual, furthermore, is acutely aware of his lack of acceptance by society and of the difficulties (social, economic, and other) arising therefrom. Each moment of chagrin, each instance of humiliation, each act of rejection awakens a rebel spirit which is seldom antagonistic to society, but only to society's offensive and unjust attitudes. And, above all, the fact of being an untouchable provokes a solidarity with and understanding of other groups of individuals who may be in analogous positions in civilization.

"Being gay has taught me one thing," a social worker for whom I have the deepest respect pointed out to me, "and that is that 'tolerance' is the ugliest word in our language. No word is more misunderstood. We appeal to people to be tolerant of others—in other words to be willing to stand them. I don't want to be tolerated, and I can't see why anyone else should be struggling to be tolerated. If people are no good, they should not be tolerated, and if they are good, they should be accepted."

In the intergroup relations, particularly of Western culture, men are far from having attained acceptance of peoples other than themselves. Tolerance—in the sense of willingness to put up with the existence of others—is still to be achieved. But what is it but a miserable compromise? In the name of humanity appeals are made to various groups to tolerate each other, when tolerance is actually hardly more desirable than intolerance. The latter is only slightly more inhumane than the former.

The homosexual, cutting across all racial, religious, national, and caste lines, frequently reacts to rejection by a deep understanding of all others who have likewise been scorned because of belonging to an outcast group. "There, but for the grace of God . . ." it is said, and the homosexual, like those who are part of other dominated minorities, can "feel" as well as understand the meaning of that phrase. The person who has felt the sting of repudiation by the dominant culture can reflect that, after all, he might have been of another religion or race or color, an untouchable in India, one of the mentally or physically handicapped. It is not for him to join with those who reject millions of their fellowmen of all types and groups, but to accept all men, an attitude forced upon him happily by the stigma of being cast out of the fold of society.

It is no wonder, then, that a true and genuine democracy so frequently pervades the activities of the homosexual group. Read the testimony of the trials of Oscar Wilde and you will find the prosecution repeatedly making sarcastic reference to the fact that a man of Wilde's social standing should have dined with a groom and a valet. In this circumstance, the prosecutor found an implication of an immoral (that is sensual) friendship. Intergroup mingling was not only unthinkable, but was suggestive of homosexual inclinations. A few years later, Edward Carpenter pointed out that it is not unusual for the employer and his clerk to cross class lines when they are united by their erotic temperaments. And today, the deeprooted prejudices that restrict marriages and friendships according to social strata—family, wealth, religion, color, and a myriad of other artifices —are conspicuously absent among the submerged groups that make up the homosexual society.

What are the sources of this democratic spirit? They are twofold: the similarity of activities and interests among those having similar sexual leanings, transcending their differences of ethnic and social backgrounds; and, secondly, a conscious rejection of the barriers and prejudices that divide humanity into innumerable antagonistic segments. It is in this latter category that we find a reaction to being gay that is strength born of handicap.

The sympathy for all mankind—including groups similarly despised in their own right—that is exhibited by so many homosexuals, can be a most rewarding factor, not only for the individual, but for society. The homosexual can—and often does—demonstrate that he harbors no bitterness, for he learns, of necessity, the meaning of turning the other cheek. He is forced by circumstance to answer hate with love, abuse with compassion. It is no wonder, then, that he can as a doctor, educator, or pacifist, show a tenderness to others, no matter how tragic their dilemma, that is seldom forthcoming from people who have themselves not deeply suffered. The humiliations of life can distill a mellow reaction, a warmth and understanding, not only for people in like circumstance, but for all the unfortunate, the despised, the oppressed of the earth.

Is the impact of being homosexual reflected in the realm of intellectual activities? The mere fact of belonging to this section of mankind, under the conditions prevailing in the current cultural milieu, compels a person constantly to search for the answers to his problems within himself. He must examine his motives, analyze his behavior. Reminded of the "baseness" and the "ugliness" of his acts, he wishes to understand what differentiates him from all others around him.

This introspective study is not limited to the sphere of sexual desires. It pervades the entire personality and all its activities. The great *why*, the infantile manifestation of curiosity that strives, in the less inhibited mind of the child, to gain the key to the ultimate riddle of man's life and its meaning, is typical of the homosexual's mentality. Unable, perhaps, to develop the extrovert qualities which require a receptive world in which to have free play; struggling to find a solution to the mystery of his own imperious desires; not suited for unquestioning acceptance of the facts of his self without an understanding of these facts—the invert finds much of his thought process consumed with inner projection. The flare-up of temper, the critical perception of a work of art, the basis of a broken friendship, the unfinished task at work, the daydream and the nightmare—whence come these facets of life, what are their hidden meanings, how do they tie in with the total personality? These perceptive abilities, sharpened by inner search, can be and frequently are applied to an understanding of all people. On the surface this seems to be confined to the ability to recognize hidden, latent, or well-disguised homosexuality behind the façade of respectability, but it also permits recognition of the concealed meaning of a poem, the delayed break of a handshake, even the condemnatory attitude of a hostile person. This ability is, in a sense, a form of self-protection.

Analytical abilities that are developed by introspection, sharpened by the search for a glimpse behind the anonymous mask, are extended to the understanding of all phases of human behavior. Because the homosexual learns that his activities, thoughts, philosophies, aspirations, are understandable only in the light of a full knowledge of the intricacies of the emotional structure; because he learns that the motives for an action may be camouflaged so thoroughly that it seems to stem from the very opposite of its actual source; because, in short, he is forced to obtain a wealth of knowledge about the personal psychological make-up, he can and frequently does apply this to the fuller understanding of others. And when to this understanding is added compassion for all individuals and groups, no matter to what tragic pass life has brought them, a rare combination of worthwhile traits is obtained.

Furthermore, the homosexual, not by inborn trait or coincidental development, but as a result of his anomalous position in society, is likely to become a skeptic and an iconoclast. Why? Because in that area of his life with which he is so vitally concerned, he is forced to reject an attitude which he finds so universally taken for granted by others. He learns that, except in a few rare spirits, the viciousness and the absurdity of homosexual practices are assumed beyond discussion. He sees that there is room neither for inquiry nor argument, and that even men who are otherwise of rational and scientific mind wish to dispose of homosexuality with rash invective or with scornful pity.

But he, the homosexual, is firmly convinced that the great mass of humanity is wrong in its judgment. Though his opinion grows out of necessity, its implications for his intellectual activity are widespread, for having come to reject a viewpoint held by so many to be beyond dispute, he must question whether many other tenets, similarly held to be beyond discussion, are not based on unthinking faith, blind passion, illogical reasoning, or lingering prejudices that at one time or another were part of the ruling mores of society.

Among many of my gay friends, no precept, no matter how dearly held, is allowed to rest unchallenged. No new thought, no matter how absurd it may seem to be, fails to receive its day in court. Whether one discusses politics or medicine, philosophy or literature, no matter how far removed from the field of sex, the homosexual brings a mind that is unusually questioning and skeptical.

Even the restlessness that permeates the homosexual's activities, his short-lived interests, his inability to complete many a task that is begun, are qualities that can be made useful both for the individual and society, for they are the characteristics of a versatile personality. If, during the course of short-lived interests and impatient investigation, an individual can acquire knowledge and develop talents in several directions, the combination of seemingly unrelated knowledge and talents becomes particularly valuable.

Indubitably, many of the qualities here so briefly outlined are absent in some homosexuals, just as they are present in many whose heterosexuality is above dispute. All homosexuals have not been able to utilize their disadvantageous position for self-improvement in every respect and in all directions. I have pointed to the struggle to excel, but many gay people are easily defeated. Their resiliency in the face of the burden they carry is insufficient to meet the exigencies of life. I have outlined the understanding that is extended to other individuals and groups that struggle, each in its own manner, against exclusion. But many gay people are deeply rooted in prejudice. They have been unable to learn the lesson that should be so apparent to them in the face of the world's bigotry and persecution. I have depicted the individual turned compassionate toward his fellowmen, but there are those whose cruelty is lustful and murderous. Self-study and insight are not always present, nor is skepticism of necessity a constructive force.

The traits I enumerate, it is true, are not to be found in each homosexual. They are a few of the several possible beneficial results that are frequently reactions to the state of being gay, particularly under the prevailing social conditions. They are cited as a guide and encouragement to those, both the straight and the gay, who can see no good emanating from these passions. And it is in the light of the intimate relationship between the fact of being homosexual and the personality and intellectual characteristics derived therefrom that one can appreciate the genius of a Leonardo, a Whitman, and a Proust.

It is not, of course, my contention that the characteristics developed in homosexuals are confined to that group. Other minorities suffering from analogous exclusion, as well as many individuals with no minority status, display the qualities I find so widespread among homosexual groups. Desirable characteristics spring from many sources, group or personal. Homosexuality and social condemnation are merely the origins under consideration here.

If the homosexual drive is utilizable for ends that both the individual and society consider desirable, and if many or all of these characteristics arise, not out of the homosexual impulse, but out of the rejection of that drive by society and the stigma cast upon those who practice (or even wish to practice) this form of love, then is this not, in effect, a plea for a continuation of repressive attitudes? Would society not defeat its own ends by lifting its prohibitions or even by relenting in its hostility? The analogy with racial and religious minorities can again be drawn. It is to the fire of protest against post-slavery conventions and aganist anti-Semitism that many of the rewarding achievements of American Negroes and of the world Jewry can be attributed, but it would be absurd to distort this fact into an argument of justification for the Ku Klux Klan or for Hitler-ism. And why? Because it is the very essence of democracy, the antithesis of totalitarianism, that justice and fair play are desirable ends in themselves. Repression and intolerance are to be condemned, no matter what lofty purpose may motivate them or what useful result may unwittingly issue therefrom.

The beneficial reaction that turns repression to the finer purposes in life is far from a justification of that course. In fact, the opposite is true, for it is a demonstration of the character, power, and intellect of the invert that gives the lie to the name-calling of his enemies and proves all the more his worthiness of acceptance by society.

The desirable ends which I have outlined must, in fact, be weighed against the needless sufferings, the dejection and humiliation, the blackmail and the court trials—all issuing from the same repressive character of modern culture. The great energy of those who have utilized the contempt of their fellows as an incentive to further creativity must be balanced against the energy expended and wasted in the struggle against this very same contempt.

There is a poetic irony in the future of the homosexual in society, for he will use the high attainments of character to struggle against the very injustices that are so largely responsible for these attain-ments, and the successful termination of repressive attitudes may erase the very achievements that were used to effect this termination. Nevertheless, I am convinced, and will presently attempt to demon-strate, that there is a permanent place in the scheme of things for the homosexual—a place that transcends the reaction to hostility and that will continue to contribute to social betterment after social acceptance.

Chapter 15

The Search for a Hero

It is characteristic of any minority having an inferior social status that it seeks at all times to identify people of outstanding achievement with the group, and it glorifies those of the minority whose achievements are worthy of recognition. It is the answer of the individual to the stereotypes portrayed in journalism and in propaganda, the need for such response arising not only with the aim of counteracting the unpleasant connotations created by the dominant caste, but also to bolster the self-esteem which is ever ebbing as a consequence of hostility. In identifying a great personality with a minority, the members of the group are actually identifying themselves to a large extent with their hero's greatness.

Thus the Jewish communities idolize such men as Spinoza, Heine, and Einstein, and even point with pride, although intermingled with misgivings, to the originality and profundity of Marx and Freud. And the Negroes not only build up the achievements of their many heroes from Crispus Attucks to Ralph Bunche, but have conducted remarkable investigations to prove that there number amongst their group such men of great caliber as Alexander Hamilton, Pushkin, Dumas, and many others.

No minority has been so needful of finding heroes who command universal respect as have the homosexuals. By identifying men and women of indisputable merit with homosexuality, the cultured inverts hope to detect a clue as to the specific contribution that being sexually in a rejected minority might have made to the creative geniuses of these people. By displaying the positive rather than the negative stereotype, they hope, furthermore, to counteract the unfavorable propaganda to which homosexuals are subject.

It is felt by many leaders of the homosexual cultural movement that if the dominant, heterosexual group can be convinced that such men as Plato, Leonardo, Michaelangelo, and Whitman were inverts, then society must either reject the men and their work entirely, which it is loath to do, or must relent in its hostility, by admitting the possibility of "good homosexuals." In fact, the acceptance of the men implies that society agrees that some homosexuals, at least, can be useful to civilization. Yet this admission would be fatal to the entire superstructure of taboo and condemnation. Thus the hero-worship and cult-formation, so evident in homosexual groups, are integral manifestations of the effort to expose the contradictory features of society's present-day attitude.

The identification of creative geniuses of the past with its own group character is a particularly difficult task for homosexuals. This is not only because of the severe stigma attached to those who admit their homosexual tendencies, but also because of the shame extending to their families as well. Consequently few of the great talents ever made open admissions, as did Gide; few consumed themselves with the subject so thoroughly in their field of creativity as to betray beyond a doubt their own predilections, as did Proust; few left such incontrovertible biographical facts, as did Symonds, Marlowe, and Francis Bacon. On the other hand, many left a heritage that was deliberately obscure, choosing to express their homosexual sentiments in a sublimated form, as did Leonardo; others, such as Whitman, motivated perhaps by self-protection, found it necessary to deny their leanings and even to denounce those who would in this manner interpret their work; others, like Tchaikowsky, were victims of a deliberate effort on the part of biographers to omit, to lie, to deceive, and to alter.

The effort to discover the homosexuals among the great minds of past and present eras is further obscured by the bisexual question. Even a man like Gide is amazed when Proust, in the privacy of his room, denied any bisexual predilection, admitting (or claiming) that his libido was directed exclusively toward males. When the homosexuals or the bisexuals of the past have married and have utilized their marriages to further obscure their true feelings, how much more difficult is the task of the analytical biographers. But when there come under study the essentially heterosexual men of fame and achievement who may have had some leanings toward the homoerotic under special conditions, as may have possibly been the case with Byron, Shelley, Tennyson, and perhaps Wagner, the area of investigation becomes particularly difficult. The line of demarcation between friendship and sexual attraction is not always strongly delineated, and the classification of human beings according to the sex of their love-object is equally difficult.

Both the homosexual and the heterosexual have been guilty of rationalization, illogical deduction, planned confusion, exaggeration, and suppression in their studies of the famous people of history. Proust is willing to declare, without equivocation, that Baudelaire was a homosexual, and he offers as his sole proof, according to Gide's report, the beautiful and sympathetic poems concerning Lesbians. Let me not pass judgment on the truth of the assertion, but only point out what meager evidence is used to substantiate the claim.

Men who have left no heritage of suspicious intrigue save their words of sympathy or friendship for some known invert, or even strong words of love for a friend (as Goethe for Winckelmann, Wagner for Ludwig, Montaigne for La Boëtie, Tennyson for Arthur Hallam), are classed by many investigators with the suspects. When these words of friendship are expressed for a homosexual, the suspicion becomes greater, for the homosexual is so unused to expressions of sympathy from without that it appears quite logical to him to believe that anyone who is somewhat understanding may be of a temperament not too far removed from his own. That this argument is completely self-defeating becomes evident, for it precludes the possibility of finding allies in the protest movement.

If the homosexuals are guilty of building their studies on a feeble foundation (for example, the interpretation of Shakespeare based merely on the dedication of the sonnets, or of Tennyson based on nothing but the words of compassionate grief expressed in his *In Memoriam*), the heterosexuals are no less guilty in arriving at the opposite conclusions. In fact the biographers who have been so anxious to leave their heroes "untainted" have lied, suppressed, and distorted in a manner that must be much more shameful than anything in the lives of their subjects. Only incompetent research could lead an honest person to a denial that Paul Verlaine and Arthur Rimbaud, the great symbolist poets of French literature, were homosexually united; and what could be more shameful than the biography of Peter Ilyich Tchaikowsky by his brother Modeste,* who was fully aware of Peter Ilyich's inversion and of the fact that his marriage was probably not even consummated, yet suppressed this and painted a completely false picture of the great Russian composer? The examples could be multiplied. It does little credit to the name of a scholar like Van Wyck Brooks, for example, that in his critical study of Symonds—and one which he declares to be "a biographical study"—he not only omitted all mention of homosexuality, which was basic to Symonds's critique of the Greek poets and of the Renaissance, but even omitted to mention, no less evaluate, several books which Symonds had written.†

Through the pages of history many names have been included in the roll call of homosexuals. A few are here enumerated in a completely uncritical spirit, for I leave to some future historian, or to many, the task of sifting the true from the false, the bisexual from the homosexual, the individuals who have repressed their sexual drive from those who indulged and enjoyed, the man for whom this love was acceptable from the one for whom it was inescapable. Most important of all, it remains to be studied what homosexuality contributed to each of these personalities, what effect it had on their philosophy, their life work, the heritage they left to mankind. Could *Leaves of Grass* have been written by other than a homosexual? Can it be interpreted except as the expression of an invert? Does it, hence, have less meaning for the average person? These are vital questions that face a biographer.

Among the great names, some of which have already been mentioned, are such outstanding military geniuses as Alexander the Great, Caesar, and Napoleon; the Greek philosophers, Socrates and Plato; Sappho, poetess from whose island of origin has come the name of woman's love for woman; Pindar, whose odes are considered among the most beautiful poems of all time; Marlowe, Shakespeare, and Francis Bacon, among many other Elizabethans; Leonardo da Vinci, Michaelangelo, and possibly Benvenuto Cellini, among the giants of the Renaissance; Tchaikowsky, Djughaliev,

* Modeste Tchaikovsky, *Life and Letters of P. I. Tchaikovsky* (New York: V. Lane, 1906).
† Van Wyck Brooks, *John Addington Symonds, a Biographical Study* (New York: Michael Kennerley, 1914).

and Nijinsky, among the Russians; Rimbaud, Verlaine, and Baude-laire, three leaders of French poetic expression; Goethe, Wagner, and unquestionably Winckelmann, the latter regarded in critical circles as the greatest German poet of his times; the critical scholars, Pater and Symonds; Walt Whitman, who revolutionized the con-cepts of poetry; Byron, Shelley, and Wilde, among the British writers; Rosa Bonheur, one of the greatest woman painters of modern times; Marcel Proust, André Gide, and many contemporary writers from America, England, and France, who cannot be named for quite obvious reasons.

The list is not exhaustive, and the names found thereon have not been chosen by the idle gossip of some uncultured but prying invert. Baudelaire, as I have noted, is placed on this list at the suggestion of a giant of French letters, a keen analytical mind, Marcel Proust; Leonardo, at the insistence of Freud; Michaelangelo, particularly through the research of Symonds. Thus in Proust and Symonds we find the burning need to have "heroes."

Why is there such a preponderance of artists, poets, and perhaps dancers, to the exclusion of scientists (save Leonardo, whose versatile mind defies classification), industrialists, and politicians (except for the military geniuses)? Why are there composers and not explorers; actors and actresses (of the present day, here unnamed, but well-known), although seldom a great inventor? Does this indicate some special predilections on the part of homosexuals? Is their talent chan-nelled in certain directions? I do not believe so. The homosexual creativity, so often freed from conventional thought, with imagination unbound and unfettered and sponsored by the need for perfection to overcome the doubt of oneself, is not confined entirely or primarily to the arts. It is present in men of science and industry, in educators, religious leaders, inventors. But certain people, through the pages of history, have left behind them a heritage that permits an undeniable interpretation of their lives. These men were either the most articulate (the writers) or the most prominent (military men, dictators, roy-alty). Who would know that a brilliant woman of the island of Lesbos was a lover of girls if she had been scientist rather than poetess, for it is precisely in her poetry that, despite frequently distorted translation, she has expressed her sentiments in undeniable fashion.

Who would know that one of the leaders of German industry was a homosexual had he not gained the prominence of notoriety for his activities and been hounded to suicide?

The writers of years past, and those of today as well, leave indisputable evidence of their predilections. Scientists, businessmen, political leaders, inventive geniuses—these men and women not only leave no such evidence, but are forced to the humiliating position of vehement denial and deliberate misinformation.

Only when a private life becomes so public that hardly a fact remains unknown can one find evidence of homosexuality. Royalty is an example, and the history of the best known of modern dynasties, the British, furnishes interesting examples. Impartial historians today assert that four of the last thirty kings who have ruled over England were primarily or exclusively homosexual.

Those who have approached this problem with antagonistic prejudices are unable to interpret in a satisfactory manner the influence of homosexuality among the peoples of the Western world. They cannot explain why this passion flourished in the unrivalled civilization of ancient Greece, and in the most creative circles of the Renaissance. Yet, many an admirer of Greek civilization hastens to dissociate himself from this great passion. One reads, not infrequently, how repugnant is "this aspect" of Greek life to some scholar or historian—a statement made by no less an historian than Lecky. But such a person not only betrays his prejudice, but is caught in a pathetic web of contradiction, for he seeks not only to understand but to admire the Greek ideal, without accepting the foundation on which it was built; he would accept the glories of Greece, without accepting boy-love, which was basic to her entire social structure.

Or take the figure of the venerable Whitman, the bearded sage of Camden, the poet-singer of freedom. There can be no question that Whitman was a homosexual. Whether he also had bisexual inclinations is doubtful, but is not pertinent to the question of how he has been treated by his biographers. The essential fact is that he knowingly harbored the homosexual urge and probably fulfilled his cravings. It is evident in almost every line of his poetry; it was clearly indicated by his correspondence and by many facts about his life. Now, how does the heterosexual world attempt to correlate this with its interpretation and evaluation of so universally admired a man as Whitman? I shall take up this matter in some detail, because it demonstrates the area of impenetrability, the dulling of even the sharpest critical faculties, when a heterosexual is attempting to keep intact his preconceived taboos and yet interpret faithfully the contributions of a homosexual genius.

A group of his biographers deny facts, suppress and ignore others, at the same time stressing as evidence Whitman's famous letter to John Addington Symonds in which he is purported to have contradicted Symonds's interpretation of the poems of "Calamus," one of the most outspoken sections of *Leaves of Grass*. A translator of Whitman, rendering his poetry into French, even takes the liberty of imparting gender where Whitman has so painstakingly avoided it; the poet had used such words as "my friend," "my comrade," "my lover," and the translator used "mon amie," "ma camarade," and "mon amante."

But as the evidence of homosexuality accumulated, the critical biographers began to refer to him as a "latent" or "unconscious" homosexual, an ill-defined term, but one with less stigma. This characterization was based on little more than conjecture. If it were accurate, Whitman would more likely have given expression to it in a negative fashion by showing a strong repulsion for the entire suggestion of comrade-love. It is largely in justification of this "unconsciousness" theory that Whitman's letter of denial to Symonds has been quoted.

What are the facts? On August 19, 1872, Symonds wrote and asked Whitman if his interpretation of "Calamus" was not justified. The letter went unanswered, but occupied Whitman's mind. He constantly spoke highly of Symonds, but even to his friend Horace Traubel, he refused to deny or affirm the implication. "It always makes me a little testy to be catechized about the *Leaves*—I prefer to have the book answer for itself."*

For eighteen years the letter, as well as several others in a similar vein from Symonds that followed, remained unanswered. Finally, in 1890, Whitman disavowed "the morbid inference," which he termed "damnable." This disavowal, Henry Seidel Canby, one of the best of the modern biographers, wrote, was entirely sincere, although "psychologically . . . he was intermediate in sex." He was not a homo-

* Horace Traubel, *With Walt Whitman in Camden* (Boston: Small, Maynard & Co., 1906), p. 203.

sexual "in the vulgar sense of the word," but he was "very definitely not the normal animal in both body and mind . . . passionate, physical love for a man was as possible for him as was the same kind of love for a woman—and in Whitman's case easier."* All of which quite evidently adds up to meaningless contradictions.

Another group of critics makes no attempt at denial. Whitman was not only a homosexual, Mark Van Doren asserts, but his sexual inversion pervades his entire work and is basic to his philosophy, which is therefore meaningless and useless to modern man. The logic of this conclusion is terrifying. Let the world reject the dialogues of Plato, the Sistine chapel and the smile of Giaconda, the *Symphonie Pathétique*, the comedies of Wilde and the camaraderie of Whitman—these and many other creations, being motivated by the homosexual urge, are hence meaningless for the normal personality. The democratic dogmas of Whitman are "wholly without meaning," are "wholly invalid," have "no serious political meaning for healthy men and women," because "half-consciously" Whitman was referring to homosexual love when he spoke of "manly attachment."†

Not only is the homoerotic temperament of Whitman openly acknowledged, but it is found to be basic to his philosophy, his poetry, his political outlook—which is precisely what I have contended elsewhere. I take issue with Van Doren's analysis, however, in the latter's rejection of Whitman's contributions, not on the basis of their inherent content, but because of their origin. Newton Arvin also concedes the homosexual motivation, but argues that personal origins (of thought, philosophy, literature) are not to be taken as the test of their validity. But, lest the reader confuse Whitman with the homosexual stereotype, Arvin adds (in manner reminiscent of those who know "a good Jew" or, worse, "a white Jew") that "Whitman was no mere invert, no mere 'case': he remained to the end, in almost every real and visible sense, a sweet and sane human being."‡ Note the implication in this remark: the mere invert, the mere case—whatever this may mean—is not a sweet and sane human being! And this characterization is made by an astute critic—not a mere heterosexual!

* Henry Seidel Canby, *Walt Whitman, an American* (New York: Literary Classics, Inc., Houghton Mifflin, Boston, distributors, 1943), pp. 201–202.
† Mark Van Doren, quoted by Newton Arvin, *Whitman* (New York: Macmillan Co., 1938), p. 273.
‡ Newton Arvin, *Whitman* (New York: Macmillan Co., 1938), p. 277.

Although Whitman's lifework is accepted by Arvin, and although the latter concedes the truth about his subject's temperament, nowhere is the contribution that Whitman made to poetry and to the evolution of our democratic thought evaluated in the light of his having been sexually inverted. And this is basic to an understanding of the rôle of the homosexual, whether genius or "mere case," in our society.

Homosexuality, maintained André Gide, "is indispensable to the constitution of a well-regulated society."* Until such a truism is understood, the work of Whitman and the meaning of his genius for modern times will be an unfathomable riddle to the investigator. Just as the homosexuals do not reject the music of Chopin, although it is imbued with the tragic romance of his love for women; or the literary influences of a Dickens or a Joyce, so is it equally absurd for the "normal man" to reject an art, a philosophy, a music, a political thought, because it came from the creative mind of a homosexual. But more than that, it is necessary to discover how Whitman's sexual make-up affected his creative genius. For instance, was he able to break the chains of traditional verse forms because his mind had been forced to question all preconceived concepts? Was he able to develop the spirit of camaraderie and true democracy because his mind found inspiration in the comradeship and close contact of man for man? Was he able to imbue America with a spirit of democracy because he found a great need for a society that would accept the non-conforming minority viewpoint? Was he able to write with immortal sympathy for the man Lincoln, and nurse on the battlefields of the Civil War, because as a homosexual he felt sympathy for the plight and suffering of his comrades in the great march for human freedom?

Not until the heterosexual critic can lay aside his repugnance, not until he can free himself of the concept of the "mere invert," can he understand Whitman, or for that matter Gide, Proust, Wilde, Verlaine, and many others. Only then can the biographer know what motivates these people. Only then can he judge whether it was because of their anomaly rather than despite it that they were able to leave this world richer than they found it; whether this legacy is meaningful for all men, although it came from men of a particular group.

In the meantime, for all the efforts to deny and to disassociate, for

* André Gide, *The Journals* (New York: Alfred A. Knopf, 1949), III, 117.

all the ridicule heaped upon those who would identify the gay lad at the bar with the genius of Whitman or Leonardo, they are of one and the same group. Neither lies nor distortion can destroy the basic unity.

The heroes of the homosexuals are many, and perhaps around them has been built a cult. If this is true, then the worshippers have merely acted as a minority, although possibly unaware of their group behavior. Some heroes are loved more than others, and some admire these people with the blindness of critical faculties that have been dulled by the wish to believe. So few have been the rewards of inversion that people will turn to any evidence from which satisfaction is derived. It took little to convince Proust of the temperament of Baudelaire, Carpenter of the leanings of Shakespeare. Thus the minority is evidently as anxious to believe as the majority to deny.

But in these heroes are found not merely justification and example. In their lives and achievements can be found an understanding of the meaning of an anomaly, an indication of its place in the scheme of things. What homosexuality has imparted to the lives of a few, it has contributed in similar manner to those less endowed with natural gifts.

How pathetic is the effort of those who would glorify a hero, yet denounce his life. These critics deny, they ignore, or they acknowledge and attempt to demonstrate the unprovable: that creative contributions have nothing to do with the accident of sexual temperament; or, if they do, that such contributions must be rejected by men of other temperaments.

It devolves, then, upon the openly acknowledged homosexuals—or upon those very few other people who approach this question with understanding and sympathy—to interpret these men, their lives, their psychology, their aspirations, their legacy, to a society that can benefit from a heritage whose origins are beyond its comprehensions.

Chapter 16

On a Five-Foot Bookshelf

It is considered by many literary historians that *The Satyricon* of Petronius is the oldest extant novel. This gives the homosexual the distinction of being the protagonist in the first novel to survive the passage of time. During the period between the revival of learning and the dawn of the twentieth century, the taboo on the portrayal of homosexuality in literature was so severe that a large part of this literature is disguised and requires keen analysis to recognize.

A more or less comprehensive list of the drama and fiction that constitute a library of homosexual literature would be impossible to compile. Many authors have employed subtleties that might have been inherent in their styles, or may have been imposed by convention, but the exact interpretation of the writings of Balzac, Henry James, and Oscar Wilde can never be more than conjectural. If one could dissociate the author from his work, it might be difficult to demonstrate the homosexual basis of *The Picture of Dorian Gray*, but when one knows that it was written by Wilde, certain phrases can be understood to have only a homosexual meaning, whether taken in or out of their context: "secret vices . . . the Duke of Berwick leaves the room of a club when you enter it . . . Why is your friendship so fateful to young men . . . Dorian, Dorian, your reputation is infamous."

Many homosexuals are so anxious to find in literature justification and clues to happiness that they interpret every manifestation of friendship as being of a sexual nature. But responsible critics, particularly avantgardists and students of psychiatric literature, have likewise found homosexuality in their interpretation of the most "innocent" classics. One critic gives a homosexual interpretation to *Huckleberry Finn*, and another to *Charley's Aunt*.

167

In *The Pupil* by Henry James, for example, a very strong attraction and mutual dependency between a young tutor and his pupil are described. In reading this story, I found little to indicate that James understood that dependency to grow out of a sexual need of the two young people for one another, and such an interpretation, it would seem to me, is not basic to an appreciation of the work. This opinion is evidently not shared by the critic, Albert Guérard, who describes the book as treating of male homosexuality.

On the other hand, there is no way of understanding the friendship between the two lovers of the Brangwen sisters in *Women in Love* by D. H. Lawrence, except that one of them found that he had a need for physical gratification with his male friend; and this is quite clearly indicated, not only by a knowledge of Lawrence's understanding of Freudianism and by such incidents as the prolonged handshake, but by the passage which ends the book:

> "Did you need Gerald?" she asked one evening.
> "Yes," he said.
> "Aren't I enough for you?" she asked.
> "No," he said. "You are enough for me, as far as a woman is concerned. You are all women to me. But I wanted a man friend, as eternal as you and I are eternal."
> "Why aren't I enough?" she said. "You are enough for me. I don't want anybody else but you. Why isn't it the same with you?"
> "Having one, I can live all my life without anybody else, any other sheer intimacy. But to make it complete, really happy, I wanted eternal union with a man too: another kind of love," he said.
> "I don't believe it," she said. "It's an obstinacy, a theory, a perversity."
> "Well—" he said.
> "You can't have two kinds of love. Why should you!"
> "It seems as if I can't," he said. "Yet I wanted it."
> "You can't have it, because it is false, impossible," she said.
> "I don't believe that," he answered.*

Friendship is the theme of a beautiful French novel entitled *Special Friendships* by Roger Peyrefitte, in which there is an undertone of a budding erotic desire between two schoolboys, but schoolboy "crushes" and particularly the similar manifestations among girls have been depicted in countless novels in which there is little room for the homosexual interpretation.

* D. H. Lawrence, *Women in Love* (New York: Modern Library edition), p. 548. Quoted by courtesy of Viking Press.

Finally, there are large numbers of books in which the homosexual plays a relatively minor but nonetheless important rôle. He (or she) is not the central character, but is an important influence in the life of that character and in the development of the novel. Such books as *Serenade* by James Cain, *Dusty Answer* by Rosamond Lehmann, and *The Rainbow* by D. H. Lawrence come to mind. Or, for that matter, *The Lost Weekend*, Charles Jackson's brilliant study of an alcoholic whose repressed homosexual memories return during his long intoxication.

Some authors have been attracted to this subject because of the importance it held for their own lives; others because they saw in it a field for the study of conflict—conflict within the individual, and of the individual with society. In addition to those already mentioned, Smollett, de Maupassant, Flaubert, Gautier, Proust, Gide, Gertrude Stein, and Thomas Mann, among many others, have written about the homosexual temperament. To these one can add many contemporary or recent writers whose permanent place in letters is not yet secure, but who are certainly among the significant literary personages of our time: Henry B. Fuller, Panait Istrati, Ronald Firbank, Wyndham Lewis, Christopher Isherwood, Jean-Paul Sartre, Jean Genêt, Gore Vidal, Truman Capote, James Cain, Radclyffe Hall, Jean Cocteau, Edouard Bourdet, Roger Martin du Gard, Djuna Barnes, Compton MacKenzie, Clemence Dane, Mary Renault, Parker Tyler, John Horne Burns, Gale Wilhelm, Blair Niles, Tennessee Williams, Evelyn Waugh . . . and the list can be extended. To these names can be added a group of several young writers who have made a contribution to the novel, sometimes drawing from their own experiences and observations; their novels are usually more important for their content than for their art form, but their final contribution to the literature of homosexuality and to an understanding of the problems of homosexuality remains to be evaluated. And, finally, there are numerous important writers—Herman Melville is an outstanding example—whose work can be interpreted in the light of concealed homosexuality.

Some of the writers mentioned have been obsessed with sexual inversion. It is either their sole or dominant theme, recurring in many of their works. Others have written on the subject in but a single work, as the brief story, "Hands," by Sherwood Anderson. For some writers, Gale Wilhelm, for example, it seems to me that the theme has inspired their finest literary endeavors; while for others, as Gore Vidal and Grace Zaring Stone, the excursion into the realm of the homosexual novel was a disappointing failure not at all comparable to their other work.

The literature on this subject would be clarified if it could be classed into two major groups: works written by those whose knowledge was acquired by a study from without; and those written by the homosexuals who have learned of the life from within. If such a classification were possible, an analysis of these works would be interesting. It would demonstrate the different degrees of understanding, the varying attitudes and approaches, brought to a subject by the in-group and by the out-group. However, much of the literature produced by writers who are motivated by a subjective approach has been camouflaged in a manner that destroys a great part of its value. A few men of letters have openly proclaimed their inclinations: Genêt, and before him Gide. A few others were well-known homosexuals who concealed little: Radclyffe Hall, Marcel Proust. But even in the early works of Gide, *The Immoralist*, for example, there is what amounts to unnecessary circumlocution, as if the author were not quite sure whether or not he ought to clarify for the reader a situation which was entirely clear to himself. Certainly Gide would not have found it necessary to use this approach had he written *The Immoralist* in his later years. And as for Proust, despite his outspoken writings on homosexuality, he chose to camouflage the theme when the word "I" was involved. It is believed by many scholars, and has been quite ably demonstrated by Justin O'Brien,* that one of the central female characters in *Remembrance of Things Past*, Albertine, is a "transposed" male, and that the narrator's infatuation for her is actually a matter of concealed homosexuality.

When homosexuals have written on the theme of inversion they have frequently used pseudonyms. If this enabled them to speak more openly, to depict more honestly, it would be a welcome step. But the pseudonym has not always freed these people of the impact of heterosexual moral judgments and standards.

One of the methods of camouflage, as utilized by Proust, has been to disguise gender by a deliberate transposition of sex. Others have

---

* Justin O'Brien, "Albertine the Ambiguous: Notes on Proust's Transposition of Sexes," *Publications of the Modern Language Association of America,* December 1949, p. 933.

written passages that can be interpreted only by the elect; their books may be read by intelligent audiences who are quite unsuspecting of a homosexual theme. This has been accomplished by several writers who have taken a leaf from Whitman, avoiding the use of gender in their amatory passages. They speak of *the partner, the dream-image, comrade, companion-in-bed, lover, body,* and the like.

But the use of deliberate avoiding of gender can serve another purpose, more worthy from a literary viewpoint—the expression of bisexuality, rather than the sponsorship of deliberate confusion through camouflage. In a book in which the central character is drawn to both male and female, John Horne Burns described the protagonist's reminiscences of amatory adventures in a skillful passage that can be interpreted only as an indication of bisexuality:

> And as the water swirled the myriad clipped red hairs out of his razor, he thought of his experiences in New York last vacation, of the remarks of his bed companions for the night, who were intrigued by his broken mouth:
> —Ooooh, broth*er*! . . .
> —Kiss me that way again. Haven't felt like that since a lobster bit me. . . .
> —Put that mouth of yours against my neck and draw blood. . . .
> He wondered if his technic as a lover had also been wrenched by his scar, for now his was a mouth more meet for prayer than for caresses.*

The reception by the literary world and the reading public of books on the homosexual theme is interesting. Unless they are works of art produced by outstanding men of letters, they are often ignored by literary reviews and journals. One reviewer doubted if the version of a certain writer was convincing and attributed this to his fortunate ignorance of the subject, but the novelist himself was hardly as ignorant as the reviewer. Another critic, writing for one of the most important literary periodicals, expressed himself as being allergic to novels on this subject—a strange admission for a reviewer to make!

For the gay readers, the novels on homosexuality have been far from satisfactory. They must, it is generally felt, be judged on three separate and distinct though interrelated levels: first, as literary efforts; second, as accurate portrayals of a phase of gay life; third, as social

---

* John Horne Burns, *Lucifer with a Book* (New York: Harper & Brothers, 1949), p. 210. The quotation is given in full; the emphasis and the ellipses are in the original.

documents on behalf of a minority group. For the general or heterosexual reader, the first of these reasons is paramount, the second he is
hardly qualified to judge, and the third is usually of no interest to
him. Therefore the intelligent heterosexual reader can say that *The
Well of Loneliness* is an overwritten literary failure, *The City and the
Pillar* is dull and sprawling, *The Fall of Valor* lacks conviction, *The
Sling and the Arrow* reads like a case history, and *The Divided Path*
is a minor study of a meaningless conflict.

With some of these judgments, a homosexual reader might be inclined to agree, with others he would take sharp issue. He seeks a
literary and artistic work, but there is no need to convince him of an
emotional structure with which he is so thoroughly conversant. Situations that seem contrived to other readers are everyday occurrences
to him. Therefore from his vantage point *The Well of Loneliness* is
primarily a social plea; *The City and the Pillar* is an accurate portrait
of a phase of gay life, but without a solution to a stated problem;
The Fall of Valor is not so much unconvincing but atypical, and possibly suffers from an inability of the author to come to grips with his
subject; *The Sling and the Arrow* is a worthless clinical case history
written by someone who is obviously (and, if you will, fortunately)
ignorant of his subject; *The Divided Path* is a portrait of a conflict
with which we are all familiar, and it offers a beginning toward a
possible solution.

What rôle can a fictional portrait of homosexuality possibly play?
It can enlighten, encourage, and offer a suggestion for the ultimate
solution of the individual's dilemma. In its efforts to enlighten, it can
impart knowledge and insight for the benefit both of the public at
large and the homosexual in particular; it can encourage the invert to
continue to function, to win his struggle for adjustment, and to accept
himself; it can offer similar aid to friends, relatives, and others who
must furnish understanding; and, finally, in suggesting a way out, it
can show all readers that the invert's life is not that of a hopeless
person doomed to defeat.

Inasmuch as the novel is usually the portrait of but one individual
or of a small group and not a panoramic picture of a larger segment
of society, its characterization can be, and often is, atypical. Thus at
least three important literary endeavors have told of the awakening
of a homosexual longing for the first time many years after maturation.

Thomas Mann handled this rather difficult subject with rare beauty and keen psychological insight in his *Death in Venice;* André Gide made it the theme of *The Immoralist,* in which the protagonist's growing guilt complex is complicated by the illness and eventual death of his bride; and Charles Jackson returned to an analogous situation in *The Fall of Valor* (after a masterful interpretation of repressed homosexuality and intoxication in *The Lost Weekend*), but there is much in *The Fall of Valor* to suggest that the professor was not as ignorant of his latent homosexuality as he led the author to believe.

But, other than to evaluate the work on the basis of its literary art, what can the homosexuals say of such a book as *Death in Venice?* It possesses, on the one hand, no relationship to the problems faced by most homosexuals, although it demonstrates the delicate line that divides two ways of life that are often considered mutually exclusive. Finally, it depicts the very commonly encountered phenomenon of homosexuality as an expression of the Greek-like love of youthful beauty.

The fictional portraits of a minority group often include a certain number of unsympathetic works. No literary excursion into the homosexual domain was, in my opinion, quite as repulsive as Dorothy Baker's *Trio.* This writer portrayed a Lesbian who had brought under her influence a youthful and innocent girl, captivating her with a remarkable display of intellectual ability as manifested in a literary document she was preparing. It turns out that the older woman is a literary thief, the document has been stolen, she has no true critical ability, and her only originality was in the creation of a theory that degeneracy is a necessary prerequisite for genius. The younger girl, furthermore, is actually in love with a man and is being held in virtual bondage in a relationship which does not appeal to her.

Now it is entirely within the realm of possibility that a literary thief might exist, although Mrs. Baker's characterization falls far short of a convincing portrait; and the thief might even be a Lesbian. But it is manifestly improper, in the conditions existing in society today, to seize upon such a character for a portrait of a Lesbian relationship. What would be said of an author who painted an equally repulsive picture of a member of some racial or religious minority? The possibility that such a person might exist could not be denied, but it would be considered irresponsible, from a social viewpoint, to depict such a character under circumstances in which he will be identified with many others in the group; and it is an abuse of literary freedom to fail to place such a person in a milieu in which he can be contrasted with the more worthy members of the minority.

Another unfavorable stereotype was portrayed in a very shallow but widely hailed drama, *The Green Bay Tree* by Mordaunt Shairp. A doddering and decadent old man has adopted an eleven-year-old boy and nursed him to a maturity of uselessness and perversity. The young man, once he seeks to re-orient his life with a woman, is restrained by the ease and luxury which his guardian-lover offers.

A relationship between an older and a younger man is not at all unusual, but it does not commence with the adoption and influencing of an eleven-year-old. Furthermore the basis of such a relationship is rarely financial; it usually has an intellectual foundation in which the older person is a teacher and guide, the youth an inspiration. Far from being unproductive and worthless, it is frequently a basis for the development of unusual talent. Finally, it is not an unwilling bondage in which the young person would follow the culturally accepted paths were he not a gigolo; rather he is an invert who, if he did not have his older friend, might be living a difficult life with many youths, or might be bewildered in the effort to adjust himself to the confusions of a hostile society.

The homosexual reader is anxious to find a fictional portrait that will be truthful yet not atypical. He seeks in literature an honest approach in which there is no need to camouflage in order to serve the public with something less distasteful, for that very attitude carries within it the concept of an acceptance of public hostility. The fictional portraits seem, probably in order to make the subjects more palatable, to have overstressed the late years of awakening and gratifying of the homosexual yearnings. Adolescent and even later years of sublimation and repression are common in these books. An exception is Truman Capote's *Other Voices, Other Rooms:* the adolescent responds to the call of a pathetic but decadent adult. But in numerous works there are years of conscious or unconscious struggle, very vague and unrecognized desires, before the consummation of the erotic urge or even its recognition for what it is. Examples include *The Divided Path, The City and the Pillar,* and *Quatrefoil.* The reader is never quite convinced in *Quatrefoil,* for example, that the ensign is as innocent of a previous knowledge of his homosexuality as the author states. There is in this situation a certain degree of tacit acceptance of the outer world's prudish concept. Homosexuality is never fully accepted by the characters as an erotic urge, but only as a manifestation of love. The theme is not only unconvincing, but in many instances evades a frank discussion of the subject.

In this vast literature it is surprising that no one should have developed a really penetrating study of the childhood influences that produced the homosexual. Adolescent conflict is abundant, but not the pre-adolescent causative developments. Some of the writers may have been led astray by their acceptance of the inborn or congenital theory, or discouraged by the difficulties surrounding the study of genesis. *The Well of Loneliness,* despite the adherence to the concept of inversion by accident of birth, offers a portrait of childhood conditions which might well be the background against which homosexuality would thrive: frigidity in the mother, overbearing love on the part of the father, a strong and athletic girl who can more easily identify herself with men than with women. An effort, all too feeble, is made in *The Divided Path* to trace the influence of childhood on the protagonist's sexuality, but the subject is not studied in detail, and plays a small rôle in the book. In Maxwell's *The Folded Leaf,* childhood influences are delineated in a profound manner, so that the reader is made to understand why each of the two schoolboys who are the central characters of the novel become dependent upon each other, but the fact is that neither of them becomes an overt homosexual, and the book can hardly be considered a contribution to the fictional portraits of homosexual genesis.

The subject of the causative factors that lead a person to the minority pathway of life was basic to a profound and powerful novel by Fritz Peters, *Finistère.* The author leaves the reader without a doubt that homosexuality is the product of divorce, the lack of love between mother and father, and the entire feeling of being rejected and unloved. But how and why the adolescent makes the transition from the loneliness of a rejected youth to his homosexuality remains unexplained. In fact, an intelligent reader is likely to gain the impression, which is certainly far from scientific fact and probably not at all intended by the author, that Michel was turning to love and affection, and that if a woman had been present, instead of a man, he would have turned his attention toward her, responding to her warmth, and never knowing how perilously close he had been to becoming a homosexual.

For the homosexual reader, the most disappointing element of the novels on the subject is the paucity of imagination and the flight from reality that characterize the endings. Suicide, murder, and other types of violent death, or emptiness and defeat, greet the reader. "There seems to be a gentleman's agreement among publishers that there shall be no happy endings to such novels," many people say, and although no such agreement exists, it is easy to understand why its existence is imagined. My own experience shows that homosexuals do not meet violent death at the hands of others or of themselves. They live out their lives with not much more dissatisfaction than do other people; some marry and have children; others form a permanent union in the romantic attachment to a friend of the same sex; others find reward in their work.

It is my opinion that some of the tragic endings of certain writers arise from the identification of the authors themselves with their protagonists. The accidental death, the murder, or the suicide of these semi-fictional, semi-autobiographical creations are the methods by which some authors, themselves homosexual and having extreme obsessions about their inclinations, persecute and punish themselves. By inflicting punishment upon their own *alter ego*, they purge themselves of responsibility for the activities of their lives. It is the child saying, "See, I am a naughty boy, and I want to be punished," and then after punishment proceeding to continue in his naughty ways. By inflicting this verdict on their fictional rather than their real selves, the authors continue to live a free life, without suffering the consequences of the physical injuries of punishment, but benefitting by the rewards of a purging chastisement. It is unfortunate, but true, that many homosexual writers have used their books to "cure" themselves of their guilt, and the reading audience becomes the unwitting confessor or the ill-paid analyst.

Many of the novels suffer from an inability of the authors to find a way of ending their stories; it is as if they do not know what will happen to their protagonists tomorrow or the day after, and they use the privilege of the creator to rid themselves of a life that has become troublesome. An ending either in violence or on a note of hopelessness is found in *Twilight Men, The City and the Pillar, The*

Invisible Glass, The Grotto, Finistère, and *Stranger in the Land,* to name but a few; whereas the sole hope in *The Fall of Valor* is to return to the almost broken marriage: homosexuality is a dead-end. A suggestion that there might be a return to a full life has been made in two first novels: *The Divided Path, Quatrefoil.* But perhaps the most significant thing that can be said about the tragedies in which these authors enmesh their characters would be to quote the words of T. S. Eliot about the tragic loneliness of the people who inhabit the world of Djuna Barnes's poignant novel, *Nightwood:*

> The miseries that people suffer through their particular abnormalities of temperament are visible on the surface: the deeper design is that of human misery and bondage which is universal. In normal lives this misery is mostly concealed; often, what is most rigid of all, concealed from the sufferer more effectively than from the observer.*

Despite the array of talented writers who have turned their attention to the homosexual theme, the body of first-rate literature on the subject is indeed small. A check list of novels, drama, and other works of literature that have been or can be interpreted in the light of a homosexual theme is given in the appendix.

The large amount of attention being shown to this subject by novelists, despite their distortions, their ignorance, their prejudices (both pro and con), is being effective in one major respect: namely, as a means of breaking through the silence that has been such a major handicap in preventing social progress of the homosexual group. If the subject is being discussed by more people than ever before, the novelists can take part credit; and because the subject is being discussed more than ever, the novelists have been encouraged to approach it without fear or hesitation.

* T. S. Eliot, "Introduction" to *Nightwood,* by Djuna Barnes (New York: New Directions).

Part Five

ADJUSTMENTS

Chapter 17

Can Homosexuality Be Cured?

It has frequently been stated that the homosexual can be cured, if only he wants to be, but that most homosexuals have no desire to be cured and therefore cannot be. This statement, repeated in slightly varying form, contains several partial truths that require clarification.

Let us first see exactly what is being said about therapy. *The Journal of the American Medical Association* has made a statement which is typical:

> Help is available and can be effective for the homosexual person who desires it. The treatment, however, is entirely psychiatric and is nearly always a prolonged undertaking, lasting, even with intensive treatment, many months or even years. For those persons who do not want to change their makeup and even those who are not highly motivated in seeking help, treatment is practically useless.*

Many types of cures have been suggested for homosexuality, and several of them I shall dismiss as having definitely not been verified. These include shock treatments (as, for instance, the use of metrazol) and hormone treatment by an endocrinologist. It has not been shown that homosexuals are lacking in male or female sex hormones; and to my knowledge, based upon conversations with many physicians—particularly specialists—as well as with patients, no hormone treatment has ever achieved the desired results. It is entirely possible, of course, that in so widespread a condition there may be a coincidence of hormone deficiency and homosexuality; in other words, if one out of every twenty males is sexually inverted, then one out of every twenty men deficient in male hormones will likewise be of this temperament.

Journal of the American Medical Association, December 23, 1950, p. 1536.

The percentage might even increase, because a predisposition to hormone deficiency can produce a somewhat effeminate child who may therefore take refuge in the homosexual life.

It is generally recognized today, as stated by the American Medical Association and quoted above, that there is only one type of "treatment" for the homosexual, and that is at the hands of a psychiatrist or psychologist. And, it is said, there must be a genuine desire to be cured before any results can be obtained.

It is my contention that, by the very nature of homosexuality, to speak of a "desire to be cured" is a superficial paradox. Where exclusive homosexuality is an important part of a person's temperament, it plays a rôle of defending the individual against a way of life which holds more terror for him than the one he is leading, and the unconscious psychological alternative to his homosexuality is not what heterosexuality would mean to others, but what it means to him. He has turned away from that path because he cannot and does not want to face it, so that it is inherently a contradiction, and by definition an impossibility, to expect him to desire it.

Many people, including numerous homosexuals who are maladjusted and unhappy, will protest. They *do* want to be cured. They seek to change themselves and never cease to struggle against their own temperaments. The life they lead is hateful and repugnant to them and is counter to their will and better judgment. Their shame is a deep abyss, a bottomless pit.

Others, however, will attest to their pride and happiness and insist that they would not relinquish their sexual leanings for anything. The difficulties are compensated for by the pleasures, and they cannot conceive of life without these pleasures.

Actually, as many psychiatrists point out, the attitudes of both groups are likely to be defense mechanisms. The former, as I learned not only from my own experience but from that of many others, are only struggling to maintain self-respect. Self-condemnation relieves them of the burden of responsibility for what they are doing and therefore makes it possible for them to continue doing it. The proud and happy ones may likewise be suffering from shame and remorse, and using their boastfulness to withstand the impact of the world's harsh judgments.

How is it possible for the homosexual not to want to be cured, it will be asked, when the advantages of being heterosexual are so obvious? These advantages are only of a social nature. For the individual involved, heterosexuality offers material "advantages" but deepgoing psychological "disadvantages."

The fact is that it is impossible for the homosexual to imagine himself living without the basic sexual urge of his life. He needs this and needs it desperately. If he did not need it so greatly, he would not be homosexual in the first place. Even those who profess their desire for cure in the most sincere manner fail to recognize that the need for homosexual relationships is a *sexual* desire; the wish for cure is a *non-sexual* desire, and therefore the individual can and does accommodate both of these desires at one and the same time.

Now it may appear, superficially, to be humane to erect a fiction that homosexuals are actually desirous of being like all other people in their sexual inclinations, but it is psychologically unsound. Furthermore, the perpetuation of the fiction of cure is far from humane; in fact, it is harmful to the homosexual, and it is based on the conception that people can be changed if they want to.

It is true that many homosexuals would like to be able to marry and cohabit with women, beget children, and live "socially normal" lives, but this does not mean that they want to relinquish their libidinous drive. Even those homosexuals who practice continence and deliberately suppress their impulses are not willing to relinquish the love urge toward their own sex. Were this impulse not absolutely necessary, it would never have existed at all. Hence, the individual cannot *wish* it out of existence. He can only pretend to others and even to himself that he so wishes, because the pretense can relieve him of self-responsibility and therefore give him a clean slate in his own eyes.

This does not mean that sexual inversion is voluntary, and that one need only exercise good judgment and willpower in order to overcome it or to choose some other pathway. Not at all. It is entirely involuntary and beyond control, because *one did not choose to want to be homosexual*.

To the heterosexual who may not be able to comprehend such an apparent contradiction, let me suggest that you imagine a society in which being as you are is a disadvantage. You might, for instance, be isolated on an island inhabited only by persons of your own sex

with the prospect of confinement to their company for the remainder
of your life. All around, you see homosexuals well adjusted to this
life. In the society in which you are placed, they are happier than
you are. It is conceivable that you might force yourself, for the sake
of release or material advantage, to enter into their relationships, but
you could not possibly wish to become one of them to such an extent
that you succeed in transforming yourself.

Given the human being as he is, and given the homosexual drive
as it exists, can a change be effected in an individual so that he issues
from psychoanalytic therapy as much a heterosexual as anyone else? I
have asked this question of dozens of physicians, and particularly
psychoanalysts, and I have searched scientific literature to find an
answer. I have questioned at least a score of men who have been
patients, and I can state that there is a considerable preponderance
of opinion and evidence that this question be answered in the negative.
There are extremely few cases on record of homosexuality ever having been cured, if by cure is meant a complete replacement of the
female for the male as the desired love-object—and how reliable the
records of cures may be remains to be determined.

The psychiatrists, when asked the above question, will frequently
avoid a direct answer. They will tell the invert, or his mother, that
he can be helped. But, on investigation, I find that their help consists
of his making a better adjustment as a homosexual, and not of overcoming the drive. Sometimes the therapist will bring about a heterosexual adjustment, leading in fact to a happy marriage, but this does
not involve a diminution of the homosexual drive. The psychiatrists
will say that there are some special cases where a more complete
change might possibly be brought about, but I find that they refer to
very young people (still in adolescence) or those who may have
drifted into a homosexual union out of lack of availability of other
outlet, rather than from a basic desire and preference. It is not my
intention to deny the strong possibilities of effecting a change in modes
of behavior under such circumstances. These cases, however, have
little to do with the problem of exclusive homosexuality in a mature
person.

It is my conviction, and I know that it is shared by many others,
including outstanding professional psychiatrists—although the latter
are not in unanimous agreement—that homosexuality is in the great

majority of people affected virtually ineradicable at this time, and that it may continue to be so in the future, not only because ineradicability may be implied by the nature of the drive itself, but also because of certain inherent difficulties that a therapist will encounter when meeting his patients who seek to renounce their inversion.

When a psychotherapist has a patient who is suffering from a maladjustment, he is faced with a choice of several possible paths to follow. He can seek to change the patient, provided he considers it feasible and desirable. Or he can aid the patient in adjusting to himself and to society without undergoing a fundamental change in his entire make-up. Or, as part of the latter adjustment, he can guide the patient into a new milieu of society where greater happiness can be achieved.

Not only is it futile to attempt to change the homosexual into a heterosexual, but it can also be very dangerous, despite the lofty motives of the physician. In his famous work *The Story of San Michele*, Dr. Axel Munthe tells of meeting a young invert who had been treated by both Krafft-Ebing and Charcot and who, in the words of Munthe, was "most anxious to be cured." The doctor attempted to guide the person, through hypnosis, to the accepted sexual path of life. A year later he heard that the man had committed suicide. "Had this unhappy man consulted me a few years later when I had acquired more knowledge of sexual inversion I would never have attempted the hopeless task of curing him."*

In the medical and psychiatric literature, there are sometimes equivocal remarks open to ambiguous interpretation, and sometimes forthright statements. Bergler maintains that homosexuals can be cured—and that he has cured some, but upon examination the ex-homosexuals have become bisexual.† He cites the fact that one of his patients has married, but this does not prove that he no longer craves sexual relations with men. London and Caprio state that "Sadger reported numerous successes in the treatment of homosexuals via the psychoanalytic approach," but they do not state whether this success resulted in the people becoming happy, adjusted homosexuals, or in their becoming free of the homosexual urge. The

* Axel Munthe, *The Story of San Michele* (New York: E. P. Dutton & Co., 1930), pp. 319–320.
† Edmund Bergler, *Neurotic Counterfeit-Sex* (New York: Grune & Stratton, 1951), p. 189.

homosexual, London and Caprio continue, "must be made to believe that he can be cured. The prognosis is good if he exhibits a genuine willingness to be cured."*

But these same authors report one case in great detail in which "the patient states that psychoanalysis relieved her of her acute anxiety states."† In another case, "her analysis in all probability enabled her to reconcile herself more adequately to her homosexual inclinations and relieved her to some degree of the guilt-producing anxiety responsible for her neurotic complaints."‡ And, finally, "As for the patient's prognosis, her analysis will perhaps enable her to reconcile herself psychotherapeutically to her homosexuality."§

The actual case histories, with the results and the aims of the therapist, themselves contradict the statements previously quoted concerning cure.

On the other hand, this question of cure has been handled in a forthright manner in a book by two prominent psychologists, who pose the question, "Can homosexuality be cured?" Here is the response:

> The word "cure" suggests disease. We have already stated that sexual inversion is not a disease, but a consequence of biologic or psychologic factors or a combination of both. In many cases the invert no more wishes to be "cured" than would a heterosexual person if his cure involved becoming an invert . . . There is no medical or surgical relief for the homosexual at the present time. Neither hypnosis nor psychoanalysis has been too successful in dealing with this problem if by "success" we mean a complete and satisfying change from a sex partner of the same sex to one of the opposite sex. Psychological treatment has enabled individuals to make a better emotional adjustment to their homosexual wishes with reduction of such symptoms of nervous strain as already described. But a complete "cure" is still very rare.‖

Now it is possible that quotation-makers can lie, just as can statisticians. But I have not sought out a quotation which fails to reflect the opinion of medical science. On the contrary, the above represents an almost universally accepted viewpoint among psychoanalysts.

* Louis S. London and Frank S. Caprio, *Sexual Deviations* (Washington: Linacre Press, 1950), p. 656.
† *Ibid.*, p. 268.
‡ *Ibid.*, p. 196.
§ *Ibid.*, p. 169.
‖ Fred Brown and Rudolph T. Kempton, *Sex Questions and Answers, a Guide to Happy Marriage* (New York: Whittlesey House, 1950), p. 238.

How can it be maintained that homosexuality is not inborn but arises from social or environmental conditions, and then deny that it is curable? I might emphasize that these two views are not merely my own: they are shared by many men of standing. The quotation from Brown and Kempton could easily be substantiated by the writings of many other authorities.

But is there a contradiction in these two views? Only on the surface. For the homosexual, because of the environmental conditions, reaches a point in his development where he desires gratification of his sexual urge with the same sex, and once that point has been reached, he cannot desire not to desire it. Furthermore, homosexuality differs from other compulsions (if it can be termed a compulsion) in that it offers both considerable pleasure and release from sexual tension. The neural pleasure obtained from the sexual act becomes a defense against change, because change would mean a sacrifice of that pleasure. The therapist seeks to increase the satisfaction, and this necessarily decreases the need for change.

It is my opinion that the failure to effect a transformation of the homosexual into the heterosexual is readily explicable. The task of the therapist is to relieve repressions, not to sponsor them. As the maladjusted homosexual finds that his feelings of guilt are diminished, that his repressions are brought out into the consciousness, he will find that he is enjoying his homosexual relations, and in fact enjoying being a homosexual, more than before. The conditions which would seem, on the surface, to be a prerequisite for cure, namely the strong desire to overcome homosexuality, therefore diminish as the therapy succeeds, and if these conditions do not disappear, then the therapy is not succeeding.

At the same time, the homosexual makes another adjustment, and that is that his fears and repugnances toward sexual union with a woman likewise diminish, and through therapy he is frequently able to effect such a union. This does not mean that he ceases to desire men, but merely that he ceases to desire them to the exclusion of women. Marriage often becomes an attractive road. But such an adjustment can only take place in an individual who has been relieved of guilt toward his homosexuality, and who has hence learned to enjoy it, and therefore marriage will not replace the homosexual side of life, but merely complement it. Any other type of cure would involve teaching the homosexual to learn to repress a desire that is very strongly imbedded in him, and obviously the analytic process, in which repressions are diminished, can hardly be expected to attain that result.

The literature of psychoanalysis contains numerous reports on the effort to aid the homosexual by convincing him that he should accept his condition. As a matter of fact, the therapists have not hesitated in bringing to the consciousness and encouraging homosexuality where it was basic and important to a patient. One could cite many such cases from the technical literature. The following is quoted from a work of the highest repute, written by men of outstanding professional reputation:

> The patient was suffering from acute anxiety in connection with unconscious homosexual tendencies. In broaching this subject matter, he described various sexual temptations to which he had been exposed as a sailor. He said that in port cities enlisted men were often approached by youths who offered to perform fellatio on them. The patient deplored the fact that he could not accept the act as most of his companions did and forget about it. He could not comply and yet he could not get the matter off his mind. In the course of this discussion it became clear that the patient considered the stranger who performed fellatio "homosexual" but the man on whom it was performed normal. The performer was a "fairy." The compliant sailor, not. This patient's attitude was quite striking because in a middle-class definition of the situation both persons would be considered partners in a homosexual act and therefore homosexuals. If the therapist followed middle-class logic in this situation, his goal would have to be to make this sailor capable of passively enjoying fellatio. The patient's disturbance arose from the fact that he unconsciously wanted to be the performer; the anxiety attached to this inhibited wish generalized to the passive acceptance of the act.*

The authors of the above passage mention what a therapist would do who followed "middle-class logic," but fail to tell us what other pathway was open for the therapist to follow. The fact is that there is none that would be acceptable. Why does the therapist not attempt to cure this latent homosexual of his urge rather than to bring it into the open and have him accept it and be happy with it? There can be only one possible answer—because the therapist considers it

* John Dollard and Neal E. Miller, *Personality and Psychotherapy: an Analysis in Terms of Learning, Thinking, and Culture* (New York: McGraw-Hill, 1950), p. 420.

so difficult to bring about such a cure that he is pessimistic about the possibilities of success.

Many people may be talking about curing homosexuals, but most professional psychiatrists are not only not attempting such cures, but are actually encouraging homosexuality in those individuals who have repressed it and who are suffering from the consequences of such repression. The following quotation is from the work of one of the outstanding American psychoanalysts:

> In another case a girl who had never been conscious of any homosexual longings attributed each of her three broken engagements to her inability to escape a feeling that, because she loved her fiancé (a different man in each case), it would somehow be unnatural to have sexual relations with him. I was summoned to see her during the height of her third depression. I found an extremely agitated patient who would not talk to me until the nurse was sent out for a walk. The patient then told me that she had just discovered to her horror that she had an uncontrollable impulse to make sexual advances to the nurse. After some difficulty I persuaded her to admit the nurse to a three-cornered conference about the matter. My reassurances not only calmed the patient but, as subsequent events proved, gave the nurse courage to yield to her own consciously but timidly held homosexual inclinations. Without any connivance on my part the two effected a permanent homosexual union. The patient got well . . .*

A sound psychiatric program must make a clear difference between the anti-social and the socially useful homosexual. The homosexual (or the heterosexual, for that matter) who molests children is of an anti-social character, and his difficulty may emanate from an adolescent fixation in which he failed to continue to mature in his relationships with people. The homosexual (or the heterosexual) who has murderous, sadistic inclinations does an enormity of harm to society and, in the final analysis, to himself. Such a person, because of his shame over his entire sexuality, may be expressing through a sadistic outlet his hatred for the object that arouses and attracts him. He obviously requires psychiatric guidance, and if the psychiatrist cannot be of help, the patient must be guarded, perhaps institutionalized.

A second differentiation must be made, namely between the

* G. V. Hamilton, "Homosexuality as a Defense Against Incest," in *Encyclopedia Sexualis;* edited by Victor Robinson, (New York: Dingwall-Rock, Ltd., 1936), p. 334.

adjusted and the maladjusted homosexual. The latter is in need of care. The purpose of therapy is not, however, to make him a heterosexual, but to transform him into a well-integrated and happy invert. That this is impeded by social conditions beyond the control of the therapist or the patient merely means that it is a problem that extends to all society and that cannot be entirely solved on the analyst's couch. In this respect it is not unlike the psychological problems that arise from racial discrimination. "If the homosexual can afford treatment," states Henry in his monumental work, "he may be helped in his adjustment by psychotherapy."* But what is the adjustment?

Self-acceptance is the basis of the adjustment of the homosexual. And for self-acceptance, the understanding of virtual ineradicability of homosexuality is basic. A person who accepts the fact that he cannot change into a heterosexual, and who from that point accepts himself for what he is, will have taken the first important step toward ceasing the struggle against himself, toward enjoying his homosexual relationships rather than fighting them, and toward building his life around a realistic program for the future.

In her brilliant paper which many people consider the outstanding recent summary of scientific knowledge on homosexuality, Dr. Clara Thompson, director of the William Alanson White Institute of Psychiatry, significantly omits any mention of cure, except to say that "it seems certain from analysis in recent years that it (homosexuality) is a problem which tends to disappear when the general character problems are solved." However, Dr. Thompson concludes her paper with remarks that leave no doubt that, if a cure were feasible (which she at no time maintains) it would not necessarily be desirable in all cases:

> Even though the specific cause for homosexuality cannot be found, the specific needs which it satisfies can be examined. Obviously it gives sexual satisfaction, and for a person unable to make contact with the opposite sex, this is important. Also, because it requires a partner, it helps cope with the problem of loneliness and isolation. The very fact of belonging to a culturally taboo group has its satisfactions. One can feel defiant, brave, and strong, and as a member of a band united against the world, lessen the feeling of ostracism. I have spoken earlier of other satisfactions, such as financial support—especially in the case of some male homosexuals—and freedom from responsibility.

* Henry, G. W., *Sex Variants: a Study of Homosexual Patterns* (New York: Paul B. Hoeber, 1948), p. 1028.

An overt homosexual way of life can play a constructive or destructive rôle in the personality. It may be the best type of human relation of which a person is capable and as such is better than isolation. This would apply especially to the mother-child type of dependencies found in homosexuals of both sexes. Or it may be an added destructive touch in a deteriorating personality. In no case will it be found to be the cause of the rest of the neurotic structure—the basic origin of the neurosis—although after it is established, it may contribute to the problems. As in the case of other symptoms in neurosis, psychoanalysis must deal primarily with the personality structure, realizing that the symptom is a secondary development from that.*

However, even if psychoanalytic therapy were possible, and even if it did succeed in effecting the type of transformation that the public would consider a cure, it would be entirely impractical, because it could not affect the lives of more than a very small minority of the minority. The great social problem would still exist. A few would escape, but very few indeed. By simple arithmetic, and using the Kinsey report or my own modifications of it, I could easily show that if every one of the physicians in the United States were to become a qualified psychoanalyst, and if every such physician did absolutely nothing for one year except work on the analytical therapy of homosexual patients in an effort to transform them, and if they each took care of fifteen patients for a four-hour-a-week one-year period, and if in so doing these physicians ceased treating every other disease and let the ailing die, there would still hardly be enough doctors for all the patients! There are less than 200,000 doctors in the United States, and all but a handful are unqualified for this work. The medical analysts number about 1,000, of whom two-thirds are still in training, and to these one can add clinical psychologists and a few psychiatrically oriented social workers.

From both practical considerations and the nature of the homosexual problem, I suggest that some modification of group therapy might be instituted to help people who are in the gay life. Group therapy consists of a gathering of a number of people in a sort of a meeting, under a guide or leader, to discuss their personal and psychological problems, their fears and their phobias, their frustrations and humiliations, in an effort to relieve themselves of the burden

* Clara Thompson, "Changing Concepts of Homosexuality in Psychoanalysis," *Psychiatry: Journal of the Biology and Pathology of Interpersonal Relations*, XX (1947), 183.

of secrecy and shame and to guide themselves by means of an interchange of intelligent opinion. Homosexual group therapy (which I am here suggesting as a possibility, although I know of no such group in existence) would have to be restricted to gay people, because the presence of anyone not sharing their impulses would inhibit the conduct of such meetings. Some ten, fifteen, or twenty people might constitute a group that would gather weekly, led perhaps by a psychiatrist or a lay therapist who should likewise be gay, and group and individual problems would come under discussion. Activities on the job, the burden of the mask, the relationships at home, the meaning of a promiscuous impulse, the effort to adjust to greater enjoyment of the physical aspects of sex, the meaning of a new novel—these and countless other problems would be analyzed. Some will object that it is absurd to suggest that the psychiatrist be a homosexual. "Must every doctor (or psychiatrist) have an illness in order to be able to treat it?" they will ask. My proposal that the leader or analyst should be homosexual stems from the social nature of this problem. Homosexuals are, for quite obvious reasons, reluctant to discuss their problems outside their own group. In short, this is a dilemma of a socio-psychological nature, and the social aspect cannot be ignored in favor of the psychological.

The popular fallacy of cure, for which the psychiatrists are partially responsible because of their failure to speak without equivocation, is extremely harmful. Whether or not a cure for homosexuality would be socially desirable if it could be effectuated is, however, another matter.

Chapter 18

Plain Words on Sublimation

As the various suggestions for a way out of the dilemma facing the homosexual are examined, it becomes clear that no easy road presents itself as an ideal and universal solution. To proclaim one's temperament and live openly is to invite insults and even to isolate oneself from the mass of homosexual society, while to hide one's identity is to invite the social and psychological difficulties inherent in living a double life. Marriage is a career open or attractive to only a certain percentage of inverts, and for them the urge to seek satisfactory sexual outlet with males is not diminished and is frequently complicated. The psychiatrist, although his guidance will be invaluable, offers at this time no hope of cure for the many, and little hope even for a few. The life of endless dissipation led by some is wasteful and, in later years, tragic, while the partnership with a single mate is difficult to achieve.

Where can one turn? Society sees that it cannot change the individual and yet will not condone his activities. With no suggestions for a way out of their dilemma, with therapy neither practical nor possible, and yet faced with relentless condemnation, some have taken hope from a new nostrum which they term sublimation.

Sublimation is a word that is frequently confused with both repression and suppression, and before sublimation can be evaluated for the homosexual, these terms require definition. Sublimation may be defined, according to Freud, as the rerouting of sexual impulses for ends that are socially useful. To quote Freud, "Energy (of the sexual instinctive forces) is turned aside from its sexual goal and diverted toward other ends, no longer sexual and socially more valuable." Suppression, on the other hand, is a conscious action by which desires, feelings, or predispositions are denied satisfactory fulfillment. Repression is a psychological process by which desires that are particularly difficult to cope with, whose very existence (no less fulfillment) is a threat to a person's state of mind, are pushed into the unconsciousness, the individual being made completely unaware of their existence.

"If you will only try to divert your feelings for men into some more useful channels—education, or psychology, or nursing, for instance," Dick's minister advised him during the course of a sympathetic conversation. At the time, Dick was about to enter college, and he was frightened. "Sublimate your feelings. Show your love for men by alleviating their sufferings, or by teaching them, or by some social or charitable work. And then you will find less need for transgressing the laws of society." The young man to whom this advice was given did become a social worker, but although he aided people with deep compassion, he still wanted a full sexual life.

Like many other homosexuals, he had been advised to suppress his urge, but suppression is frowned upon in modern psychology. Sublimation is a word that is more appealing to the individual. But can suppression be effective, is it desirable, shall it be practiced by homosexuals? These are the questions I shall seek to answer.

There are times in life when a person chooses to suppress an impulse. For social or other reasons, he decides not to indulge himself. The temptation to drink, smoke, or eat sweets can be met with a conscious realization that indulgence under given circumstances can bring forth results more harmful to the person than denial. It is a matter of weighing the two pathways on a scale.

Many inverts will express deep regret at their inability to "sublimate" their desires. They feel that the need for homosexual relationships is something beyond their control; they are guiltless and blameless. But the same cannot be said, they contend, about the fulfillment of their desires.

Sublimation and suppression . . . how unlike they sound. Yet the two words have something in common, at least on the surface: the denial of fulfillment. But where sublimation implies that an impulse is, in a sense, actually satisfied by new and devious ways that are useful to society, suppression leaves the individual completely unsatisfied. Sublimation implies a self-acceptance of the impulse and subsequent diversion; suppression, a struggle against the impulse—not merely against its fulfillment. And many people who express a wish that they could "sublimate their homosexual feelings" are actually stating that they would like better to be able to control or suppress them.

Is suppression desirable for an individual and for society? That depends entirely on what is being suppresssed. If there is a violent hatred that takes the form of an urge to kill, it is necessary to suppress this desire because its fulfillment not only is socially destructive, but leads to greater unhappiness for the person than would its suppression. If the desire for alcohol is so great that continual indulgence is causing deathly illness, then its suppression is better than its fulfillment for the individual concerned.

Many people have pointed out that, aside from the consequences of the social stigma, homosexuality does no one any harm. It remains for each person who feels a need for sexual expression of this type to decide for himself whether he obtains a greater degree of happiness by denying himself this pleasure or by seeking it for himself.

In some cases, suppression of a desire is necessary in order to maintain good social rapport with other people. The invert who is attracted toward someone who is not of similar inclination—toward one who can neither understand nor return his affection—is forced to suppress this desire. To do otherwise would lead to very unfortunate complications. Under such circumstances, the homosexual must find another outlet.

The history of modern psychiatry is filled with case histories that relate of the nefarious and destructive results obtained by those who sought to repress their desires, and particularly their homosexuality. The father of modern psychoanalytic theory and practice, Sigmund Freud, has emphasized that paranoia is closely interlinked with the repression of homosexuality. Such repressions are not merely in the form of denials in which the appetite is frustrated, but take the form of total banishment from the consciousness; the patient is unaware that there is anything homosexual in his make-up and would in fact be horrified at the suggestion. Freud writes:

From these observations, which were continually corroborated, we drew the conclusion that persecutory paranoia is the means by which a person defends himself against a homosexual impulse which has become too powerful. The conversion of the affectionate feeling into the hate which, as is well-known, can seriously endanger the life of the loved and hated object then corresponds to the conversion of libidinal impulses into anxiety, which is a regular result of the process of repression.*

As I have pointed out in my chapter on the cure of sexual inversion, many of the outstanding psychotherapists, as Dollard and Hamilton, far from urging suppression on their patients, or tolerating repression, have actually urged them to accept their homosexuality and fulfill their hitherto repressed desires. In the case cited by Dr. Hamilton the desire had not been previously recognized. In other words, repression of homosexuality had been comp'ete and, so to speak, "successful," but the patient was paying a terrible price for it. It was not homosexuality that Dr. Hamilton fought in his manic-depressive patient, but only its repression.

The full and complete repression of the homosexual urge is one of the most common sources of many personal and social ills. If more people knew and admitted that they were homosexuals and then came to grips with the problem, perhaps there would be less insanity, less depression, less suicide, and even less murder. Much of man's sadism is an outlet in the form of hatred for a carnal desire that is only repressed successfully by being camouflaged in this manner. I can think of no presentation of this theme in fiction more poignant than D. H. Lawrence's profound short story *The Prussian Officer*, in which the officer, attempting to repress his longings for the handsome young orderly, imposes upon the latter a regime of unbelievable cruelty, finally leading to a dual tragedy.

Now, what of sublimation? Civilized man lives in a world in which the gratification of appetites, sexual and other, must be held under control. The ideal love-object cannot always be obtained; in fact, at times there is sexual need with no satisfactory outlet. Daily lives cannot be interrupted because there arises at a particular moment the need for sexual pleasure. No matter how satisfactory is the sex life, no matter how frequent the indulgence, a part of man's sexual energy must be directed to other channels, and when these channels are socially useful, that desire is said to have been sublimated.

The important thing to remember about sublimation is that it is not at all incompatible with gratification of the primary sexual aim.

---

* Sigmund Freud, *A General Introduction to Psychoanalysis* (Garden City, N. Y.: Garden City Pub. Co., 1938), p. 368.

It does not take place only under conditions of denial and suppression. Two men living happily together may find an outlet for their energies not only in their love-making, but in their compassion for fellowmen, in work that is philanthropic, literary, or educational. Friendships that are called "platonic" may be sublimations of strong carnal desires.

The difference between sublimation and suppression lies not only in the utilization of the resultant energy—that is to say, whether it is destructive or constructive for the person involved and for his relationships with a social community. Another discernible difference is found in the degree of denial necessary in order to effectuate this transfer of energy. Suppression is only effective if it is complete, and it reaches its fullest and most complete form (and its most dangerous) when the individual is no longer aware of his impulses—in other words, when the desires are forced into the unconscious, or repressed. In order to bring this stage about, the individual creates all sorts of delicate and neurotic conditions, ranging from paranoia to sadism. When the repression is incomplete, there is a double danger in that it not only leads to the destructive ends of repression, but leads to remorse and guilt feelings to the degree that it has failed. Repression of homosexuality, particularly in women, can result in sexual frigidity, which is destructive of the warm relationship with a husband and often permeates to a frigid relationship with children. In their study of psychosomatic aspects of frigidity, Drs. William S. Kroger and S. Charles Freed found latent (repressed) homosexuality a factor causing frigidity in women and stated that such latent homosexual condition "is present much more frequently than was formerly recognized."*

Sublimation means warmth. It is, in many respects, the very opposite of suppression. It arises, not out of shame or guilt, but out of a desire to make the total personality—sexual and other—serve useful purposes. And sublimation is most successful when there is no repression at all—in fact, when the full needs of the individual, including the sexual appetite, are being gratified. The person fulfilling his desires, not being frustrated, fully aware of and accepting his personality in all its facets, can redirect the remainder of his energies into the best possible course.

Suppression implies continence; sublimation implies temperance.

* *Journal of the American Medical Association*, June 10, 1950, p. 532.

The continent way of life is the road of futility. It is predicated upon the assumption that homosexuality is bad and suppression is good. But neither of these two concepts has been proved.

Much of the world's great art and literature has been the product of the total personality of the creative homosexual. It did not require the denial of his homosexual nature, or a continent restraint from sexual practices, for Tchaikowsky to be able to compose the *Symphonie Pathétique.* In fact it is very doubtful whether it would have been possible for him to find expression for this tragic musical theme if at every turn in his life he had been struggling to flee from his true nature. On the other hand, not all people can cope with sexual temperaments that are so urgent in their demands that they leave little time for other pursuits. So far as the homosexual is concerned, he is often wasting more time and energy fighting against sex than participating in its pleasurable pursuits.

Those who call for suppression (or repression) do so without scientific sanction for their cause. I have failed to find a single reputable work emanating from a man of standing in modern psychiatry that advises the homosexual to repress his desires. And those who speak of sublimation not only are frequently misusing the word but are actually hypocritical, for they would be the first to denounce a really successful sublimation of a homosexual urge. It is in the light of the confusion of terms, and of the findings of modern science, that the advice on sublimation of two eminent psychologists can be cited—men who are tearing down some of the myths that have been so carefully constructed. Here is some plain speaking on the subject:

> Actually, the amount of sexual tension which most people are capable of tolerating is very slight, and sublimation, even if it represented the popular notion of what it means, could only take care of a very small fraction of the drive. Prolonged abstinence runs counter to the biological structure of the human machine. . . . Much nonsense has been written about this process of channelization, called "sublimation," for which no conclusive scientific evidence has been advanced.*

It is a far cry from these words to the futile and hopeless advice

* Fred Brown and Rudolph T. Kempton: *Sex Questions and Answers: a Guide to Happy Marriage* (New York: Whittlesey House, 1950), pp. 57–58.

given by a homosexual who is attempting—in a book which has
fortunately had little influence—to reconcile his sexual temperament
with the traditional position of the Roman Catholic Church:

> The positive and universal rule of the Catholic Church is that the
> sex impulse can be licitly indulged only in marriage, and then only
> without interference with the natural physiological consequences. To
> this teaching I assent, and believe, moreover, that it is productive of
> the greatest good for the greatest number.*

In urging the denials of temperance, rather than those of suppression, it is not my wish to mimic the moralists whose ethics I dispute.
Temperance is demanded by the exigencies of social living. It will
free much of the total energy of the personality for sublimated
purposes. But, and this is perhaps the most vital of all, a temperate
and disciplined indulgence in homosexual affairs will heighten im-
measurably the pleasures obtained from every experience in which
gratification is obtained.

By choosing one's partner with greater care, the sexual act becomes
free—at least in the minds of the participants—of the stigma of degradation which society seeks to place upon it. The periods of denial,
the refusal of many opportunities that are placed in one's path, may
bring greater meaning, enhanced pleasures, to physical acts of making
love, provided, of course, that the denials are not so frustrating
that they become destructive of energy.

Much social and personal good has emerged from sublimated homosexuality through the years of history, but it has been a sublimation of
an impulse that was known, recognized, and accepted by the individual; and it was the sublimation of an impulse that at the same time
was being physically satisfied and not denied.

* Anomaly: *The Invert and His Social Adjustment* (2nd ed.; Baltimore: Williams
and Wilkins, 1948), p. 83.

Chapter 19

Till Death Do Us Part

Is marriage the answer to the problem of the struggle for adjustment of the homosexual in a hostile world? This is a question which almost every gay person has asked himself on numerous occasions and which he can answer only for himself.

How many homosexuals get married? What are their reasons for marriage? What types of mates do they choose? How much is known about their lives? What pattern of behavior do they follow after their marriage? These are a few of the questions that challenge the investigator.

What does marriage hold for a young gay man who is about to renounce the life of a bachelor? Why does he enter matrimony? What adjustment does he seek to make? How many of those who come to the church, who come to be best man or usher or perhaps spectator, know what has transpired in life for the youth who is about to be the groom?

No aspect of homosexualism is quite so difficult to investigate as marriage; none is so deeply enshrouded in veils of secrecy. Kinsey found that the homosexual activities of married men were more difficult to unravel than almost any other phase of sexual relationships.

It is my conviction, based not upon statistical study but upon conversation and observation, that most people who are either completely or mainly homosexual never get married, whereas most people who are more or less equally hetero- and homosexual, as well as those whose proclivities are more toward attraction to the opposite rather than the same sex, do get married. The protagonist in Vidal's *The City and the Pillar*, traveling through a particularly promiscuous stage, finds that most of his one-night mates are married; and it is common practice, when an acquaintanceship is made between two homosexuals, for one of them to ask the other (especially if the latter is past the age of thirty), "Married?"

There are several reasons why the homosexual is attracted to marriage as an institution, just as there are several reasons why he fears marriage and is revolted by the thought of becoming a groom. His reasons for seeking marriage are in many respects similar to those motivating other human beings, with the exception of the peculiar rôle of sex as a special problem.

It would seem from my observation that first and foremost is the homosexual dominated by a desire to have children. This wish is likely to be stronger in the invert than in others, and certainly it plays a greater rôle in a decision to get married. Is there a hidden motive in this strong wish to become a parent? Is it a desire to grasp something firm, real, permanent, in a life of dismal emptiness? I posed these questions in a discussion with an orthodox Freudian. He replied that many male homosexuals seemed to have a strong mother instinct, actually desiring to give birth, and expressing this consciously as a wish "to have children," unaware that beneath the surface they want to become a mother, not a father. But my friends are not troubled by a need to be analytical about their longing. "Life is such a mess, and a kid would just about make it perfect." Thus did one person express in simple terms the feelings shared by many.

The homosexual is, furthermore, simultaneously frightened by fly-by-night, unstable relationships and attracted by the seeming permanence of marriage as a family institution. Despite the high rate of divorce among the general populace, the homosexual notes that the majority of marriages endure, and many seem to be happy, especially when they are viewed from without. The dream of the gay youth, still perhaps in his teens, that one day he would find a perfect mate from his own sex, becomes more and more ephemeral as the years pass by. Each night in itself is fun, but collectively the nights, in the eyes of many, add up to nothing, and a sense of aloneness grips the individual. Marriage, home, children—this represents an anchor to enable one to build a life of stability.

If instability and aloneness are frightening at the moment, much more so is the fear of the future. Nothing is so pathetic as the spectacle of a man of fifty or sixty, his youthfulness gone but not his youthful desires, his gaiety in the past but not his gay self, seeking companionship of any sort no matter where it be found. Out of desperation he pays for his pleasure, frequently without the joys of even a pretended reciprocity of feeling.

The gay young man looks into the mirror of life and sees in the older person himself at the twilight of a wasted existence. He recoils from the image and with fear in his heart sets out to steer a course that will lead to another end. Where to turn, he asks, and one of the pathways seems to be that of marriage.

Then there is the young man who has not accepted his self. Even while participating in sexual activities with another male, he refuses to be resigned to this way of life and cherishes the hope that he will escape. A few years earlier he had thought that his tendencies would be outgrown. Now, in maturity, he looks to marriage for aid in effecting a complete change in his habits. How this is to be accomplished is not quite defined in his mind. The day of marriage will be a breaking point; the vows will be chains which cannot be broken. A self-imposed discipline with iron rigidity will start the moment he becomes wedded. That moment is in the future, and therefore the present becomes more acceptable, less painful, for it takes on the aspect of a temporary expedient, a passing phase.

I have known at least two youths who married under these conditions. Herbert had known that he was a homosexual from the time he was a child of twelve. After maturity, he had had, from time to time, some relationships with women, but although successfully consummated, there was little excitement or pleasure and no longing whatever for their repetition. Alone, either immediately following these affairs or a day or two later, his reawakening urges brought fantasies of male contact. Consequently he harbored no illusions; marriage would mean a suppression of his true self, but it was a road that he felt he had to choose in order to bring stability to his emotional life.

And Allen? How different his pattern! An intelligent youth (in fact both boys had graduated from college with the highest honors of the class), he found it necessary to impose illusions not only upon others but upon himself. He lived a homosexual life before marriage but always created the fiction among his friends, which he sought to believe himself, that this was a temporary substitute, motivated by the attraction of a special friendship, but one in which his masculinity was carefully preserved. He deliberately confused playing the male rôle with a man with being a heterosexual. In this way it was possible to have an intimate relationship with a male, which he craved, and to retain a concept of himself as being in all respects normal. Thus in the intimacy of relationships he was always the male, although a moment of slight intoxication might relieve the repressions and bring those caresses which began to border on forbidden paths.

Allen associated with a group of homosexuals, yet almost boastfully spoke of the relationships with his fiancée. He sought to hide from even the most intimate friend the fact there was more than one man in his life, and he insisted that his affair with this man arose primarily out of the other's need and aggression, and was reciprocated only out of special affection. Transgressions with other males were hidden from all, not only because they would jeopardize the greater love, but because they would characterize him as an invert. In his own mind he relegated them to non-importance—something easy to find, the answer to a need that comes upon one with suddenness and curiosity, a momentary pleasure that goes in and out of life and that would no longer be required once he was married.

To his gay friends, Allen would say, "If I were that way . . ." and he would be indignant when a common acquaintance would be referred to rather facetiously as "the last straight man on earth." He would delight in humor which victimized the homosexual. For Allen, marriage would be the day of change, just as it would for Herbert, each thought.

Other reasons for marriage are to be found, one of which is simply that the homosexual develops a deep and sincere love for a girl. The sentiment he feels is strengthened when he finds it reciprocated, and his doubts are removed by an aggressive affection on the part of the woman. She offers him confidence where before he was beset by self-doubt; she removes the fear of rejection which had characterized his unconscious feelings toward women; and she opens the way for a life of warmth and mutual devotion. In many respects his attitude parallels the not infrequent awakening of an affection in a man, previously conventional in his sexual life, for another male. Surely each of us has within himself a latent germ of love for both man and woman, and just as, under special conditions and under the influence of a particularly strong attraction, latent homosexuality is brought to the surface (*see The Immoralist, The Fall of Valor, Death in Venice, Serenade*, and other portraits in fiction), so too is the latent heterosexuality, once repressed in fright and fear, brought to the fore by contact with the proper mate.

The corollary of this particular reason for marriage is found in the individual with little or no knowledge, or perhaps only a vague and restive fear, of his homosexual self. "I was married, and I really thought I was happily married," Les told me. "Now that I think back, I begin to see signs that I was gay, even in those days. I was always curious about homosexuals, but extremely vicious in my condemnation, preoccupied with telling people what I thought of queers, queens, fairies, fags, and any other names I could think of. And at the same time I loved the company of male athletes, liked the smell of their locker rooms, the excitement of watching their beautiful bodies swimming in the nude at the Y." At the age of twenty-five, Les was inducted into the Army, soon discovered that many of his companions were finding sexual outlet with other soldiers, and before long had his first experience. A short period of doubt and then Les made his choice. "It was the only path I could take. I knew that I had secretly been wanting this and waiting for it for many years and that it could never be sacrificed for a return to the life I had left behind."

Others look to marriage for companionship, find difficult the formation of friendships with meaning, are aware that marriage cannot and will not change their basic drives. Males are exciting, they fulfill a great and overpowering need, but frequently the relationships are shallow in the formative period and replete with inherent difficulties later on. Lovers seem to come and go, and family ties no longer retain the hold that they formerly had. Whether or not one will have children, whether or not one will succeed in the escape from the homosexual life, it becomes necessary for many, as the years go by, to bind themselves to another individual with whom they can share the intellectual joys and the emotional travails of life. To find a companion who will always be at one's side, with whom one will entertain and travel and read, for whom one will care in an hour of need and who will reciprocate that care—this is the meaning of marriage for some. To achieve this with another male would be desirable but, for many, difficult if not impossible, and eventually they look to marriage as the answer.

For some, perhaps few in number, who are in somewhat prominent position and aware that there is considerable gossip about their names, marriage is looked upon as a "front," an artificial façade to demonstrate to the world that the whispered doubts and sneering questions are ill founded. Marriage is the pretense, the hypocrisy, the almost perfect silencer of talk which is slanderous although truthful. For even post-Kinsey America has little realization of the widespread nature of bisexual activities, and it continues to classify people in the public mind as homosexual or heterosexual. Few people outside of the gay world realize how many of these homosexually-inclined bisexuals marry, and how much homosexuality is practiced or desired among married men. In *The City and the Pillar*, there is such a character, a prominent movie star who is prevailed upon by his studio to marry in order to protect his reputation and appease the suspecting public.

There is possibly a certain amount of marriage among homosexuals for social position or monetary gain, or in order to please one or both of the families directly involved. From my experience and observation, I would say that such motives have been somewhat less prominent than among the general population and much less important than the others I have mentioned. The motive for embarking on a course of marriage is seldom the political, social, or economic gain to be derived therefrom; but the motive determining the choice of a particular mate in that marriage may frequently be such.

Finally, with no strong feeling against marriage, with a vague doubt as to the desirability of it and yet an urge to explore its possibilities, with a hope that it may contribute in many respects to solving some of the problems of life, the individual frequently finds himself drifting aimlessly toward an alliance from which he finds it increasingly difficult to extricate himself. Commitments are made with but a half-realization that they have been put into effect, and these lead in turn to new and greater commitments. A web is woven, and it becomes easier and perhaps more desirable to save face by attempting the marriage than to hurt and humiliate many others by disrupting it on the eve of its occurrence.

Human motivation is complex, and the causes for a single course of action are usually plural. Thus the reasons for marriage are not easily defined, nor can they be separated from each other. In every marriage in which a homosexual participates, not one but several of the motives we have enumerated are present, many of them hardly in the consciousness of the individuals. The wedding vows are taken for a variety of intermingled, mutually dependent, and yet somewhat contradictory (even mutually exclusive) reasons. Such is the paradox of the homosexual in the face of an institution which was not created for him, which did not evolve with a view to integrating him in it, and which can never offer him more than a marginal life. It is, in short, an institution in which he seeks to a find a place despite its disadvantages to him.

In order the better to proceed with an investigation of the possibilities of success and the patterns of behavior in marriage, and in order to contrast the urge for marriage with the rejection of it, I shall summarize the various causes leading to the day of nuptials that I have mentioned above:

1. Desire for children.
2. Need for permanent family relationship.
3. Inability to create permanent relationship with male companion or lover.
4. Fear of loneliness of older years.
5. Desire or hope to escape from homosexual life.
6. Deep affection for girl.
7. Latency or repression of homosexuality.
8. Hope of finding companionship in marriage; disappointment at inability to find it outside of marriage with male friends.
9. Desire to create façade of married life, and hope to find protection against gossip and its concomitant evils.
10. Aspiration for economic and social gain.
11. Desire to please family.
12. Inability or unwillingness to take strong stand in order to put an end to drift toward marriage.

It would seem, then, that if the motivations are so strong, all homosexuals would eventually get married. Nevertheless, as stated, I believe that most of them do not. The reasons for shunning marriage are likewise multiple and perhaps more apparent.

The sexual block against union with the woman is unquestionably the strongest psychic motive for avoiding marriage, and it continues even after such a union has been effected for the first time. Many homosexuals have never had sexual relations with a member of the opposite sex; others, who may have had such on rare occasions and under special circumstances, do not want to undertake an obligation to repeat an activity which may have been loathsome or which, at the very least, left them indifferent.

In addition to apathy or actual antipathy toward heterosexual relations, and closely intermingled with it, is to be found a grave fear and searching doubt as to one's abilities and accomplishments. Fear, psychological in origin, inexplicable though it may be, of an act for which there can be no deleterious consequences to one's physical self, can be as overwhelming as a more understandable fear of falling bombs or burning buildings.

On the one hand, the individual fears impotence, doubts his own ability to consummate, and on the other hand such fear and doubt become the very cause of impotence, thus justifying and bolstering the apprehension.

In order the better to avoid embarrassment, and in order to determine one's own capabilities, the homosexual is frequently led into a premarital relationship with a complete stranger. Inhibited against approaching a friend and fearful that failure will lead to chagrin and disclosures, he goes outside his social world—generally to the prostitute. There the expected repulsion is magnified, and if the union is not effected, the invert obtains the fixed idea, which consciously may depress him but secretly he will cherish, that he is impotent and therefore must banish from his mind any thought of turning his life toward the path of heterosexualism.

This, in fact, was my own experience, only to find soon thereafter that it was not unique; that many of my gay friends had discovered their supposed impotence under similar conditions. It is at this point that a resolution, or perhaps a resignation, to eternal bacherlorhood is taken. The road of marriage is thus seemingly closed, although efforts to proceed with marital union and its consummation, under more desirable conditions or with the aid of psychiatric care, may result in success for some, as it did for myself.

Some homosexuals, as I have already noted, succeed in finding a

mate and lifelong companion from their own sex and their own
set; others, always searching for such a love, postpone a decision
regarding marriage in the hope that it may prove unnecessary.

One of the most important among the conscious reasons for
rejecting marriage—although I deeply suspect it may hide other
motives—is that such a union must of necessity be incomplete, would
lead to infidelities, and would be unfair and unethical. "I would not
want to be running around while my wife or my kid's mother is at
home," a typical friend, George, remarked, "and I know that I
couldn't stop running around just because she would be at home."
Thus George, with little difficulty, reconciles homosexualism with the
standards of ethics he has set up for himself, but adultery he considers
unforgivable. "And is it perfectly all right for you to spend the
night with another man while you're living with Larry?" I asked
George, to which he shrugs his shoulders and answers, "That's
different."

Is George genuinely concerned with the ethical standards when a
woman is involved, although he is able to disregard them when he lives
with a man? Or is he perhaps inwardly fearful that a betrayal of the
vows to a wife would be equated to the betrayal of his mother by
his father? Is George merely resigned and accommodated to the
unavoidability of transgressions when two men are living together, or
does he feel that standards for married couples must be on a different
plane? I ponder over his remarks and wonder whether sex for him,
within his unconsciousness, is not something dirty—as it is and must
be to a certain extent for all people in modern civilization. I wonder
whether he finds it permissible to have indulgences with men but
not with women because the latter are the last worldly symbols of
something pure, something to remain untouched and unsullied?

Whatever the recondite motives, George will avoid marriage and
be somewhat scornful of his friends who enter into a sacrament which
they cannot fulfill. The need for marriage is strong within him, but
in others the burning needs that drive one to the altar are not as
great. Some have found in their literature, their art, their business
activities, their many achievements, the counterpart of the companionship and the home life. They have sunk their roots: they do not
find life at all empty or lonely. Marriage is given little consideration

because it answers no great requirement; it fills no gap that has not already been filled by other phases of life.

Another motive given for the rejection of marriage is that one suspects an hereditary trait (or even taint) and could not possibly have children for fear that they, too, would be gay. This fear is strengthened by casual observations of brothers, particularly twins, uncle-nephew relationships, and others. Although I personally do not concede the hereditary nature of the homosexual desires, and have expressed an opinion on the subject in the chapter on the genesis of inversion, I find it rather widespread although not deeprooted. "Is this not an admission that you are really ashamed of what you are, that you accept the outer world's judgment and therefore would not want your child to be like you?" I asked a friend when, on the eve of his marriage, he spoke to me about hereditary traits. "I concede nothing," he answered, "except that life is difficult enough without adding complexities to it. Homosexualism is a great burden to carry in our society, and I would not wish it on any child of mine."

If some avoid marriage because of the hereditary doubts, others are reluctant to relinquish a freedom that bachelorhood has offered them. To come and go as one wishes, never to have to take another's life into consideration in planning, vacationing, traveling, working, spending, loving—this is the positive aspect of the life of aloneness that so many homosexuals live. The game of marriage is one of diminished individual liberty; the prize is permanence, home, companionship. Each must decide for himself whether the prize is attainable; if so, is it worth the game?

And, finally, marriage as a front, for the sake of appearances, does not appeal to certain people who are actually contemptuous of pretense. Particularly if they have achieved some economic freedom, they have little respect for the hypocrisy that marriage forces upon them. On the other hand, they raise their head and are proud of their gay selves, and in defiance demonstrate their being to all the world.

Thus, counteracting the numerous motives that can and do lead to marriage are the many deterrents:

1. Revulsion against or apathy toward sexual union with a woman.
2. Fear of the heterosexual act, and fear of impotence in such an act; or actual proof of impotence.

3. Success in finding a male life-mate or permanent lover.
4. Hope of success in finding such a person.
5. Abhorrence of adultery, which appears to most gay people to be a necessary concomitant of marriage.
6. Substitution of artistic, industrial, and other activities for companionship of marriage.
7. Rejection of fatherhood because of the fear of hereditary nature of homosexual trait.
8. Inability or unwillingness to relinquish freedom of bachelorhood.
9. Rejection of marriage as a front; desire to live as one truly is.

Assuming, then, that the considerations in the earlier part of this chapter have outweighed those just described, and the individual is about to marry, what are his thoughts and plans; what does he reveal to the bride; what type of woman is likely to be the partner in the marriage; what patterns of behavior is he likely to follow?

Chapter 20

A Galaxy of Gay Husbands

Having decided to embark upon the road of matrimony and perhaps having chosen the mate and the date for the significant step, each individual is faced with fundamental conflicts. What will marriage mean in the way of change, sublimation, repression, accommodation, disclosure, and pretense?

It would seem rather obvious that many homosexual men would marry similarly inclined women, thus solving the problem of the search for companionship, the struggle against aloneness, and finding at the same time a protection in marriage, building around it a home and perhaps a family, and making it unnecessary either to conceal or to relinquish an integral part of one's life. Nevertheless, few such marriages occur; here and there one encounters such a union, but it is rare; in my opinion, it would be in the overwhelming minority were it possible to make a statistical study of all marriages in which the groom is a homosexual.

Nevertheless it is unquestionably true that most homosexuals give some thought, from time to time, to the desirability of entering into such a marriage. A psychiatrist of my acquaintance recently delivered a lecture on homosexualism, discussed the adjustment to be found in what he termed a "front marriage" (referring to the type now under consideration), and spoke in a rather sanguine manner about its possibilities. Within a few days, he later related to me, several dozen letters arrived, many giving data on age, education, and other vital facts, asking if the psychiatrist would offer the name of a Lesbian who would like to enter into such a pact.

If such a front marriage is so attractive, why is it so infrequent? I have already observed that in my opinion there are relatively few

Lesbians as compared to the statistical estimates of male homosexuals and the homosexually-inclined male bisexuals. Whether or not the estimates are valid, it is nevertheless true that there is little inter-mingling between the male and female homosexual societies. At the parties, at the bars, among one's friends and friends' friends, it is rare to meet Lesbians. The gay person in a large city like New York or Chicago may in the course of ten years have met hundreds of males of acknowledged, obvious, known, or admitted homosexual penchant, and among them may have acquired a circle of a couple of dozen per-manent friends, yet will have met few females and may number but two or three as part of this intimate circle.

Whether the Lesbians be few in number, as I contend, or whether for social and psychological reasons they seldom cross paths with the gay males, the fact is that such intermingling is sufficiently uncommon as to offer little possibility for laying the necessary groundwork for marriage. For instance I have often heard some such dialogue as the following:

"Have you ever thought of marrying a Lesbian?"

"Yes, but frankly I don't know one."

The front marriage is not quite as universally appealing as it would seem, and even if, as some people believe, Lesbianism were as common as male homosexuality, and even if the males and females in this sub-merged world freely intermingled, such marriages, in my opinion, would not be frequent occurrences. For the Lesbian cannot offer a hope for an avenue of escape that so many homosexuals are seeking; the Lesbian, by her very nature, seldom arouses the response of warmth, affection, self-confidence, that the gay youth, although not necessarily an escape-seeker, nevertheless desires from marriage. Finally, he cannot visualize the Lesbian as a likely homemaker, wife, and mother.

I have known of three such marriages. One faltered over the ques-tion of offspring, but this was merely an excuse. There was little that bound the man to the woman. They were, at times, hardly more than apartment-sharers. When she refused to bear a child and insisted that her career could not be relinquished, he packed his things and left.

The wife in the second marriage was also repelled by the thought of pregnancy and the burden of child-carrying, but the years of rearing and the rewards thereof were appealing to her. The couple found in adoption a suitable compromise; they were investigated, there were delays, and then an infant was obtained. Into this hope there is the radiance that is brought by the growing youngster, and at the same time both husband and wife have a circle of friends with whom they can show their concealed tendencies.

The third gay-Lesbian front marriage continues the mad, party-giving revelry of the promiscuous life, supplemented by a companionship which usually seems to cover the needs of the participants. The two of them make the rounds of bars alone and together; on each other's shoulders they cry about their latest loves and their newest frustrations, their great and their ephemeral crushes. Here is the gaiety from which this life derives its name, with the fastness of the Prohibition era, and the hangover of loneliness somewhat less severe because there is not only a certificate but a companion, someone who was here last year and will, almost certainly, be here on the morrow. "I don't know what my marriage means," this husband said to me. "I just don't know."

But others are better acquainted with the purpose, meaning, accomplishments, shortcomings of marriage. Turning inward, they have mercilessly evaluated it and have arrived at inescapable conclusions.

The patterns of sexual behavior of gay husbands seem to be primarily determined by the degree of inclination toward the heterosexual side of their natures; secondly, and directly related thereto, by the extent of compulsion toward the homosexual; and, finally, by the extent to which the guilt feeling exists, by the nature of the conflict over the homosexual way of life, and by the amount of gratification obtainable without fulfilling the homosexual urge.

Not very frequent but most important, there are those who consciously suppress the homosexual drive, and who are successful in effecting total suppression. Convinced that, if not wrong on a moral-ethical plane, it is an antisocial and destructive force for the life of the individual, the man seeks marriage in the hope of escape. The wedding date becomes the complete and critical turning-point; the marriage is the act from which no return must be made. All former associations will be destroyed and the life will be forgotten. Willpower must triumph, and if the desire is ineradicable, then fulfillment is not inevitable. He will now find his time occupied with work, ambition, achievements, home. All warnings of psychiatrists against suppression are ignored. Life offers no alternative. Bachelorhood is lonely. Marriage and a double life are unworthy.

Can such a path be followed for any great length of time? With a few people it can, and if its toll be not too heavy, if it offers satisfaction of a self-respect that was formerly lacking, it may even result in a new peace of mind, a new freedom from torment. For some people the torture of desiring and not having may be less than the torture of having failed in a great effort to overcome their homosexuality. The torment of frustration may be of little consequence when balanced against the new quietude that life offers. But suppression will certainly bear its fruit. What is wrong with these people, as any psychiatrist can point out, is not their homosexuality but their sense of guilt.

Adjustments of this type, if such they can be called, do not come easily. After Steve married, he found it necessary to cease visiting the gymnasium, where the sight and smell of naked male athletes excited him. He avoids New York because knowledge of the whereabouts of gay bars is a temptation he cannot risk. He seldom ventures forth on a social engagement or even a business trip without his wife, whose very presence is a self-imposed discipline that has a salutary effect on his inclinations.

Only a short time ago we sat for hours in the car and discussed the subject of the gay life—Steve's first discussion of this sort for several years, his first evening out without the mask. "I am a homo, through and through," he said, "but I've decided that, come hell or high water, I won't give in. It may be a happy life for the next guy, but it's not for me!" So Steve walks out of a movie because he will suddenly, as if from nowhere, find himself tortured by the handsome face of a Hollywood hero shown in magnificent close-up on the screen; and should the subject of homosexualism ever arise in the course of social conversation, he will use abusive language, speak of perverts and degenerates, hoping thus not merely to strengthen the impenetrability of the mask but to convince himself all the more that the road of suppression is the sole one for him to follow in life.

By what standards can the course of life chosen by Steve be judged? Shall it be by the legal and ethical standards as defined in the prevailing moral codes? On such a basis, the ethics of civilization would applaud him for his continence but would despise him for the urge that thrives within his very being. Only on the surface and in the narrowest sense of the word is he conforming, for modern culture rejects the person who feels an attraction to one of his own sex as completely as it rejects the man who gratifies this urge.

Has Steve—and those other married men who are consciously avoiding an outlet they desire—found a greater happiness, a more genuine peace of mind, than he would if he were living a double life, or perhaps "married" to a man instead of a woman? His answer is evident from the life he is pursuing. Despite his admittedly strong if not overpowering inclinations, he would feel so guilty, frustrated, and defeated were he to fulfill the love-longing within him that he could find no peace. Either direction—suppression or gratification, continence or indulgence—means internal difficulty. He has chosen the path which means the lesser difficulty for him.

What of Steve's contribution to society? Is he a better individual, more capable of directing his vitality, energy, initiative, imagination—the sum total of his personality traits and intellectual talents—to the benefit of our social organism because of the life he has chosen? Or would his accomplishments be enhanced by fulfillment of his desires for one or several males?

Steve did not hesitate in replying to this last question. "Each person will have to answer for himself. For me, the matter is of no importance. I am not interested in society, and society is not interested in me. I am trying to find a way to live with myself in a very bad situation. I am trying to make the best of things, and that is the only point that interests me."

Will Steve finally break down? Will a moment of intense attraction a weakness during a semi-intoxicated revelry, a reaction from a quarre with his wife (such as punctuate all marriages), or a response to an insistence from a man—will some such moment arrive, resulting in the downfall of this fragile structure upon which a marriage is built? No one can predict. The years have thus far brought no such climax, although it has come within perilous proximity, always however staved off by contrived situations and planned defenses. If, despite precaution, willpower, and suppression, despite flight from oneself and protection with another, Steve fails in his resolution, what will the reaction be? I fear for the turmoil within this man on the morrow of such an event. I fear for the marriage so carefully constructed, so delicately protected, yet so fragile in its inner foundation.

If, as previously stated, a large number of homosexuals marry, and if few marry Lesbians, and few follow the path of continence toward other males, what patterns of behavior remain for the majority? Most married homosexuals continue, with or without the wife's knowledge, with or without her consent, to gratify their sensual needs with men. In what appears to me to be a minority of such marriages, the wife—although herself not homosexually inclined—has some knowledge of her mate's activities, usually because he has told her about his life before the marriage. Such a revelation may have been prompted by the fear of marriage, the misgivings on the very eve of it or as the date approached, the hope that perhaps a breaking-point could be reached, a safety exit opened. Or, in others, the wish to reveal was motivated by a yearning for the acceptance that comes with full understanding. Very likely these two forces interplay: the need for acceptance of the true self, the hope to drop the mask, and—should rejection be the sole reaction—the alternative of the disrupted courtship.

Such a confession is often greeted by ignorance, incredulity, and ego-driven conceit. The woman is unable to believe that she will not be able completely to win the man in competition with another male. Seldom have I heard of women who were discouraged by such a revelation; rather they are so filled with love, tenderness, and what they mistake for understanding, that they are able to delude themselves into the belief that homosexuality was only a temporary substitute, a childlike stage which the sweetheart and intended groom will soon have left behind.

The day of nuptials, however, is seldom the turning-point. It solves nothing in the psychic drive of the individual, and in but a few instances is it able to permit even the change to complete suppression. The overwhelming desires continue and, whether with one friend or many, whether in the home or away, the husband finds occasion to obey the imperious sensuality that orders him to find pleasure with a male companion.

Three such marriages come to my mind. In two, the subject is discussed more or less openly. As Lewis puts it, his wife knows "when, where, with whom—everything but how—that's where I draw the line." In the third, there is a tacit understanding, a mutual knowledge always left unspoken. The evenings out with "the boys" and the "business trips" are never questioned. Despite acceptance, a sense of delicacy pervades the subject. The mask is not removed. It is worn thin and hardly serves as a disguise.

Many of these men follow a pattern of sexual behavior which is extremely common among homosexuals. They develop a relationship with one woman (in this case, the wife; in others, a sweetheart), and their sexual life with this woman is quite satisfactory. Usually these men have never had a sexual relationship with any woman except the one, in contrast to the many and the short-lived affairs with men. On a rating scale, from the viewpoint of activities, they might be considered more or less completely bisexual; that is to say, they have about as much sex with many men as with one woman. But, from the viewpoint of desire, they are never aroused except by the one female, and they would have to be considered almost entirely at the homosexual side of a rating scale.

Without going into the psychological conditions that make possible a response to one woman but to no other, let me emphasize that this is a frequent occurrence, that it can be an effective aim of psychotherapy, and that it can offer a key to the understanding of adjustment through marriage.

But what of the other partner in the marriage? What motivates these wives who do not seek gratification with women or with other men to accept infidelities as a part of married life? An accommodation seems to take place in such cases. The wife is convinced that her primary place as object of permanent affection is unchallenged; she accepts the fact that her husband has a particular need that requires satisfaction, and that, if gratified from time to time, will never interfere with his rôle as a man, husband, father, friend, and lover.

How shocked was young Bernard, still in his upper teens, when he visited the home of his married lover-friend, found him away, and in conversation with the wife discovered that his relationship with the husband was fully known to her. Embarrassed, responding to the self-protecting reflex, and perhaps from a sense of loyalty to his lover, Bernard was vehement in his denials, laughing in ridicule at the thought, even pretending to be insulted by such accusations. But the woman merely laughed in turn. "I know what he needs," she said, "and I know that he's a better person if he has it. It's a weakness that has taken hold of some people. And I'm glad he finds his pleasure with a friend like yourself whom he really likes."

But few women can accept marriage under such conditions. Most wives insist upon a veil of ignorance, whether their husbands' infidelities be with women or with men. So that, finally, there is another pattern of marriage, and that is the double-life in two completely separate worlds which most married homosexuals inhabit. It consists of being the good husband at home, true as any, loving and faithful; and, away from home, the invert. These married men seemingly struggle to unify in one entity two ways of life whose totality they find both attainable and desirable. Keeping their wives in ignorance of their cravings, they find a better balance in fulfilling their needs than in struggling against them.

From the vantage-point of my own prejudiced position, which would quite naturally bring me in contact with those whose patterns most closely follow my own, it would appear that most married homosexuals are not suppressing their inclinations and are not divulging their extra-marital activities to their spouses. This observation must be qualified, of course, because those who travel in the submerged world would have very little opportunity to meet the totally suppressed married invert. In a sense, we married homosexuals who not only acknowledge our male-directed desires to ourselves but also gratify them resemble that very wide group of straight married men who supplement what may be a very happy home by flirtations, occasional or frequent, in some instances confined to one person over a long period of time, in others to promiscuous pick-ups—flirtations motivated perhaps by necessity, perhaps by some lack at home, or perhaps merely culminating without plan from an unexpected opportunity.

The married homosexual is usually well adjusted to his dilemma and perhaps finds one of the best compromises known to the group. He admittedly accepts his life as a conscious accommodation, but precisely because he is aware of his shortcomings, he strives all the more to contribute to the building of a successful union with his wife. He offers her care and compassion and understanding. He seeks to compensate for that area of his being which is reserved and unattainable by becoming all the more outgoing in the areas in which he can establish rapport. He sees the social disorganization in the lives of so many of his fellow-homosexuals and is driven, as a result, to strengthen the bonds of his home life the more.

Many gay husbands keep their two lives completely separate. Not only are physical experiences but even friendships reserved for business trips and for their nights out. An entire circle of acquaintances and friends is unknown to the wife and in turn this circle does not know her—a situation patently possible only in a large metropolis, or if the husband's sensual activities are indulged in only when he is out of town. An address or a telephone number is rarely disclosed to a friend in the life, since fear of blackmail is a major factor in the behavior of some of these homosexuals.

But separation of the two lives is not always possible, and results more frequently in a deprivation of the true affections and genuine friendships that arise from mutual attachments among gay men. Other gay husbands bring their circle of friends—save those who may be quite apparent to anyone—to the home, and the two lives are intermingled in all respects, except that the gratification, when it does take place, is arranged for elsewhere. That one aspect of the group life is kept from the wife. Thus she becomes, unknowingly and unwittingly, a part of the group, just as many other straight people have been brought or have drifted into the gay society. In the circle she is often loved and finds many of the friends inspiring and charming, though she would be aghast if the entire scene were unveiled before her. Occasionally a suspicion may becloud her mind —the preponderance of bachelors, the strength of a special comrade-ship between two people, the momentary mannerism that can so easily betray—but the entire thought runs counter to preconceived notions of taboo. Both husband and friends, adept at concealment, erase the doubt from her suspecting mind.

Over a period of many years—nay, over a lifetime—such a marriage continues, occasionally to falter because of a single false step, but more frequently to develop a bond of strength comparable to that of the most successful marriages devoid of an analogous problem. Into such a home the husband brings a sense of gratitude and compassion that compares favorably with the less understanding virility of the average male; toward his wife he feels a sense of responsibility that may derive from doubts as to whether his course of life is ethically justifiable, but which nevertheless results in a firmer union.

To the home he brings a love for children, a sensitivity for their acute needs and inner desires. In short, a marriage of this type, far from being doomed, has many valuable features.

Does the married life, with its numerous restrictions, with its proscriptions upon the very form of sexual pleasure which is most ardently desired, fulfill the needs of the homosexual? As previously demonstrated, not all gay men have either the need for marriage or the capability of fulfillment of the marriage vows. A certain degree of bisexuality is required. If, on the other hand, a man's bisexual drive is weighted in the direction of attraction toward women, his problems are outside the province of this book—if, indeed he can be said to have problems at all. The married men here under consideration, while capable of sexual relations with women, are homosexuals by definition: that is, their primary desires are toward gratification with other males.

It is one of the most curious aspects of this group life that a gap, sometimes as unbridgeable as that between the straight and the gay, separates the married and the bachelor homosexuals. Their lives intermingle, but their paths hardly unify to the extent that their interests, hopes, joys, and travails are cut of one and the same pattern.

The married man looks simultaneously with envy and pity at the bachelor; and the latter, fully acquainted with his friend's motivations and activities, is contemptuous of his double-life, denounces his hypocrisy, yet envies the home, security, and family that have been obtained in the accommodation. This is not to imply that any actual enmity exists between the two. Often they are the best of friends, and sometimes the friendship includes love. But the submerged group life accepts with hesitance and deep reservation the married man. He is not one of them. His protestations are to no avail. All self-avowed declarations, fully believed though they may be, do not open the magic doors, do not remove the invisible panels that separate the worlds.

So that the married man is a part of no world at all, precisely because he partakes of two disparate ones. Living in two societies that commingle without intermingling, he seeks to belong to both and therefore falls short of full integration in either. Wherever he turns, he is a minority—not only in the world at large, but even in his small world of escape.

The married homosexuals I have known never for a moment regret the home, the family life, the mutual care and tenderness, the pursuit of common interests that have arisen from the union with a woman. They regret most of all the mask, the fact that it cannot be discarded even with the one with whom the burdens of life are being shared. But if these men could look into the inner selves of other husbands, would they not find that all people wear masks, even in the presence of their most intimate companions?

Part Six

OUTLOOK

Chapter 21

The Society We Envisage

What does the homosexual want? He cries out against the injustice of society, yet offers no alternative. He finds the discrimination and the calumnies a manifestation of the grossest intolerance, but he fails to offer the world at large a pattern for a better social organization in which he could be integrated.

This is not at all surprising, for the development of such a plan would, by its very nature, imply freedom of discussion. It is only from the exchange of opinion in a free press and by all other methods of communication that a subject of this type, wrought with so many unknowns and paradoxes, can reach adequate solution.

What does the homosexual want? The question cannot be answered because each person can speak only for himself, and his reply will be prejudiced by his religious and ethical background, by his philosophy of life, and by the degree of happiness he has been able to achieve. The actress whose predilections are almost public knowledge and are no impediment to her stardom and public acceptance is hardly likely to feel the same need for social reorganization as the lonely, the wretched, and the frustrated. A deeply religious Roman Catholic invert who professes that there is no justification for any sexual pleasure outside of the sacrament of marriage can hardly share aspirations for social change with two men who are living together in a happy physical and spiritual union.

The homosexual society, such as it is and to the extent that it exists at all, reflects differences of opinion on the social solution of this question just as does any other group of people on any problem confronting them. There is no single, quasi-official, universally accepted version of the social organization envisaged by homosexuals, any more than there could be a single opinion of college professors on loyalty oaths, of university students on the accomplishments of education, of physicians on socialized medicine.

But the homosexual viewpoint is less well developed than that of other groups on other questions because of the virtual impossibility of having an exchange of opinion through the usual channels of thought expression. First, the facts themselves on which an opinion must be based are difficult to obtain and, once found, are difficult to communicate to others. There are very few reliable statistics, and even the words of experts are usually based on the most atypical homosexuals, namely those who fall into the hands of the law or who are seeking help from a psychiatrist.

Even were the facts more readily available, an expression of opinion requires a free and open debate, and American society is hardly more advanced in this respect that the totalitarian lands. There is, of course, no interference with the effort to discuss the subject by word of mouth, provided the discussion remains within the homosexual group. It is almost impossible to have, except in a few and rare circles, a full interchange of opinion between people of all sexual temperaments in which each viewpoint is defended ably and each argument refuted honestly.

Homosexuals have had little opportunity for the development of a well-defined outlook. Within the homosexual group, there is little uniformity of opinion, and perhaps even less so than would be found in another minority group. One person can therefore do little more than express his personal viewpoint, reflecting only what he himself envisions for the homosexual group in the supposedly Utopian situation, but in this reflection there are distilled the arguments, viewpoints, contradictions, and philosophies of many others with whom discussions have been held over a period of many years.

There is probably only one thing on which homosexuals would in general agree with regard to the attitude of society, and that is that the present situation is unjust and that change is necessary. The injustice is not so much before the bar, nor in the effort to obtain employment, but is found above all in the general social attitude of the heterosexual society. No one can prevent an individual from expressing hostility toward another, provided he stays within the law and neither libels nor physically harms his enemy, but when this hostile attitude is officially sponsored by all possible means among the entire population, it is no longer the private affair of a single person.

The homosexual, first and foremost, wants recognition of the fact that he is doing no one any harm. He wants to live and let live, to punish and be punished when there are transgressions, and to go about the ordinary and everyday pursuits of life, unhindered either by law or by an unwritten hostility which is even more effectual than the written law.

This is a far-reaching program, requiring the modification of attitudes over a period of generations, and it is only natural that it must fall upon those most concerned with this problem—the inverts—to take the initiative in remolding public opinion.

However, the invert is not alone in feeling that the present situation is unsatisfactory. The dominant group in our society tacitly understands and is ready to concede that it has no proposal for bettering a situation which is obviously unjust. It would like—in a manner similar to the attitude of many white persons on the color question —to "wish" the problem out of existence. It dreams of a world in which the problem does not exist, hopes that the problem will not touch the lives of individuals personally related to oneself, and just does not think, talk, or write about it. But its dreams are in vain.

The dominant society cannot offer a cure for homosexuality. It urges in a weak, ineffectual, and ignorant manner that willpower be exerted, but willpower solves nothing. It talks of suppression and sublimation, while its own scientists scoff at such a proposal. It damns in the harshest of terms in the hope that damnation will be a deterrent, but again there is failure. It passes laws that make felons of homosexuals, but ignores its own laws and admits that it cannot put homosexuals behind bars. It concedes that homosexuals must earn a living, and banishes them from employment. And, as society always does when it is in a blind alley, tied by tradition and folkways to a system which is unreasonable and which does not answer the needs of the people, it uses silence as the answer. It hides its head in the sand, pretends that the problem does not exist, and forbids discussion, save in professional circles.

But the problem does exist, and it will be discussed. Furthermore, it is not a problem created by the homosexuals. A sociologist writing on racial minorities—and again the parallel is inescapable—has stated that there are no minority problems. There are only majority problems. There is no Negro problem except that created by whites; no Jewish problem except that created by Gentiles. To which I add: and no homosexual problem except that created by the heterosexual society.

There would be no economic dilemma for the invert were he not excluded from practically all jobs unless he hides his identity. There would be no blackmail problem for the homosexual except that he cannot live happily after exposure, because the world which has learned of his temperament will inflict severe sanctions. There would be no ethical problem of being a lawbreaker except that the laws have been codified in such manner that he cannot be a homosexual without at least aspiring to break them. And thus the problems of the homosexual could be enumerated, and it could be seen that they are majority problems—not minority ones!

Even the psychological aspects of the homosexual's dilemma primarily involve adjustment to a hostile world. There would be no need for the invert to feel guilty, to suffer remorse, to be forced to suppress hatred toward his love-object, if society did not condemn so bitterly. He would not be faced with the paradoxical problem of attempting on the one hand to be proud of himself and on the other to deny his temperament, if it were not so difficult to live in a world that demanded such denial.

It is a majority problem, but only the minority is interested in solving it. The fundamental dilemma is that it must rest primarily upon the homosexuals, being the most interested party, to take the initiative in bringing about change, but until such change is effected, anyone taking such initiative is open to pillory and contumelious scorn.

The homosexual is thus locked in his present position. If he does not rise up and demand his rights, he will never get them, but until he gets those rights, he cannot be expected to expose himself to the martyrdom that would come if he should rise up and demand them. It is a vicious circle, and what the homosexual is seeking, first and foremost, is an answer to this dilemma.

It is an answer that I contend can be found and one which happens, by the most fortunate of coincidences, to be identical with the needs of society at large and with the historic task of the democratic forces of our generation. The answer is to be found in the liberalization of our newspapers, radio, and theater, so that homosexuality can be discussed as freely as any other subject and within the confines that circumscribe any other type of discussion. Already a beginning has been made in the very large interest shown in the subject by novelists, and in the occasional portrayal of homosexuality on the stage. A few popular magazines in the United States have at least mentioned it. In the larger cities serious articles have appeared even in the newspapers, and in one case an entire series of articles, written in a penetrating and not unsympathetic manner and without any evasion of terms, appeared in a New York newspaper.

This discussion may prove to be an opening wedge. There will be more articles, books, and further utilization of other means of thought communication, and out of this will come the interchange of opinion, the conflict and the controversy, which alone can establish truth.

And all of this is good for society, good particularly in this era, when no greater threat to the democratic way of life and to everything that has evolved in modern civilization, both Western and Eastern, appears than the suppression of all differences of opinion, the repression of all controversy. At this moment in history, when the forces of totalitarianism seek to extend the conspiracy of silence and the distortions of truth to all phases of life—to science and politics and human relations—the homosexuals (including even those few who are mistakenly in the camp of the totalitarians) are seeking to extend freedom of the individual, of speech, press, and thought to an entirely new realm. While others wish to narrow the confines of allowable differences of opinion and permissible discussion, the homosexual seeks to broaden them. This is not because he is a greater lover of liberty, but because he is fortunately placed in that historic position where his liberties have been denied and he seeks to regain them.

Thus, as the first answer to the society we homosexuals envisage, we seek freedom of thought and expression on this question. This involves not only the right to publish books and magazines without interference from the police, but the right to employ the main channels of communication, the leading newspapers, magazines, and the air for the expression of a viewpoint in the spirit and traditions of American freedoms. It may be the right of one editor or publisher to express his own viewpoint, as he does on things political, and to exclude the opposition from his press, but when his outlook coincides with that of all of the major editors, and when those who differ fear to open their pages because of reprisals by church, government, or advertisers, then there is a totalitarian control of the press by a particular group and hence a denial of freedom to the other. This is indubitably the situation so far as the rights of homosexuals are concerned today.

If the day of free and open discussion arrives, and if, during the course of such discussion, the struggle for it, and as a consequence of it, the social stigma attached to being a homosexual begins to be lifted, there will automatically come about a happier milieu in which the individual can live, love, thrive, and work. Part of that happier relationship will be found in the dropping of the disguise.

Many homosexuals consider that their greatest fortune, their one saving grace, has been the invisibility of the cross which they have had to bear. The ease with which they were able to hide their temperaments from the closest friends and business associates, from their parents, wives, and children, made it possible to partake of the full benefits and material and spiritual advantages life offers to the heterosexual. Many such people—and I include myself—have constantly striven to perfect their technique of concealment.

Actually, the inherent tragedy—not the saving grace—of homosexuality is found in the ease of concealment. If the homosexual were as readily recognizable as are members of certain other minority groups, the social condemnation could not possibly exist. Stereotype thinking on the part of the majority would, in the first instance, collapse of its own absurdity if all of us who are gay were known for what we are. Secondly, our achievements in society and our contributions to all phases of culture and social advancement would become well-known, and not merely the arsenal of argument in the knowledge of a few. The laws against homosexuality could not be sustained if it were flagrantly apparent that millions of human beings in all walks of life were affected. Blackmail, naturally enough, would be non-existent as a problem facing the invert.

It is a chimera, but worthy of speculation. If only all of the inverts, the millions in all lands, could simultaneously rise up in our full strength! For the fact is that we homosexuals are defeated by the self-perpetuation of the folkways which inflict severe punishment on those who protest against these folkways. Again, the circle is vicious.

We need freedom of expression to achieve freedom of inversion, but only the free invert is in a position to demand and to further freedom of expression. And what are we to do in the meantime?

A few individuals, well-placed because of their position in society, their economic freedom, their universally acknowledged attainments, can speak up and further their cause. Others can, with discretion, spread enlightenment to a few intimate and trustworthy friends. And still others can utilize their knowledge or talents by disseminating truthful information and by bringing the subject before the public, but behind the veil of pseudonymity.

But once there is freedom of expression and once the invert is fully accepted and is an object neither of calumny nor sneer, an object neither to scorn nor to pity, how will he fit into our social and family life? Is it proposed that society recognize and sanction marriages in which both "bride" and "groom" are of the same sex and in which the two parties to such a union have the same rights and obligations as in any other marriage?

Most of the problems concomitant with being homosexual would be automatically solved if there were no discriminatory attitudes on the part of society. Many homsexuals would marry and have children, attracted by the family life which such a prospect offers, but there would be no shame of the homosexuality, no concealment from wife or from offspring. Others would form unions with males, as they do today, but without social ostracism; they would bring their friends to social functions and might adopt an orphan child or a nephew of an overcrowded and overburdened family. Others would live the lives of bachelors, perhaps have many loves or few, and as the years pass would probably show less interest in the pursuit of the sexual object than in cultural activities.

In all such matters the homosexual's life would parallel that of the heterosexual. Some people require a mate; others do not. Some pursue sex relentlessly; others organize a life in which the physical gratification of their impulses plays a rather minor rôle.

What the homosexual wants is freedom—not only freedom of expression, but also sexual freedom. By sexual freedom is meant the right of any person to gratify his urges when and how he sees fit, without fear of social consequences, so long as he does not use the force of either violence, threat, or superior age; so long as he does not inflict bodily harm or disease upon another person; so long as the other person is of sound mind and agrees to the activity. This means that both on the statute books and in the realm of public opinion all sexual activity is accepted as equally correct, right, and proper so long as it is entered into voluntarily by the parties involved, they are perfectly sane and above a reasonable age of consent, free of communicable disease, and no duress or misrepresentation is employed.

This is, for our society, a radical proposal. It has been expounded in the remarkable works of Guyon,* among others, and its full exposition would be beyond the realm of this book. But it is radical only to expound and defend this theory, for sexual freedom is actually being practiced on a very wide scale in modern life, despite its being condemned by school, church, newspapers, and government. Adultery, fellatio between husband and wife, homosexuality, premarital fornication—all are so common that it is rare to find the individual who has not indulged in one or several of these forms of sexual activity quite frequently.

However, on the law books these are punishable acts, and in the realm of public opinion even more so. The result is that modern civilization adopts a hypocritical attitude and attempts to force an extreme feeling of shame upon the individuals who live what to them is a normal and natural life.

The homosexual often feels that the source of his difficulty lies in the fact that he is born into a hostile world, and this hostility is inherent, he believes, in that he lives in a heterosexual society. He is, in my opinion, entirely wrong in this concept. The root of the homosexual difficulty is that he lives, not in a heterosexual world, but in an anti-sexual world.

The anti-sexual nature of modern civilization is apparent wherever one turns. In the description of the virgin birth, the term "immaculate conception" is used, and thus an inference is made that all conceptions that take place by means of sexual intercourse are not immaculate and are therefore unclean. Any humor pertaining to sex

* René Guyon, *The Ethics of Sexual Acts* (New York: Alfred A. Knopf, 1934 and 1948) and *Sexual Freedom* (New York: Alfred A. Knopf, 1950).

is called a "dirty joke." It is "lewd" to fail to conceal the sexual organs, and the strongest epithets in the English language—and in many other languages—are synonymous with having sexual intercourse. Even the more progressive educators teach the children about birds and flowers and something about the physiology of sex, but skirt the fact that the higher animals, and particularly man, indulge in sex for the pure joy of the thing. In modern anti-sexual society, the heterosexual is tolerated only because he is necessary for the propagation of the species, but the virgin and the chaste are glorified as pristine purity. If we homosexuals lived in a predominantly heterosexual and not an anti-sexual society—as witness the American Indians and the South Sea Islanders—we would not be in constant conflict with our fellowmen nor with ourselves.

Some will object that there is a basic contradiction. Have I not, throughout this book, decried the attitudes of the heterosexual society, of the heterosexual-dominated society? Is the reader now to be informed that that heterosexual society is non-existent? The fact is that it is only apparently a heterosexual society. The anti-sexual culture pretends that it is heterosexual, in order the better to suppress all sex for pleasure!

The heterosexual's conflicts in our society are also deep; sexual maladjustment is by no means the sole property of the homosexual in modern life. But the lesser stigma attached to adultery and pre-marital relationships, the ease of concealment of fellatio when it takes place with the opposite sex, and, finally, society's acceptance (albeit reluctantly) of sex in the conjugal relationships—these facts place the heterosexual in a preferred position in the anti-sexual setup.

The homosexual then, to summarize, desires freedom of expression, aspires to recognition of his temperament without discriminatory attitudes or punishment, and will find all of this possible only when he is able to proclaim his true nature. Such a program will be possible only in a culture that proclaims sexual freedom—the right of adults to enter into any voluntary sexual arrangement with each other without fear of reprisal by society. At the same time the embracing of such a guiding policy of sexual freedom will hasten the liberation of the homosexual from concealment and from silence.

The homosexual, thus, has two historic missions to perform. Whether he is a democrat or a totalitarian by political conviction, he is historically forced to enter the struggle for the widening of freedom of expression. And, whether his religious and ethical convictions are those of the continent or the libertarian, he is historically compelled to enlist in the legions fighting for liberalization of the sexual mores of modern civilization.

It is interesting and heartening to note that in the two greatest totalitarian regimes of our century veritable reigns of terror against homosexuality were instituted, despite the collaboration of certain homosexuals in the establishment of these regimes. The purge of Roehm by Hitler can be understood only in this light—that no free, deviating, unassimilable viewpoint was tolerable in Nazi Germany, no matter how obsequious it might be to the Hitler regime.

After the Russian Revolution, the laws against homosexuality were repealed. These Tsarist laws were denounced as the remnants of the bourgeois concept of sex, and a new era of sexual freedom was foreseen. In the years that followed, as the totalitarian stranglehold on all channels of thought expression was strengthened, the old bourgeois and Tsarist laws were restored. Abortion was illegalized, divorce made increasingly difficult to obtain, and the law restoring homosexuality to a crime, placing it in the same category as other social crimes, was signed by Kalinin in March, 1934. This is a significant date, for it was the period of the heightened struggle against the Old Bolsheviks, the last great effort of the Stalin regime to bring about a complete system of thought and action control. "The mass arrests of homosexuals," writes Wilhelm Reich, "led to a panic . . . It is said that there were numerous suicides in the army."* Since that time, there have been several reports that homosexuals have been involved in anti-Stalinist conspiracies.

Today, Russia is much more backward than the rest of Europe and America in its attitudes toward the sexual non-conformist, just as it is in the attitude toward all non-conformists. There is no room except for orthodoxy, and that includes things sexual as much as things political. In the socialist state the homosexual lives in dread. Even the few channels open to him in the United States are closed in Russia. With medieval severity he can be seized and pilloried.

How can one account for Russian and Nazi cruelty on this ques-

* Wilhelm Reich, *The Sexual Revolution.* (New York: Orgone Institute Press, 1945), p. 209.

tion? Only in this way—that in a totalitarian state, there was no room for a group of people who, by their very sexual temperaments, could never be assimilated, must always remain apart with their own ways of life, their own outlooks, their own philosophies.

And it is this inherent lack of assimilability that is the greatest historic value of homosexuality. Any minority which does not commit anti-social acts, which is not destructive of the life, property, or culture of the majority or of other minority groups, is a pillar of democratic strength. So long as there are such minorities in our culture, whether of a sexual or religious or ethnic character, there will be many broths in the melting pot, many and variegated waves in the seas. No force will be able to weave these groups into a single totalitarian unity which is the unanimity of the graveyard.

Thus on three scores, homosexuality—fortunately but unwittingly —must inevitably play a progressive rôle in the scheme of things. It will broaden the base for freedom of thought and communication, will be a banner-bearer in the struggle for liberalization of our sexual conventions, and will be a pillar of strength in the defense of our threatened democracy.

Chapter 22

A Problem for Everyone

With but a few exceptions, the general hetereosexual population is either completely indifferent to the fate of the homosexual or in fundamental agreement with the prevailing attitudes of society. In one major respect, then, the homosexual problem differs from that of all other minorities: namely, in the failure to find allies outside the ranks of those most directly and personally affected. This failure derives from a multiplicity of sources: the suspicion falling upon the ally; the psychological rôle of hostility as an aid in the repression of tendencies that are considered abnormal; the inability of homosexuals to defend their viewpoint and appeal for support; and the belief that this is a problem which does not affect the average man and which therefore need not arouse his interest.

The struggle to change the prevailing moral codes insofar as attitudes toward homosexuals are concerned has not always been without allies. In Germany, during the last years of the nineteenth century, a movement for legalization and acceptance of homosexuality was organized under the leadership of Magnus Hirschfeld and continued to function until after the establishment of the Weimar Republic. This movement agitated and organized toward the end of breaking through the barriers of silence and of bringing the homosexual society out of the depths of submerged semi-legality. It published a journal, *Jahrbuch für sexuelle Zwischenstufen*, and it called not only for a repeal of certain statutes, but for a change in the attitudes of all people. Although centering a great deal of its attention on the theme of legislative reform, the Hirschfeld circle unquestionably recognized that this was not of major importance in and of itself, but could be employed as a rallying plea around which a general struggle against injustice might be waged. The basis of its appeal was humanitarianism.

Similar movements have existed elsewhere in the world, although the German group achieved strength and influence that were unmatched in other countries. A British circle functioned for many years under the leadership of Edward Carpenter; it published a few pamphlets and was held in high repute in British intellectual circles.

The twenty-three volumes of the *Jahrbuch* that appeared in Germany under Hirschfeld's editorship are extremely interesting, mainly because they constitute the first effort in modern times to publish an avowedly homosexual magazine (the word *homosexual* appeared on the title page as part of the journal's subtitle).

The Hirschfeld movement made a strong effort to organize support among legislators, writers, scientists, and all those who would respond to a call for understanding and sympathy. During the latter years of its existence, the group drew up a petition to the Reichstag; and after considerable effort, signatures were obtained from several hundred distinguished men and women. The names on this list are today little known in the United States. The signatories were physicians, professors, writers, and others prominent in Germany in the years immediately following the First World War. But to those who were familiar with the German culture of the times, the list was surprisingly strong for the quality and standing of those who signed the appeal. A few of the names would be known to any American reader—Heinrich Mann, Thomas Mann, and Albert Einstein.

The Hirschfeld appeal argued that the prevailing social conditions and the laws which reflected them were designed to make a minority suffer without contributing anything whatsoever to society at large. A social injustice required rectification, and it was in support of this call for human sympathy that outstanding German intellectuals were rallied.

Since the decline of the Hirschfeld and Carpenter movements, little has been done in an organized fashion to arouse the interest of the public at large in the plight of the homosexual. As has been noted, a handful of writers have treated the theme sympathetically, but although millions of Americans are today unquestionably aware of the difficulties faced by the homosexual, they are either indifferent to his fate or are actually in favor of severe treatment. This is but one of many manifestations of the general decline of humanitarianism as a worthy end in itself.

There was a period in modern history when the fact that a cause was humane would be considered its sole necessary justification. Today, whether it be to send food to an area where famine is rife, or to give blood for boys on a battlefield, or to aid the colored peoples, the positive and selfish gain to be derived therefrom must be stressed in order to arouse wide popular support. Humanitarianism, in and of itself, is dismissed as maudlin sentimentality or as ineffective propaganda, and the plea for compassion is confused with the plea for pity, which is an invitation for contempt.

Even the advocates of racial equality have centered their main argumentation on the evil effects of race hatred on the welfare of the majority group. In the United States, the champions of equality argue that America's prevailing racial codes are weakening this country's position in global and particularly Asiatic affairs; they contend that these codes permit an economic exploitation of the poor whites; and they point out, as did Myrdal, that the American folkways have created a deep psychological problem for the white man, who seeks to believe in the American tradition of fair play, democracy, and sympathy for the underdog, and yet finds these tenets in sharp conflict with his own attitude toward and treatment of the Negro. However, without denying the truth of these arguments and their efficiency in the struggle to find allies, the fact is that they are entirely irrelevant, for racial equality is a desirable end in itself, to be achieved even if it did not mean a betterment of the position of America in world affairs and of the white man in America.

Herein lies one of the tragedies of this era—that humanitarianism, the plea for the betterment of human conditions for purely unselfish motives in order that people may be happier, is becoming a forgotten cause in the conflict of forces and in the struggle to survive in the modern world.

I contend that this humanitarian plea, this deep compassion of man for man, must be revived if the values of the democratic world are to survive and be meaningful, and it is upon the basis of a democratic Christian humanitarianism that the sexual majority must be called upon to rally to the support of the minority.

However, this does not mean that there is no other reason for the average person to take an interest in the cause of homosexuals and to support their aspirations. No minority group lives in a vacuum. It functions in a society in which it is in constant contact with the majority. It touches, moves against, influences and is influenced by the majority. The interrelationships are significant for people in the dominant as well as the submerged group.

Because of the size of the homosexual minority, and because of the non-hereditary and involuntary nature of the drive which character-izes this group, no one in the world is exempt from the very strong possibility that homosexuality already exists or is likely to exist in one's most immediate family or in the family of one's closest friends. How much tragedy in the lives of parents, how much anxiety and appre-hension among brothers and sisters, might be averted if social hostility were unknown. Most of the severe problems brought into focus in the life of the homosexual—humiliation, disgrace, pretense, and the struggle to believe in oneself while denying one's nature, to name a few—are primarily the result of hostility, and the diminution and even-tual disappearance of this hostility will impart a greater degree of happiness not only to some unknown people, but also to the child growing into maturity and to the child not yet born.

For every homosexual in the United States, there are approximately three to five others in the immediate family who are directly concerned with that person's life and happiness. And when the homosexual inci-dence is multiplied by a figure of three or four or five, an enormous minority is reached. Only a movement to ameliorate the conditions in which the homosexual finds himself in society can guarantee these families freedom from the intense suffering they experience when they discover the anomaly of a child.

But even if this situation never enters a man's home, he is inescapably concerned with the social ostracism, because all oppressive attitudes toward any minorities (unless the latter be socially destructive forces) contain the seeds of oppression toward other groups and toward all groups. When the Veterans Administrator is permitted to deny to the homosexuals the privileges afforded under the G. I. Bill of Rights, a precedent is set by which conforming to the moral codes becomes the criterion for government benefits; and when his actions go vir-tually unnoticed and unchallenged, then sovereign powers have been seized by a man who was not delegated such powers by the legislators, and the precedent becomes usable against other individuals and groups. When a state court interprets a law in such manner as to allow a man to be convicted of a crime on the basis of the uncorroborated testimony of an accomplice, the possibilities of corruption, blackmail, and other evils are apparent, and their repercussions will affect the heterosexuals as much as the homosexuals.

When a witness can be humiliated and intimidated by being asked when on the stand (or by being warned in advance that he will be so interrogated) entirely irrelevant questions about his private homosexual life, which admittedly has nothing to do with a case at issue, and when no action is taken against those responsible for such intimidation and blackmail, then the possibilities arise that witnesses will be queried—as indeed they have been!—on their extramarital and premarital sex lives, entirely extraneous though these matters may be to a point at trial. No witness becomes free from the frightening specter of a government that will pry into every angle of a man's personal affairs, trail men and women to gain information on their sexual activities, and confront witnesses and defendants with irrelevant facts in order to prevent unfavorable testimony; or if intimidation is unsuccessful, then to blemish their characters and impeach their credibility. The use of this technique by the American government in major cases is most frightening, but the heterosexual must realize that it is a technique whose use is not confined to homosexuality.

And thus I could continue. The setting up of a government commission to investigate why certain groups should not receive employment not only represents a step in the usurpation of a psychiatric rôle by legislators in no way competent to handle such matters, but demonstrates the bias and prejudice with which an official body can set out to investigate a problem—and these are matters which do not start or stop with homosexuals. Unless the population at large puts an end to such practices, they will be extended—as indeed they have been—to other groups of people.

It is no creditable reflection on the caliber of an official United States government body that it presents specious arguments for banning homosexuals from employment, some of these arguments demonstrating a sociologically bankrupt mind on the part of the investigators. (For example: *homosexuals tend to congregate together*, a statement which ignores the reasons and responsibilities for this tendency; which does not prove that there is anything nefarious about such congregation; and which could just as truthfully be made about heterosexuals as a reason for banishing them from employment). But the important lesson to be learned is that such methods of investigation, such argumentation, such presentation of findings without permitting the opposite viewpoint to be aired, can be and have been utilized against any group of people in society. For this reason, a threat to the freedom of all people is contained in the methods utilized against a few.

All minority problems are actually majority problems, I have already noted, but this is not only because the majority is responsible for the existence of the problems. It is also because the majority suffers, indirectly and often unknowingly, from the oppression inflicted upon the minority. All legal and governmental measures that have been taken against homosexuals can be and have been used against heterosexuals as well, and can be used against every group that is not in all respects acceptable to the dominant majority, and against every individual whose life does not conform to the prevailing moral codes of the United States. It is therefore essential to be on guard against government oppression, to take issue with the unfair laws and the interpretation of these laws, because unchallenged they remain a threat to all Americans. But the most important fact is this: that social hostility made these laws and their interpretations possible, and that only a change in social attitudes will effect a change in governmental and judicial regulations.

It may, on the surface, seem outrageous to many in a community to propose that magazines, publishing houses, newspapers, forums, lecture halls, and other educational and cultural media offer facilities for the presentation of the homosexual viewpoint, but if this minority is not to be allowed the freedom to express itself in a legal manner, then what is to prevent similar oppressive measures against the anti-puritanical heterosexuals, against atheists and other anti-religious nonconformists, and against political groups whose propaganda may be embarrassing to a church or state?

The unhappiness that has sprung from anti-homosexual traditions has not been exclusively that of homosexuals. Quite the contrary, much of the suffering, directly or indirectly, knowingly or unknowingly, has been by heterosexuals. One of the most successful techniques of modern tyrants has been to exploit widespread prejudices for political purposes. Among these is the social hostility toward homosexuality—so universal that it must go without effective rebuttal. Both Stalin and Hitler have utilized the bias against homosexuality as a smoke screen to cover up their own deficiencies, to rally the outraged populace against opposition, to arouse the fury of hatred by linking personal and political opposition with this sexual practice. These dictators were carrying on in the traditions of those who had linked homosexuality with heresy and sorcery in the Middle Ages; whereas here in the United States the charges of sex perversion in the government were used as a basis for an attack upon the foreign policy of the Truman Administration, when support for such an attack could not be obtained on the basis of the logic of relevant argumentation.

A healthy social attitude must be based upon a recognition that homosexuals have become scapegoats, and that society as a whole is not only responsible for this situation but also suffers therefrom. America has learned through sad experience that having any minority in society that is easily available as a defenseless scapegoat, whether of racial or sexual or whatever origin, is as menacing to the welfare of those who are not condemned as it is for those who are. A scapegoat may be sent to prison or even to death, but the failures and shortcomings which made it necessary to inflict such punishment continue unabated, with opposition often effectively silenced.

It is, in fact, not the homosexuals who suffer most in the crusade against their modes of life, for they conceal their inclinations. But it is in the course of the persecution of homosexuals, and in the fortification of the suppression of their activities, that censorship, antiquated divorce laws, and outmoded moral codes are foisted upon people who are blinded by hatred from giving them proper evaluation. The cry of sexual perversion that is raised is like the traditional "red herring" in things political; it is used to inhibit any effort to effect a re-orientation in man's thinking on all things sexual.

The failure of the homosexual to attract allies is attributable in the first instance to the disadvantage of becoming an ally; to the inability of the invert to break through the taboos and express his viewpoint before a wide and general audience; and, finally, to the failure to demonstrate to the population that this is a problem having repercussions far beyond the lives of those most directly affected. But, above all, the failure can be traced to the omission of even the humanitarian appeal, which has not been effectively expressed in the United States. The fact is that in democratic Germany, and to a lesser extent elsewhere on the Continent, the appeal for human sympathy found a hearty response. If, on the one hand, ordinary human beings following the majority pathway of sexual practice can be made to understand that they themselves suffer grave disadvantages from the social attitude of condemnation of the homosexual; and if, on the other, an appeal is made to the American traditions of fair play and equality of opportunity, I am personally convinced that American attitudes will change.

At a time when man's sympathy for his fellowman is at a low ebb, I believe that humanitarianism as the foundation of the struggle for the rights and freedoms of the homosexual must take precedence over all other pleas. The rectification of the social evil of hostility is a desirable end in itself, and if presented in the light of modern scientific and sociological findings, can rally to its cause men of high standing and influence in American life. But this is not to exclude the very real truth that anti-homosexual attitudes affect millions of people because they inflict a cruel and unusually difficult type of punishment on members of their families, or will inflict such hardships on those close relatives in years to come; and because such oppressive measures are in the last analysis a threat to the freedom of all people.

The removal of the scapegoat rôle of a minority, without removing that minority, is a socially necessary end for the defense of the rights of the majority, and the reconsideration of society's attitude toward the phenomenon of homosexuality must bring with it a simultaneous reconsideration of sexuality itself. In fact, in this anti-sexual culture it is entirely possible that there is no such thing as a persecution of homosexuality; there may be only a persecution of sexuality.

A call for the re-evaluation of attitudes toward the homosexual is actually (and cannot be separated from) an appeal for re-orientation on sexual life in modern civilization. In such an evaluation, it will be seen that it is to the advantage of every man in society that a change in general sentiment takes place. If, in arousing the population to the need for such a change, there is a revival of a spirit of humanitarian sympathies, that too will be beneficial to all men and women.

Chapter 23

A Discussion with Parents

Every year thousands of people who have previously been unaware of homosexuality as a problem affecting their lives become painfully awakened to the realities of the world of marginal men. The homosexual had hitherto been someone to sneer at on the street, had been an unenviable character in a joke, or the subject of gossip repeated with gleeful malice. Now the homosexual was the son in the home, the beloved boy going to high school or college, and still he was the despised individual. How could these two concepts be one?

"Millions of people are queer," it had been said, and if the family moved in sophisticated and educated circles, it had undoubtedly heard this repeated. But "millions" is an abstraction, a problem involving others, far removed from one's own life. These millions were, perhaps, human beings, but like the inhabitants of concentration camps in a far-off land, or the miserable inmates of a leper colony, they were millions untranslatable into plain, ordinary, everyday young men and women like one's own children.

The awakening sometimes comes gradually, sometimes with rude suddenness as a shock from which it is well-nigh impossible ever to recover. And frequently the awakening is never full and complete; there remains in the minds of many parents a half-suspected feeling that is deliberately shut out from the mind, never exposed to verification, never subject to affirmation or denial.

Actually the relationship between parents and the mature (or maturing) homosexual offspring constitutes one of the most important, most troublesome, and least discussed phases of gay life in America.

It is quite evident that any strain or rupture between parent and child is a source of discomfort to all concerned, regardless of the degree of adjustment that each makes. The family unit, in a world of changing and unstable relationships, offers an anchorage, an opportunity to sink one's roots and gain direction.

To the homosexual, however, there are three additional reasons why a complete understanding with parents (or brothers and sisters) is indispensable. First, as already demonstrated in my summary of psychiatric opinion on the origin of the homosexual drive in the individual, there is frequently an extremely strong psychological attachment between the homosexual and at least one of his parents, or in some cases a sibling. This was demonstrated in fiction most ably in *The Well of Loneliness*, in which Stephen, the heroine, bestows a disproportionate share of her affection on her father, a kind and compassionate individual, while she feels completely removed from her mother, a woman of uncommon frigidity.

The loss of a parent, whether through death or voluntary disassociation, is always particularly difficult and initiates one of the saddest periods that any human being must go through in life. But people who have formed an attachment so strong that it pervades their entire being and is at the root of their rejection of the culture around them—they find such a loss many times more unbearable. Two brothers whom I have known well for a long time were on the surface equally attached to their mother, equally hurt to the quick by her death, but demonstrated completely dissimilar patterns of behavior thereafter. Only a few months had passed before Lawrence was his happy-go-lucky old self, attending movies, dating girls, the mother already a vague but cherished memory, the wound healed though fresh. But William, a year his junior and a homosexual, had not adjusted to his loss a decade after his mother's death. To this day he cannot hear her name or see her photograph without a choking sensation in his throat; he cannot look at a calendar, he admits, without searching through tear-filled eyes for the date that marks the anniversary of her death.

So strong can these attachments to a mother or father be that they can reach unbelievable and even neurotic degrees. Consequently it is essential to the welfare of the homosexual youth to preserve the strong bond that frequently exists between him and his parents.

In the second place, the homosexual needs the protection and the friendship that can be offered by a family far more than do most other people. His problems are deepgoing; they are not easily solved; nor can they often be brought elsewhere. His must be an orientation in a hostile world, and the friendship and advice that may be found at home can be of immeasurable aid. His problems will be those of every minority group member: to choose between the ease of moving within one's own circle and the advantages of penetrating into the world at large—or to seek a *modus vivendi* in both; they will be problems of education, earning a living, exposure, blackmail. But, much more vital throughout his life than any of these material and easily expressible dilemmas, will be the fundamental question that he must answer at all times when he examines himself in the mirror of life—can he find self-pride and self-justification in the face of the cultural impact of opposition, ridicule, and debasement besetting him from all sides? It is to the warmth, security, and permanence of a family's love that one needs to turn under such circumstances.

Finally, the gay youth desperately yearns for the acceptance of his self in a world not only of hostility but also of rejection—a society that attempts, with neither success nor reason, to force rejection of oneself upon the individual. Accept yourself, his psychiatrist advises, but how hard this is if acceptance cannot be found at home.

Many parents are completely unaware of the homosexual side of their children's lives, just as wives and husbands are ignorant of such activities on the part of their spouses. The young person, whether bachelor or married, maintains so perfect a pretense, always on guard against exposure, always careful to wear the mask, that the parent is baffled. Even the slightest modicum of suspicion is absent. Such a parent often reflects the hostile attitude of the world toward the sexual invert and may even find occasion to express such unfriendly sentiments in the presence of the son.

"Degenerate," I heard the mother of one of my friends state in his presence when the name of a prominent homosexual was mentioned. I writhed within, wondering what the son was thinking at that moment. Later I asked him, and he explained that he ignored such remarks because his home meant so much to him that he was unwilling to jeopardize it. "There is not nor could there be any common ground on the subject between my mother and myself," he explained, and then added, "and I don't know if I would be comfortable if there were."

All people could not accept such an adjustment. Some would feel that they were imposters, living a falsehood, unwanted if their true selves were exposed.

But so complete an ignorance of the facts is not universal. In many instances the homosexual has become suspect. Here and there a remark has been let pass, a friend slightly more obvious than others has been brought to the house, eyebrows have been raised and malicious tongues have wagged and left their evil behind them.

And the parents watch with dread, seeking to find, to seize upon and believe any evidence that their suspicions are ill founded. With the infinite capacity of the human mind to believe what it wishes to believe, the parent seeks to console himself with a conviction that the son is not unlike other young people. And perhaps he succeeds in this self-delusion, but to what avail?

And the son, ever on guard, becomes in turn suspicious that he is suspected. He carefully selects the books that he brings into his home, becomes more guarded than ever about his friends, will not even divulge his telephone number to some, and may on occasion join a hostile conversation.

Thus subterfuge is literally forced upon the homosexual. On the one hand, the mask must be worn because he fears that its removal will deeply hurt the persons he loves so dearly. Seeking to spare their feelings, he finds a deliberately fostered ignorance to be the best method of accomplishing his aim. And, on the other hand, he fears reprisal from his parents in the form of condemnation, complete rejection, and perhaps banishment from their lives.

Finally, there are the parents who are certain of the homosexuality of the child. The latter may be obvious, or the parent may have become familiar with the facts because of an unpleasant incident at school, or in some cases the young person may find it necessary for his peace of mind to go to a mother or father and voluntarily discuss the situation.

Within the framework of these various patterns of relationships, each in common practice in literally hundreds of thousands of homes, there are innumerable variants. No two families have worked out their problems in the same manner; to categorize always results in vague generalizations.

Parents often come to psychiatrists, social workers, churchmen, educators, and others, and with great hesitancy confess their predicament, asking for advice. Or, frequently enough, they approach these mentors, stating, "I have a friend"—or a sister, or a neighbor (many subterfuges are employed)—"whose son has a homosexual tendency. What can I advise her to do?" The sister or neighbor is clearly a fiction, the word "tendency" a euphemism, the entire approach thus being cushioned in order to find a formula that will hide the shame.

Sometimes these questions are well directed, and the advice is intelligent. More often, one gets a deep sympathy (for the parent) but neither orientation nor help. All of these people and many more should be questioned and their counsel weighed. But unfortunately, with the exception of a few psychiatrists, they are woefully ignorant of the homosexual problem, and without knowledge how can they be of help?

Let us suppose your son is a homosexual and you are bewildered by it. Perhaps, as a homosexual, I can offer some helpful advice on how to deal with him. But first I must urge you to lay aside all preconceived notions—your hatreds, revulsions, and prejudices.

If you have followed the pages that have gone before, you will know certain facts about homosexuality that bear repeating—that it is common, that many homosexuals are really bisexual (as are many people who consider themselves heterosexual, too), and that a deep-rooted homosexual drive cannot be whipped or banished from your child. But, most important of all, you must know and remember that lectures from a clergyman can do little good, and may possibly do great harm, to a person in your son's predicament; and treatment at the hands of a physician or psychologist is more likely to adjust him to his homosexuality than to turn him away from it.

I know one parent who openly boasts of the good thrashing that he gave his fifteen-year-old boy when he discovered "the awful truth" about his life. Filled with anger and hatred, boiling over with a temper that had never before asserted itself so strongly, the father, aided by his eldest son, mercilessly inflicted such torture upon the youngster that medical aid had to be called to heal the bruises. But other wounds had been made that no doctor could ever assuage.

And what had the father accomplished? Nothing save that he had demonstrated how normal a person he was. He had made no effort whatsoever to understand the boy or to arrive at an acceptable solution of his problem. A father of that type must have been extremely guilty in his feelings toward his son; he must have felt that he had somehow failed, or that the world would consider that he had failed. To express disapproval to the youth in such a violent manner was both pointless and unnecessarily cruel, but he was forced to express it to himself. The whipping must have left the father with the conviction that he was good and pure and therefore free of responsibility for the wayward son. Of father and son, the latter was the greater sufferer, but perhaps the former had the greater problem.

To banish your son from his home is but a slightly refined and more civilized form of whipping. It, too, contributes nought to solving either the youngster's problems or your own. It does nothing but demonstrate that in a choice between respectability in the eyes of the world at large and the love of your child, you are prepared to sacrifice the latter in favor of the former.

What attitude then, can you assume toward your son? It should hardly be necessary to reiterate that the family unit is a cornerstone of modern culture, and that in such a unit, for which you have assumed your responsibilities and in which you have brought up your child, there is an obligation on your part, both social and biological in origin, toward those whom you have created and reared. The mother or father who abandons a youth in a period of distress can hardly be justified in the eyes of an impartial moralist.

But double is your duty as the parent of a homosexual, for from the time your son was cradled and weaned, through the years of puberty and adolescence, his care and rearing have been your obligation, and the essential responsibility—albeit unwitting—for his development into a gay youth is yours. True, you did not choose his path, but neither was it his choice. Your son awoke to it, as though it were inborn, and from it he is unlikely ever to escape. But it was primarily you, the parents—through your conduct of home life, your behavior patterns, your affection or lack of affection, your education or lack of education—who laid the foundation for the inverted sexuality of your son.

Therefore it is not only unjust but immoral for you who have forced your child upon a certain path now to reject him because you abhor that path.

Some parents—and they are very few—respond with sympathy and understanding to the knowledge of their child's problem. They are aware of the difficulties that the child is going to face in life. In these rare cases the parents dread the instability of homosexual friendships, the economic, social, and educational discrimination, the life-long humiliations. Most parents reading these words will seek to identify themselves with this group, but many only use the difficulties of the invert's life as an excuse to hide their fundamental complaint. For the majority of parents are little interested in such unselfish considerations. They fear the gossip, the wagging of evil tongues, their own humiliation because they have a "queer" child. For this reason they rise up in violent indignation, denouncing the youth's habits as evil, unnatural, perverted.

To those of you who can do nothing other than dissociate yourselves from your child's inclinations, I suggest you search within yourselves for the reasons and then try to foresee the results of your denunciation. I do not see how you can find justification for whipping and banishment. Those of you who wish to aid your child are likely to have no preconceived ideas as to what form such aid should take. If your concept of aid is not necessarily confined to bringing about a change in the entire psychological and sexual make-up of your child, perhaps your efforts will be crowned with success—not only for the child, but for yourselves as well.

Thus, at the very start, you must establish an orientation. Do you honestly desire to obtain clarification on that course which will give your son the fullest possibilities in life within his reach, in order that his be a happy life in every sense of the term; or are you seeking self-justification and vindication for a road of brutal action? Are you searching for the courage to face the world with the truth, or are you seeking the subterfuges that will enable you to turn to lies and false pretensions? Finally, are you seeking advice only on how to change your child, or on how to make your child a happy person?

This last question is the crux of the problem. To some of you the answer will be most obvious—the two are not only not mutually exclusive, you will maintain, but they are mutually interdependent. They are not two questions, some of you will say, but one; for you are convinced that the road of future happiness lies in but a single direction—to change the course that life is taking for your child.

Not only is such not necessarily the case, but even were this true—that genuine happiness can never be found save in the heterosexual world—it would be entirely irrelevant. The fundamental truth which you, the parents, must accept is this—that neither prayer nor medicine nor whipping nor sympathetic therapy are likely to remove the homosexual drive from the person in whom it has taken root. You must accept the condition of your son or daughter as having finality. Banish entirely from your dreams any thought that on the morrow your offspring will see the light. Cease forever your suggestions of marriage, your disapproving attitudes and remarks. From this point on, your course of action will not be difficult to determine.

Should your son or daughter be sent for psychiatric care? This largely depends on the age of the youngster and his attitude toward the need for the advice of the psychiatrist. If the lad is in his formative years and can be brought to a physician with ease, such a consultation can do no harm, provided the physician is qualified to handle the matter. A family doctor, however, despite the confidence which he enjoys, may do nothing but frighten a young person with a series of half-truths and admonitions, may speak sternly of unnatural practices, and seek in this manner to foster a greater guilt in the individual. But neither fright nor guilt will help; in fact, they will increase the difficulties concomitant with homosexuality without relieving the homosexual drive one iota.

Other physicians, and particularly accredited psychiatrists, will handle the matter with finesse, searching for motives, seeking to discover whether the individual is traveling through a stage or is manifesting the symptoms of sexual inversion.

You parents, however, must be prepared for the professional opinion that the child cannot and must not be changed from the basic pattern of his sexual life, but can only be adjusted to it so that this pattern does not become an impediment to his search for happiness. And you must also be prepared to be shut out of the relationship developing between psychiatrist and patient. The confidences between the two must never become the property of a third person.

All of this does not mean that you can draw up a chair and say, "Son, I've made an appointment for you to see Dr. Jones. He's a first-class psychiatrist, and he'll straighten you out about messing around with men." You can only suggest a visit to a psychiatrist after you have established a satisfactory parent-child relationship.

The very first problem, most difficult of solution, is to "reach" your youngster, to establish a mutual confidence and a rapport with him. So strong is his assumption of your disapproval that he has created a wall around himself, and although moving within your midst, he is protected through a retreat into his own world. His is at one and the same time a secret and a shame. He has created a sort of self-contrived and deliberately schizophrenic pattern in which he has laid aside his homosexual self in all dealings with you. With remarkable care and through the means of ingenious rationalizations he lives two selves simultaneously, and one of them has been placed completely outside the scope of your reach.

That these two selves are really one, thoroughly interwoven and mutually interdependent, he may inwardly realize, but this does not dismay him in the efforts to hide one and put forward the other.

Thus, the exterior person walking within your midst demonstrates complete apathy toward homosexualism. His inner self has answered the universal taboo against discussion by establishing a taboo of its own. It is he, this exterior personality, this false front, sometimes the only part of your son that you can ever know, that prohibits any mention of sexual inversion.

It is a cruel shock to this young person, filled as he is with efforts to accommodate to a hostile world, to awaken and find that you have learned his secret. So accustomed is he to lifting his head and facing you with a false personage, so much is he convinced that this is a necessary and involuntary function for which he is free of all responsibility, that the revelation of his secret leaves him with a great burden of shame. Already in a quandary as to whether his activities are sinful, he is now overwhelmed with a new sense of guilt for having brought sorrow to you.

Yet unless the wall of pretense is removed, the youngster cannot possibly establish a relationship based upon mutual acceptance and understanding. How can this be accomplished without your informing the youth that his secrets are known and shared? How can the traumatic disturbances inherent in such a revelation be avoided?

It is ironical that the problem in a family relationship has at this point become completely reversed. Instead of your son maintaining a secret which he cannot reveal to you, you are now maintaining information which you find it difficult to convey to your son.

As a first prerequisite, you must carefully avoid all sly insinuations and none-too-subtle hints, remarks that do nothing but build up suspicion and increase the sense of guilt. "Why don't you go out with Dora, she's a nice girl?" is the kind of question which demonstrates a lack of understanding and an interference into the private life of an individual that is both absurd and useless, since the desired results cannot possibly be forthcoming. When the subject of a marriage arises and a father remarks, "Well, I hope Joe will be the next one," he cannot accomplish the ends in mind but can only increase the unhappinesses of the listener, who must reproach himself for his inability to bring happiness to his parents.

On the other hand, if you are sincerely devoted to your son's welfare, when someone inquires about the possibilities of marriage, you might reply, "There are many roads to a full and complete life. Some choose marriage, others do not. Joe will make a choice of his own. Whatever it is, I am with him."

While you are attempting to establish this mutual rapport—attempting to reach your invert son—you may be able to direct the subject of conversation toward homosexualism from time to time. Whether starting from music or literature or art, whether discussing a lurid newspaper story or a current political scandal, it is not difficult to drift toward sexual inversion as a topic of conversation. Then, almost pointlessly, you might remark that society can improve its attitude, learn that each contributes toward a better life in his own way; or you can offer the opinion that punitive measures have never been known to solve a psychological dilemma.

The young man may perhaps be puzzled by this unexpected display of tolerance, but he can soon learn that it is sincere. "I would not want my son to be a fairy," a man disdainfully said to his brother in the presence of a bewildered youngster, frightened and ashamed that his homosexuality had been divulged. But the father of the youth rose to the occasion, and replied, "I want my boy to live a full life, to respect the rights of others, and always to have understanding for others—even for those who cannot understand him."

During this period of the establishment of mutual confidences, the secrets have not yet been told, but the road for their exposure is being paved. Deliver telephone messages without comment, make your son's friends feel welcome in your home despite a suspicion of their proclivities, invite them to spend the night—even suggest a weekend or a vacation with a special friend.

After several months have elapsed, it will become increasingly apparent to the youth that his secret is shared, but he will no longer be ashamed of his activities. Shame and secrecy, mutually dependent as protection for each other, will gradually be removed, and with their removal, a great burden will be lifted from his shoulders. The son will then be better able to assimilate his two lives and, accepted and loved for what he is, will feel the utmost relief that all is known.

At this point, there has been no open and complete revelation: a very vague air of secrecy continues to veil the subject, and the new status can easily become, and frequently does become, a permanent one. A full discussion may never take place. A gay companion at lunch will often say to me, "My parents know, and I know that they know, but nothing has been said. We've never talked about it and never will, but there is a silent understanding."

To reach a stage of discussion beyond the outward appearance of acceptance is a difficult step to take, but an important one. Actually there is no complete acceptance so long as there is a forbidden area of discussion. "I have my life to live, my mother knows what it is, and she respects it, but we never talk about it," Raymond said to me one day when outlining the relationship at home. "And this is the way it should be. It is perfectly satisfactory, and I wouldn't want to change it in any respect. In fact she wouldn't either, I imagine."

For Raymond, this stage seemed to be perfectly satisfactory, but was it? Could he genuinely feel that his mother accepted him if he could not discuss the burning question of homosexualism with her? Could he find within the shelter and protection of his own home the relief of life without the mask, merely because his mother knew his secret, when he could not share with her his hopes and aspirations, his love and his pain, his humiliations and his struggle to lift his head and find a road in life?

We who are gay can aid in establishing this home relationship, but only if the ground is fertile. The great burden of demonstrating that we are accepted for our true selves lies on our parents' shoulders.

Too many rebuffs have come from teachers, relatives, and those who called themselves friends. We are rightfully suspicious; we see an enemy until, beneath the surface, he has proved himself a friend.

By patient and continuous display of sympathetic interest in all phases of your son's life and all facets of his character, you can prove yourself a friend. And in the many days and years of life when we who are gay seem to be walking alone, when despite the warmest of friendships and the most exciting of romances, we seem to be, like a spaceship in time, abandoned in the universe, the unshakable love of our mothers and fathers will give us strength and courage.

It was my effort, in the course of this book, to shed some light on the homosexual problem. It was my hope that the subjective approach to the individual and the group might provide further knowledge of the homosexual's psychological make-up and of his relations with his fellowmen and with organized society. Writing as a homosexual, I have addressed myself not only to the general reader, but to the sociologist, teacher, psychologist, jurist, and parent with the aim of enabling them possibly to see and to appreciate the viewpoint of those of us who stand so close to them, yet separated by infinite distance.

But, by and large, directly and indirectly, this book was addressed to all the gay people in America. Even when I addressed your parents, I was doing so with you in mind, hoping to alleviate the ill feelings and misunderstandings engendered between them and yourself. In my opening pages I explained that I share with you one of the great problems and secrets of your life, and that this unites us by an invisible bond that makes of us a group, a minority. I did not indulge in self-righteous moralizing, did not pretend that I had "sublimated" my feelings, or that I saw anything "fine" or "noble" or "pure" about such sublimation. I have lived like you and loved like you, have had my moments of hope and of despair, and have played at love with the corner pick-up, and found greater meaning to love in a more enduring passion. At times I felt that I had been tricked by fate, and then I would pray for a chance to taste of the joys of life again in a reincarnated being devoid of this omnipresent love-longing for men.

The story of my life is unlike yours, but only as each of us is an

256

individual unto himself. You may have found adjustment and acceptance of yourself more difficult, or less so; you may not share my opinion of the psychological origin of our anomaly or of the true nature of the condemnatory attitudes of the hostile society. Our points of difference are, however, rather minute. We are placed, by circumstances beyond our control, into a single unity, are judged as one, and we have problems and aspirations in common. My story is yours, just as your story is mine, no matter how divergent our paths of life, no matter how sharp our disagreement on the specific aspects of life.

But now I wish to close by addressing myself only to you. You are, let us say, a youth in his late teens or early twenties, and you are bewildered by the realization that you are a homosexual. It did not come about in a day or in a moment; you had been aware of inclinations and even practices for many years. But back in your mind you had had an idea that these were "boyhood" trends that would be outgrown or take a secondary place. Then there simultaneously developed two thoughts, first creeping in only as suggestions or perhaps vague possibilities, but gradually impressing themselves on your mental outlook: one, that you were what you learned was called gay, fully and completely so, and utterly beyond your control to change; and, secondly, that the attitudes you would encounter in a society that discovered your inclinations would in many respects be more severe than if you were the most vicious criminal. You would meet the sneer, the laugh, the epithet, the contempt, the threat. And, you could not help but wonder, perhaps justifiably so!

Where shall you turn? First, I urge you, turn inward and accept yourself. For better or for worse, for good or for evil, for right or for wrong, be it an ailment, a neurosis, or a natural manifestation—accept yourself. This is easy to say, but how difficult to accomplish! Once and for all, relinquish the thought that, in this world or in another, you will ever be different. You are what you are, and what I am—a homosexual. This is inescapable. You will not outgrow it, will not evolve in another direction, will not change on the couch of an analyst. Next year, next decade, you will be gay, just as you are today, and as you must be until the last breath leaves your body.

Accept yourself, and then you can decide on the road of adjustment. Your reverie about the straight guy who is your brother or cousin or who works at the next bench is only self-pity. You may camouflage a truth you are not yet ready to face, but the truth is the only road to freedom for you.

Once you have accepted your homosexuality as an irrevocable part of your personality, your road to happiness will not be so difficult, although it is not an easy road to travel. Look around and see the millions like us. They are in the bars, at parties, on street corners, in shops and offices, in the chairs of professors, on judges' benches, fighting on the battlefields, or languishing in jail. They are hiding behind the respectability of marriage or are living openly as lovers. But they are literally millions, in all lands and at all times. I am not suggesting that in these numbers there is inherent strength, for strength requires more than mere numbers—courage, self-interest, weapons in the struggle for change. But you can take heart from the fact that you do not march down the path of life alone, that you can meet friends and comrades in all walks of life. You are not an abandoned stranger lost in the waves of the sea, nor a lone star that has been misdirected in the skies.

Self-acceptance and the realization that the number of those like yourself is legion—these will lead to a third phase of your problem, an understanding of the destructive nature and uselessness of the guilt feeling which you may harbor for being gay and for indulging in gay love. Always beware lest you have accepted the values imposed on you by those who are hostile to your way of life. If you carry within you, even to the slightest extent, the feeling that you are doing something wrong, then you will succeed only in preventing yourself from partaking of the pleasures of your actions. Guilt feelings will never change you; they will not stay your hand in action, but will only bring remorse when you should be feeling joy, and will engender hatred toward your beloved when you should feel tenderness.

To divest yourself of the feeling of guilt, you must first of all re-evaluate your entire way of life. This involves a realization that your impulses have never been anti-social. They are the manifestations of your particular personality, which is not peculiar unto you any more than it is singular in the world.

Once you are able to accept this view of yourself, you will be on the road to accepting it for others whom you will meet, and particularly for your love partners. After a lovemaking episode, you will no longer say, nor feel like saying, that you hate yourself for what you have done. And you will not feel any such hatred for your companion. On the contrary, after the physical expression that has united your bodies and given such delights, you will feel gratitude for your lover's part, pride and joy in your own, tenderness for the comrade, and desire to repeat and to continue.

You can now recognize the meaningless hypocrisy of the talk about "pure love" and love "without gross indecencies." These are the concepts imposed on you by the hostile world, which does not adhere to these false ideals although it would inflict them on us. They who pray before the altar of virginity and make Hymen their pagan god have attempted to separate love from sex by creating a paradox termed "pure love." By this is meant an affection devoid of physical desire, which evidently is the "impure" form of love. But there is nothing in the realm of nature which demonstrates that physical culmination of love is unclean or impure. A love that you may feel for a companion is pure if it is selfless, devoted, reciprocated, and brings in its train the fulfillment of its promise. This does not at all exclude the physical aspects of such a relationship; in fact, it prescribes rather than proscribes them.

You will be faced with the question, sooner or later in life, of whether you can possibly build a permanent "family unit" with another person of your own sex. You will, on the one hand, be discouraged by the instability of such relationships and by the drive toward promiscuity which seems to pervade our group, including yourself. On the other hand, you will feel dismayed at the prospect of traveling through the years ahead of you alone. "Marriage," either to one like yourself, unrecognized by all but a few, or to one of the opposite sex, seems increasingly urgent. The impulse to continue sowing your wild oats strongly asserts itself, but not without warning that it is a hopeless dead-end in life.

Can you become one of those who succeed in building with another a life of voluntary association, mutual companionship, and sexual fulfillment? This requires, first, acceptance of the propriety and high character not only of yourself and your companion, by both of you, but specifically of your homosexuality and his. If there lingers in the back of your mind some doubt as to whether this activity might not be a depravity on your part or his, or both, the relationship will carry within itself the seeds of its own destruction.

Furthermore, you must choose your companion with the care that you would choose a wife in legal marriage, and you have an advantage in that there can be a try-out period in which nothing is lost. If you find a person who is intellectually stimulating, who is kind and who inspires kindness, who possesses sincerity of purpose, and who is physically attractive and fulfills your physical needs, then surely the basis of a permanent relationship will have been constructed. If you have interests in common, find joy in the same friends, and both respect each other's separate interests and activities, you have a bond as firm as that of a great many legal marriages.

Your own "marriage," however, will suffer from the ease with which it may be ruptured, the lack of economic pressure to hold it together, and the tendencies toward the temptation of infidelity that may descend upon you or him. If you feel, from time to time, a curiosity over joys untasted, there is no need for self-flagellation. This is a natural impulse that comes over all human beings, no matter what their sexual proclivities. You may find that such indiscretions are something "to get out of the system" and that they have nothing to do with the deeper relationship of love that you have established. They are no threat to the continuation of that love, whether they last for a few fleeting moments or for several days of infatuation. And, out of kindness, you will wish not to utilize such affairs to arouse the jealousy of a partner to whom, in the depth of your heart, you know that you will return.

In any human relationship involving more than one person, there must be give and take. Something in the way of individual liberty is relinquished in favor of the advantages of group living. It is for you to decide whether the gains to be made in interweaving your life with that of another person are worth the effort and the sacrifices. It seems to me that they are, but you alone can judge for yourself.

Having made such a decision, you may find that it conflicts with the indiscriminating and imperious nature of your sexual impulse. All of us, those in our group and in the hostile world, are animal-like at heart, easily aroused, desiring many, but living in a civilization whose rules require discipline and self-control. Those of us who have rejected a certain portion of these rules cannot live by the laws of the jungle. We cannot hope to gratify every desire, to welcome every temptation, and at the same time reap the benefits of a social life founded on quite opposite principles.

Controlling your impulses so that you can withstand temptations that will lead you into difficulty, so that you can channel your love-life in the directions most satisfying to you, will, in the final analysis, bring greater sensual pleasure to your sexual activities. In place of the excitement of novelty, you will have the understanding of the experienced. In place of curiosity over the unknown, you will have the rich assurance of acceptance from the lover who awaits you.

During your life many people are likely to advise you to get married. Some will do so, ignorant of your homosexuality; others, ignorant of the ways of homosexuality. Perhaps your parents, knowing not what problems you face, may urge marriage upon you. They can be ignored, for their lack of knowledge is hardly their fault. But others who learn of your being gay will offer the gratuitous advice of the amateur: "All you need is a woman!" You know, as well as I, that a woman will never solve the problem of your desire for men, and all of the advice and argument can do no more good than the old-fashioned whipping-post. On the other hand, you yourself, for a variety of reasons that have been here reviewed, may decide to embark upon a course of marriage. If it is possible to do so with a mate who understands your nature and who will not consider it a threat to her position, the possibilities of a successful marriage are not at all remote.

No one can properly advise you whether or not to get married The thought may be deeply repugnant to you, and you may be unable to carry out the wedding vows and consummate the marriage If, however, you do take a wife, do so with the knowledge that through infinite patience, understanding, and compromises such a union can be a great success.

Greater than the dilemma of marriage will be that of self-imposed secrecy. If you belong to that large group of homosexuals whose inclinations are not at all apparent and you therefore find it possible to pretend that you are straight, you will see the advantages of so doing. The roads of social and economic progress will be open for you as they could not possibly be if you were known to be gay. The contempt of humanity will be spared you, and in its place you will find the embracing arms of a welcoming world. But it is not you, as you know yourself to be, who are welcome.

Whether or not you should enter that world, wear the mask, pretend to be what you are not, even partake of a viewpoint that is hostile to yourself, you alone must decide. But there is nothing morally or ethically wrong in wearing the mask. If anyone must feel guilt for the pretense, it is those who have literally forced it upon you. The mask is not an admission that your inner nature is sinful; it is merely a recognition that it is universally considered sinful—two entirely different concepts.

If you must wear this mask, you will have to live a life of deep secrecy, or perhaps you will be forced to pursue simultaneously two different modes of life in two hostile and irreconcilable worlds. In the straight group, you will learn to recognize your own and to find among the others those few enlightened souls who are free from prejudice. Their friendships will prove stimulating and encouraging to you as they have been to me, but in general I have had to learn, by severe lessons in experience, that few straight people can be entrusted with a knowledge which they are incapable of understanding. Friendships that seemed to be deeply woven in the fabrics of our lives, with individuals indebted to me and even to a great extent dependent upon me, were on at least two occasions rudely disrupted when my fair-weather friends learned that I was gay. They are friendships discarded with relief, but not without hurt. One way of sparing yourself this hurt is by concealing the secret of your nature within the confines of yourself and your gay world. But in doing so, you miss one of the most fruitful relationships that a gay person can have, and that is the deep friendship and mutual understanding between one of us and one of "them"—between the straight and the gay, the bridge from the in-group to the out-group.

It is possible, although rather rare, that some unscrupulous person, probably himself straight or perhaps a "two-way" man, may attempt to play the blackmail game with you. Do not fall into any traps, for these persons are most easily frightened. You can go to a lawyer or directly to the police and explain, in self-righteous words and with great indignation, that you are a virtuous and law-abiding citizen threatened in this manner by a youth whom you befriended with a drink in a bar—and no more! You need not fear your lawyer or the courts, for only the would-be blackmailer is threatened by them. These people can be dealt with summarily without resorting to extra-legal violence and without exposing yourself to the suspicions of the community.

It would be foolhardy, although quite understandable, if you were to feel hatred toward society at large or toward those individuals most vicious in their attitudes toward you. "Forgive them," it is written, "for they know not what they do." Let us take heart from the words of a great and compassionate teacher; we, too, can turn the other cheek.

Let us, in all humility, remember that we could so easily be among the vilifiers were it not for the accident that placed us with the outcasts. What understanding would we have offered to the gay world if we had ourselves been straight? And can we look back with a clean slate on our record of our relationships with all other minorities? Have we at every turn of the road and under the most adverse conditions offered other groups the understanding that was denied to us?

To fight back in self-defense is necessary, but retaliation born only of resentment is futility. If we are convinced of the propriety of our actions, then we can offer only pity to those who have been the perpetrators of centuries of calumny and misrepresentation. We should know that their need for hatred arises out of a deep sense of insecurity; that their disgust comes from a fear that there is the germ of the gay impulse in them. Their condemnation is a disease, and we cannot help but be sorry for those who are ill, although their ailment does great harm to many. It is bitter irony that many of these people must some day discover that their children are gay, and that they must display hatred toward those they love most deeply. To the human being reduced to this tragic condition, we must display a compassion born of deep sympathy.

If there is one lesson, useful to yourself and to society, that you can learn from your experience, it is that all human beings are brothers and merit treatment as such. Just as you have longed to be made to feel welcome in the great brotherhood that is mankind, so you must extend this hand of love toward others in less fortunate position than you, toward those struggling with other handicaps, vilified and calumniated by society, whether they be men of other colors or worshippers at other temples.

You will be faced with the question of whether to seek professional advice. Many who have no understanding of people such as ourselves will tell you to "see a doctor and get straightened out." If you feel that you have a deep problem in the acceptance of yourself as an invert, if you cannot enjoy the sexual delights toward which you are driven, if you are remorseful and depressed following sexual pleasure, reproachful toward yourself and your partner, then professional help is certainly needed. Your failure to accommodate to your condition can be corrected. But beware of ignorant people, of quacks, of incompetents, including some who have medical degrees. And beware, also, of the doctor who will betray your secrets to a parent or to an older brother or sister.

Fortunately most physicians will respect your confidences and will not overstep the bounds of their training. They know their limitations. They are not psychiatrists, and many realize that they are not as well equipped to "treat" you as is a clinical psychologist without a medical degree.

In the hands of a good psychiatrist many of your difficulties can be overcome. If your problems are of such a grave nature that you cannot cope with them and if you have the wherewithal to obtain aid, then certainly you should take your story to the best available analyst or competently trained physician or psychologist.

With him, I strongly urge honesty. Only complete and unashamed frankness will lead to an understanding of your dilemma and a solution satisfactory to you. I personally know a homosexual who was visiting a psychiatrist once a week for over a year and who had never told him that he was an invert! Such a course of action is indeed futile.

An analyst is a helpful person to you if the burden of secrecy is heavy in your heart. Perhaps you feel a deep need to pour out of yourself all that you think and feel. Perhaps the mask is stifling all life, and you want to be yourself. I am deeply sympathetic, for I know that this is how I feel when I pretend, day after day, to be what I am not.

There is another place to remove the mask, and that is in the company of those like ourselves. Do not fear the group life of the gay world. It has its superficialities, its jealousies, its promiscuity, even some violence. It has the sad character of a marginal life of outcasts, with the tragedies of many who are ill-adjusted. But it has many compensations. In such company you can find gaiety, humor, intellectual challenge, artistic temperaments, perseverance against odds, honor, comradeship, and love. Friendships can be deep, and loyalty can be unswerving.

In the gay life you can be yourself and form friendships with those who know what you are and who accept you and love you, not despite this or in ignorance of it. The group life is not a thing of shame, a den of iniquity. It is a circle of protection, a necessary part of a minority society. By shunning it, you shut yourself off from one of the most rewarding parts of being gay, but not from the fact of being gay.

Filled as you are with ambition, anxious to utilize the abilities with which you are endowed, you will find yourself in a most contradictory position. On the one hand, you have rebelled against the injustices to which you are subjected and you wish to raise your voice to make this a better world for those like us. But, on the other hand, your voice of protest will make it all the more difficult for you ever to be able to effect these accomplishments which might reflect favorably on you and therefore on this minority group. Few of us are in a position to influence public opinion on homosexuality, and those who rise to such high stature would, in fact, lose much of their influence if they were to attempt to use it for this cause.

How, then, can you aid your group if you join the millions of silent ones? Of what help can you ever be as you sit, not complacently but effectively silenced, behind the mask? There is no single formula by which this question can be answered. However, by making known to a select few who admire your personality or achievements that these were inspired by homosexuality, you may influence some small measure of public opinion.

Furthermore, your line of work may make it possible for you to contribute, in what is seemingly a small way, toward changing society's attitude or toward alleviating the suffering of even a single homosexual. As physician, lawyer, writer, professor, psychiatrist, child-guidance counsellor, journalist, or in many another line of endeavor, you may be able to make some contribution. Alone, you cannot change the world, but the combined efforts of many will surely effect a beneficial change.

Sometimes the future may look bleak to you. This is not rare. It looks threatening to all mortal human beings at times. Let us not blame our sexual inclinations for difficulties inherent in life itself. All those who love life and cling to it live through their years with an awareness of its inevitably finite character. We are frightened by the unknown nothingness of death and dismayed by the futility of the efforts that will come to nought in the grave. The burdens of all of us are heavy, and the gay not significantly more so than the straight.

We are here, for a short stay on earth, to enjoy the process of living. Life can be as full, as rich, as joyous, for us as for anyone. The challenge we face must result only in equipping us for the struggles to meet all of the problems of human existence.

The future belongs to those who will have it. It is yours and mine, and it belongs to all worthy men of good will. I am confident that you, like so many others who are gay, will utilize the years ahead to good advantage, undismayed and undefeated, inspired by the knowledge that your temperament can make you a better person and this a better world.

APPENDICES

APPENDIX A

United States Government Documents Relating to Homosexuality

(The following letter, reproduced in full, was sent to the author of this book, in reply to a communication requesting information on the offical attitude of the Civil Service Commission with regard to employment of homosexuals by the government. The second paragraph of this letter implies quasi-official approval of the findings revealed in Document No. 2.)

UNITED STATES CIVIL SERVICE COMMISSION
WASHINGTON 25, D. C.

May 3, 1951

In reply to your recent letter, you are advised that the regulations of the Civil Service Commission for many years have provided that criminal, infamous, dishonest, immoral or notoriously disgraceful conduct, which includes homosexuality or other types of sex perversion, are sufficient grounds for denying appointment to a Government position or for the removal of a person from the Federal service.

The Civil Service Commission's handbooks and Manual containing internal instructions are not available for general distribution. However, in connection with the purpose of your inquiry you may desire to refer to U. S. Senate document No. 241 published December 15, 1950. This is an interim report submitted to the *Committee on Expenditures in the Executive Departments* by its Subcommittee on Investigations pursuant to Senate Resolution 280 (81st Congress). This document is entitled *Employment of Homosexuals and Other Sex Perverts in Government* and is available at the U. S. Government Printing Office.

Very truly yours,

/s/ James E. Hatcher
James E. Hatcher, Chief
Investigations Division

(The following document is reproduced only in part. The missing sections, shown by asterisks, deal only with the arrest of homosexuals in the District of Columbia, method of dismissal from government service, etc. All parts of the document dealing with reasons for homosexuals being barred from government employment are reprinted here in full.)

Document No. 2. Employment of Homosexuals and Other Sex Perverts in Government.
Interim Report submitted to the Committee on Expenditures in the Executive Departments by its Subcommittee on Investigations pursuant to S. Res. 280 (81st Congress).
A Resolution Authorizing the Committee on Expenditures in the Executive Departments to Carry Out Certain Duties.

Introduction

The Senate Investigations Subcommittee of the Committee on Expenditures in the Executive Departments was directed, under authority of Senate Resolution 280 (81st Cong., 2d sess., adopted June 7, 1950), (see Appendix I), to make an investigation into the employment by the Government of homosexuals and other sex perverts. This resolution was the result of preliminary inquiries made earlier this year by a subcommittee of the Senate District of Columbia Subcommittee on Appropriations composed of Senator Hill of Alabama and Senator Wherry of Nebraska. The reports and testimony of that subcommittee were of considerable value to the Investigations Subcommittee in the conduct of this inquiry.

An investigation on a Government-wide scale of homosexuality and other sex perversion is unprecedented. Furthermore, reliable, factual information on the subject of homosexuality and sex perversion is somewhat limited. In the past, studies in this field, for the most part, were confined to scientific studies by medical experts and sociologists. The criminal courts and the police have had considerable experience in the handling of sex perverts as law violators, but the subject as a personnel problem until very recently has received little attention from Government administrators and personnel officers.

The primary objective of the subcommittee in this inquiry was to determine the extent of the employment of homosexuals and other sex perverts in Government; to consider reasons why their employment by the Government is undesirable; and to examine into the efficacy of the methods used in dealing with the problem. Because of the complex nature of the subject under investigation it was apparent that this investigation could not be confined to a mere personnel inquiry. Therefore, the subcommittee considered not only the security risk and other aspects of the employment of homosexuals, including the rules and procedures followed by Government agencies in handling these cases, but inquiries were also made into the basic medical, psychiatric, sociological and legal phases of the problem. A number of eminent physicians and psychiatrists, who are recognized authorities on this subject, were consulted and some of these authorities

testified before the subcommittee in executive session. In addition, numerous medical and sociological studies were reviewed. Information was also
sought and obtained from law-enforcement officers, prosecutors, and other
persons dealing with the legal and sociological aspects of the problem in
10 of the larger cities in the country.

The subcommittee, being well aware of the strong moral and social
taboos attached to homosexuality and other forms of sex perversion, made
every effort to protect individuals from unnecessary public ridicule and
to prevent this inquiry from becoming a public spectacle. In carrying out
this policy it was determined at the outset that all testimony would be
taken by the subcommittee in executive session. Accordingly, all witnesses appearing before the subcommittee testified in executive hearings.
In the conduct of this investigation the subcommittee tried to avoid the
circus atmosphere which could attend an inquiry of this type and sought
to make a thorough factual study of the problem at hand in an unbiased,
objective manner.

It was determined that even among the experts there existed considerable
difference of opinion concerning the many facets of homosexuality and
other forms of sex perversion. Even the terms "sex pervert" and "homosexual" are given different connotations by the medical and psychiatric
experts. For the purpose of this report the subcommittee has defined sex
perverts as "those who engage in unnatural sexual acts" and homosexuals
are perverts who may be broadly defined as "persons of either sex who
as adults engage in sexual activities with persons of the same sex." In this
inquiry the subcommittee is not concerned with so-called latent sex perverts, namely, those persons who knowingly or unknowingly have tendencies or inclinations toward homosexuality or other types of sex perversion, but who, by the exercise of self-restraint or for other reasons do
not indulge in overt acts of perversion. This investigation is concerned
only with those who engage in overt acts of homosexuality or other sex
perversion.

The subcommittee found that most authorities agree on certain basic
facts concerning sex perversion and it is felt that these facts should be
considered in any discussion of the problem. Most authorities believe that
sex deviation results from psychological rather than physical causes, and
in many cases there are no outward characteristics or physical traits that
are positive as identifying marks of sex perversion. Contrary to a common
belief, all homosexual males do not have feminine mannerisms, nor do all
female homosexuals display masculine characteristics in their dress or
actions. The fact is that many male homosexuals are very masculine in
their physical appearance and general demeanor, and many female homosexuals have every appearance of femininity in their outward behavior.

Generally speaking, the overt homosexual of both sexes can be divided
into two general types; the active, aggressive or male type, and the sub-
missive, passive or female type. The passive type of male homosexual,

who often is effeminate in his mannerisms and appearance, is attracted to the masculine type of man and is friendly and congenial with women. On the other hand the active male homosexual often has a dislike for women. He exhibits no traces of femininity in his speech or mannerisms which would disclose his homosexuality. This active type is almost exclusively attracted to the passive type of homosexual or to young men or boys who are not necessarily homosexual but who are effeminate in general appearance or behavior. The active and passive type of female homosexual follow the same general patterns as their male counterparts. It is also a known fact that some perverts are bisexual. This type engages in normal heterosexual relationships as well as homosexual activities. These bisexual individuals are often married and have children, and except for their perverted activities they appear to lead normal lives.

Psychiatric physicians generally agree that indulgence in sexually perverted practices indicates a personality which has failed to reach sexual maturity. The authorities agree that most sex deviates respond to psychiatric treatment and can be cured if they have a genuine desire to be cured. However, many overt homosexuals have no real desire to abandon their way of life and in such cases cures are difficult, if not impossible. The subcommittee sincerely believes that persons afflicted with sexual desires which result in their engaging in overt acts of perversion should be considered as proper cases for medical and psychiatric treatment. However, sex perverts, like all other persons who by their overt acts violate moral codes and laws and the accepted standards of conduct, must be treated as transgressors and dealt with accordingly.

Sex Perverts as Government Employees

Those charged with the responsibility of operating the agencies of Government must insist that Government employees meet acceptable standards of personal conduct. In the opinion of this subcommittee homosexuals and other sex perverts are not proper persons to be employed in Government for two reasons; first, they are generally unsuitable, and second, they constitute security risks.

General Unsuitability of Sex Perverts

Overt acts of sex perversion, including acts of homosexuality, constitute a crime under our Federal, State, and municipal statutes and persons who commit such acts are law violators. Aside from the criminality and immorality involved in sex perversion such behavior is so contrary to the normal accepted standards of social behavior that persons who engage in such activity are looked upon as outcasts by society generally. The social stigma attached to sex perversion is so great that many perverts go to great lengths to conceal their perverted tendencies. This situation is evidenced by the fact that perverts are frequently victimized by blackmailers who threaten to expose their sexual deviations.

Law enforcement officers have informed the subcommittee that there are gangs of blackmailers who make a regular practice of preying upon the homosexual. The modus operandi in these homosexual blackmail cases usually follow the same general pattern. The victim, who is a homosexual, has managed to conceal his perverted activities and usually enjoys a good reputation in his community. The blackmailers, by one means or another, discover that the victim is addicted to homosexuality and under the threat of disclosure they extort money from him. These blackmailers often impersonate police officers in carrying out their blackmail schemes. Many cases have come to the attention of the police where highly respected individuals have paid out substantial sums of money to blackmailers over a long period of time rather than risk the disclosure of their homosexual activities. The police believe that this type of blackmail racket is much more extensive than is generally known, because they have found that most of the victims are very hesitant to bring the matter to the attention of the authorities.

In further considering the general suitability of perverts as Government employees, it is generally believed that those who engage in overt acts of perversion lack the emotional stability of normal persons. In addition there is an abundance of evidence to sustain the conclusion that indulgence in acts of sex perversion weakens the moral fiber of an individual to a degree that he is not suitable for a position of responsibility.

Most of the authorities agree and our investigation has shown that the presence of a sex pervert in a Government agency tends to have a corrosive influence upon his fellow employees. These perverts will frequently attempt to entice normal individuals to engage in perverted practices. This is particularly true in the case of young and impressionable people who might come under the influence of a pervert. Government officials have the responsibility of keeping this type of corrosive influence out of the agencies under their control. It is particularly important that the thousands of young men and women who are brought into Federal jobs not be subjected to that type of influence while in the service of the Government. One homosexual can pollute a Government office.

Another point to be considered in determining whether a sex pervert is suitable for Government employment is his tendency to gather other perverts about him. Eminent psychiatrists have informed the subcommittee that the homosexual is likely to seek his own kind because the pressures of society are such that he feels uncomfortable unless he is with his own kind. Due to this situation the homosexual tends to surround himself with other homosexuals, not only in his social, but in his business life. Under these circumstances if a homosexual attains a position in Government where he can influence the hiring of personnel, it is almost inevitable that he will attempt to place other homosexuals in Government jobs.

Sex Perverts as Security Risks

The conclusion of the subcommittee that a homosexual or other sex pervert is a security risk is not based upon mere conjecture. That conclusion is predicated upon a careful review of the opinions of those best qualified to consider matters of security in Government, namely, the intelligence agencies of the Government. Testimony on this phase of the inquiry was taken from representatives of the Federal Bureau of Investigation, the Central Intelligence Agency, and the intelligence services of the Army, Navy and Air Force. All of these agencies are in complete agreement that sex perverts in Government constitute security risks.

The lack of emotional stability which is found in most sex perverts and the weakness of their moral fiber, makes them susceptible to the blandishments of the foreign espionage agent. It is the experience of intelligence experts that perverts are vulnerable to interrogation by a skilled questioner and they seldom refuse to talk about themselves. Furthermore, most perverts tend to congregate at the same restaurants, night clubs, and bars, which places can be identified with comparative ease in any community, making it possible for a recruiting agent to develop clandestine relationships which can be used for espionage purposes.

As has been previously discussed in this report, the pervert is easy prey to the blackmailer. It follows that if blackmailers can extort money from a homosexual under the threat of disclosure, espionage agents can use the same type of pressure to extort confidential information or other material they might be seeking. A classic case of this type involved one Captain Raedl who became chief of the Austrian counterintelligence service in 1912. He succeeded in building up an excellent intelligence net in Russia and had done considerable damage to the espionage net which the Russians had set up in Austria. However, Russian agents soon discovered that Raedl was a homosexual and shortly thereafter they managed to catch him in an act of perversion as the result of a trap they had set for that purpose. Under the threat of exposure Raedl agreed to furnish and he did furnish the Russians with Austrian military secrets. He also doctored or destroyed the intelligence reports which his own Austrian agents were sending from Russia with the result that the Austrian and German General Staffs, at the outbreak of World War I in 1914, were completely misinformed as to the Russian's mobilization intentions. On the other hand, the Russians had obtained from Raedl the war plans of the Austrians and that part of the German plans which had been made available to the Austrian Government. Shortly after the outbreak of the war Captain Raedl's traitorous acts were discovered by his own Government and he committed suicide.

Other cases have been brought to the attention of the subcommittee where Nazi and Communist agents have attempted to obtain information from employees of our Government by threatening to expose their abnormal sex activities. It is an accepted fact among intelligence agencies that espionage organizations the world over consider sex perverts who are in possession of or have access to confidential material to be prime targets where pressure can be exerted. In virtually every case despite protestations by the perverts that they would never succumb to blackmail, invariably they express considerable concern over the fact that their condition might become known to their friends, associates, or the public at large. The present danger of this security problem is well illustrated by the following excerpt from the testimony of D. Milton Ladd, assistant to the Director of the Federal Bureau of Investigation, who appeared before this subcommittee in executive session:

The Communists, without principles or scruples, have a program of seeking out weaknesses of leaders in Government and industry. In fact, the FBI has in its possession information of unquestionable reliability that orders have been issued by high Russian intelligence officials to their agents to secure details of the private lives of Government officials, their weaknesses, their associates, and in fact every bit of information regarding them, hoping to find a chink in their armor and a weakness upon which they might capitalize at the appropriate time.

The subcommittee in pointing out the unsuitability of perverts for Government employment is not unaware of the fact that there are other patterns of human behavior which also should be considered in passing upon the general suitability or security-risk status of Government employees. There is little doubt that habitual drunkards, persons who have engaged in criminal activities, and those who indulge in other types of infamous or scandalous personal conduct are also unsuitable for Government employment and constitute security risks. However, the subcommittee, in the present investigation, has properly confined itself to the problem of sex perverts.

* * * * *

Conclusion

There is no place in the United States Government for persons who violate the laws or the accepted standards of morality, or who otherwise bring disrepute to the Federal service by infamous or scandalous personal conduct. Such persons are not suitable for Government positions and in the case of doubt the American people are entitled to have errors of judgment on the part of their officials, if there must be errors, resolved on the side of caution. It is the opinion of this subcommittee that those who engage in acts of homosexuality and other perverted sex activities are unsuitable for employment in the Federal Government. This conclusion is based upon the fact that persons who indulge in such degraded activity are committing not only illegal and immoral acts, but they also constitute security risks in positions of public trust.

The subcommitee found that in the past many Government officials failed to take a realistic view of the problem of sex perversion in Government with the result that a number of sex perverts were not discovered or removed from Government jobs, and in still other instances they were quietly eased out of one department and promptly found employment in another agency. This situation undoubtedly stemmed from the fact that there was a general disinclination on the part of many Government officials to face squarely the problem of sex perversion among Federal employees and as a result they did not take the proper steps to solve the problem. The rules of the Civil Service Commission and the regulations of the agencies themselves prohibit the employment of sex perverts and these rules have been in effect for many years. Had the existing rules and regulations been enforced many of the perverts who were forced out of Government in recent months would have been long since removed from the Federal service.

It is quite apparent that as a direct result of this investigation officials throughout the Government have become much more alert to the problem of the employment of sex perverts in Government and in recent months they have removed a substantial number of these undesirables from public positions. This is evidenced by the fact that action has been taken in 382 sex perversion cases involving civilian employees of Government in the past 7 months, whereas action was taken in only 192 similar cases in the previous 3-year period from January 1, 1947, to April 1, 1950. However, it appears to the subcommittee that some Government officials are not yet fully aware of the inherent dangers involved in the employment of sex perverts. It is the considered opinion of the subcommittee that Government officials have the responsibility of exercising a high degree of diligence in the handling of the problem of sex perversion, and it is urged that they follow the recommendations of this subcommittee in that regard.

While this subcommittee is convinced that it is in the public interest to get sex perverts out of Government and keep them out, this program should be carried out in a manner consistent with the traditional American concepts of justice and fair play. In order to accomplish this end every reasonable complaint of perverted sex activities on the part of Government employees should be thoroughly investigated and dismissals should be ordered only after a complete review of the facts and in accordance with the present civil-service procedures. These procedures provide that the employee be informed of the charges against him and be given a reasonable time to answer. Furthermore, in view of the very serious consequence of dismissal from the Government on charges of sex perversion, it is believed that consideration should be given to establishing a board of review or similar appeal machinery whereby all persons who are dismissed from the Government on these charges may, if they so desire, have their cases reviewed by higher authority outside of the employing agency. No such appeal machinery exists at the present time.

Although 457 persons who were arrested by police authorities in sex perversion cases in the District of Columbia during the past 4 years indicated that they were employees of the Government at the time of their arrest, information concerning the great majority of these arrests did not come to the attention of the Civil Service Commission or the other agencies of Government until April of this year. This deplorable situation resulted from the lack of proper liaison between the law-enforcement agencies and the departments of Government. The subcommittee is gratified to report that this situation has now been corrected. Since April information concerning Government employees arrested on charges of sex perversion in the District of Columbia and elsewhere has been promptly reported from the FBI to the Civil Service Commission and the employing agencies of Government in order that appropriate action may be taken in each case.

The subcommittee also found that the existing criminal laws in the District of Columbia with regard to acts of sex perversion are inadequate and the subcommittee has drawn up proposed amendments to the District Criminal Code which should materially strengthen these laws. It was also discovered that most of the homosexuals apprehended by the police in the District of Columbia were booked on charges of disorderly conduct. In most cases they were never brought to trial but were allowed to make forfeitures of small cash collateral at police stations. This slipshod method of disposing of these cases with little or no review by the prosecutive or judicial authorities was corrected after the subcommittee brought this situation to the attention of the judges of the municipal court in August 1950.

Since the initiation of this investigation considerable progress has been made in removing homosexuals and similar undesirable employees from positions in the Government. However, it should be borne in mind that the public interest cannot be adequately protected unless responsible officials adopt and maintain a realistic and vigilant attitude toward the problem of sex perverts in the Government. To pussyfoot or to take half measures will allow some known perverts to remain in Government and can result in the dismissal of innocent persons.

In view of the importance of preventing the employment of sex perverts in Government the subcommittee plans to reexamine the situation from time to time to determine if its present recommendations are being followed and to ascertain whether it may be necessary to take other steps to protect the public interest.

(Documents 3 to 8 are extracts from laws and official regulations. No. 3 indicates the conditions laid down by Congress for eligibility to benefits under the G. I. Bill of Rights, and No. 4 and No. 5 show the interpretation of that provision by the Veterans Administration. No. 6 and No. 7 provide for exemption of the decisions of the Veterans Administration from

court review, and No. 8 provides the conditions for eligibility under the National Service Life Insurance Act.)

Document No. 3. Servicemen's Readjustment Act of 1944 and The Act Providing for Vocational Rehabilitation of Disabled Veterans.

SEC. 1503 (38 U. S. C. 697c). A discharge or release from active service under conditions other than dishonorable shall be a prerequisite to entitlement to veterans' benefits provided by this Act or Public Law Numbered 2, Seventy-third Congress, as amended. Act of June 22, 1944.

Document No. 4. Veterans Administration Instruction No. 2, Sections 300 and 1503, Public No. 346, 78th Congress (Servicemen's Readjustment Act of 1944)

Subject: Legal Bars Under Section 300, Public No. 346, 78th Congress, and Character of Discharge Under Public No. 2, 73d Congress, as Amended, and Public No. 346, 78th Congress.

1. The acceptance of an undesirable or blue discharge to escape trial by general court martial will, by the terms of section 1503, Public No. 346, 78th Congress, be a bar to benefits under Public No. 2, 73d Congress, as amended and Public No. 346, 78th Congress, as it will be considered the discharge was under dishonorable conditions.

2. An undesirable or blue discharge issued because of homosexual acts or tendencies generally will be considered as under dishonorable conditions and a bar to entitlement under Public No. 2, 73d Congress, as amended, and Public No. 346, 78th Congress. However, the facts in a particular case may warrant a different conclusion, in which event the case should be submitted to central office for the attention and consideration of the director of the service concerned.

3. The usual appellate procedure will be applicable to this class of claims.

4. Of course, a claimant may apply to the War or Navy Department for a review of his discharge under section 301, Public No. 346, 78th Congress, with a view of having the nature thereof changed so as to make him eligible for benefits from the Veterans Administration.

/s/ Frank T. Hines
FRANK T. HINES,
Administrator of Veterans Affairs.

April 21, 1945.

Document No. 5. Veterans Administration Regulations and Procedures.

1064. Character of Discharge Under Public No. 2, 73d Congress, as
      Amended, and Under Public Law 346, 78th Congress

(A) To be entitled to compensation or pension under Veterans Regula-
tion No. 1 (a), as amended, the period of active service upon which claim
is based must have been terminated by discharge or release under conditions other than dishonorable. In other words benefits under Public No. 2,
73d Congress, and Public Law 346, 78th Congress, are barred where the
person was discharged under dishonorable conditions. The requirement
of the words "dishonorable conditions" will be deemed to have been met
when it is shown that the discharge or separation from active military or
naval service was (1) for mutiny, (2) spying, or (3) for an offense involving moral turpitude or willful and persistent misconduct; Provided, however, That where service was otherwise honest, faithful, and meritorious
a discharge or separation other than dishonorable because of the commission of a minor offense will not be deemed to constitute discharge or separation under dishonorable conditions. (October 31, 1946)

* * * * *

(D) An undesirable or blue discharge issued because of homosexual acts
or tendencies generally will be considered as under dishonorable conditions and a bar to entitlement under Public No. 2, 73d Congress, as
amended, and Public Law 346, 78th Congress, as amended. However, the
facts in a particular case may warrant a different conclusion, in which
event the case should be submitted to the Director, Claims Service, district office, in field death cases, to the Director, Veterans Claims Service,
Central Office, in field living cases, or to the Director of the Service concerned in Central Office cases, for attention and consideration. As to the
effect of alienage see R&P R-1001 (J). (October 19, 1949).

Document No. 6. Section 11, Public Law 866; 76th Congress

Notwithstanding any other provisions of law, except as provided in
section 19 of the World War Veterans' Act, 1924, as amended, and in
section 817 of the National Service Life Insurance Act of 1940, the decisions of the Administrator of Veterans' Affairs on any question of law
or fact concerning a claim for benefits or payments under this or any
other Act administered by the Veterans Administration shall be final and
conclusive and no other official or any court of the United States shall
have power or jurisdiction to review any such decisions.

Document No. 7. Title I, Public Act No. 2, 73d Congress, and Laws
Supplemental Thereto, as Amended, Granting Bene-
fits to Veterans and Their Dependents.

SEC. 5. All decisions rendered by the Administrator of Veterans' Affairs
under the provisions of this title, or the regulations issued pursuant thereto,
shall be final and conclusive on all questions of law and fact, and no other
official or court of the United States shall have jurisdiction to review by
mandamus or otherwise any such decision.

*(Document No. 8 is reproduced here because of its significant omission
by Congress of the homosexual from the list of those who are not entitled
to insurance benefits as veterans.)*

Document No. 8. National Service Life Insurance Act of 1940, as
Amended and Appendix. Revised as of September 1,
1948.

SEC. 612. Any person guilty of mutiny, treason, spying, or desertion, or
who, because of conscientious objections, refuses to perform service in
the land or naval forces of the United States or refuses to wear the uniform of such force, shall forfeit all rights to insurance under this part. No
insurance shall be payable for death inflicted as a lawful punishment for
crime or for military or naval offense, except when inflicted by an enemy
of the United States; but the cash surrender value, if any, of such insurance on the date of such death shall be paid to the designated beneficiary,
if living, or otherwise to the beneficiary or beneficiaries within the permitted class in accordance with the order specified in section 602 (h) (3).

APPENDIX B

Extracts from the Statutes of the Forty-Eight States

The following are extracts from the statutes and penal codes of the forty-eight states of the United States. In each case the statute quoted is the one which defines sodomy, crime against nature, or buggery, and provides punishments upon conviction. The laws here extracted do not cover disorderly conduct, solicitation, prostitution, corruption of minors, and other crimes.

The quotations from the laws are printed in the larger type. Interpretations of these laws are shown in the smaller type. Where the interpretations have been given by a court, this is indicated by the legal citation at the end of the paragraph.

ALABAMA. 14 38. Any person who commits an assault on another, with intent to . . . commit the crime against nature, shall, on conviction, be punished by imprisonment in the penitentiary for not less than two nor more than twenty years.

The statute does not declare what constitutes the felonious assault or felonious attempt. These must be ascertained from the common law. Simpson v. State 59 Ala. 1, 8.

Any touching of another person in rudeness is an assault and battery. Siegel v. Long 169 Ala. 79.

14 106. *Crime against nature.* Any person who commits a crime against nature, either with mankind or with any beast, shall, on conviction, be imprisoned in the penitentiary for not less than two nor more than ten years.

It is not necessary to prove emission, but penetration must be proven. As in rape, it must be proven that the "res was in the re," but to no particular depth. Tarrant v. State 12 Ala. App. 172.

ARIZONA 43–406. *Sodomy.* Any person who shall commit sodomy, or the crime against nature, with mankind or beast, shall be punished by imprisonment in the state prison not more than five (5) years nor less than one (1) year. Said crime may be committed by the penetration of the mouth or rectum of any human being by the organ of any male person; proof of emission shall not be required, and any sexual penetration, however slight, shall be sufficient.

43–407. *Fellatio and cunnilingus.* Any person who shall wilfully commit any lewd or lascivious act upon or with the body of (or) any part or member thereof, of any male or female person, with the intent of arousing, appealing to or gratifying the lust or passion or sexual desires of either of such persons, in any unnatural manner, shall be guilty of a felony and imprisoned not less than one (1) year nor more than five (5) years.

ARKANSAS 41–813. *Sodomy or buggery.* Every person convicted of sodomy, or buggery, shall be imprisoned in the penitentiary for a period not less than five (5) nor more than twenty-one (21) years.

The testimony of the prosecuting witness must be corroborated if that witness were an accomplice, but if witness did not consent, the witness was not an accomplice and testimony need not be corroborated. Hummel v. State of Arkansas, 196 S.W. (2d) 594.

41–814. *Sufficiency of evidence in crime against nature.* Proof of actual penetration into the body shall be sufficient to sustain an indictment for the crime against nature.

The fact of penetration may be proven by circumstantial evidence, provided the inferences deri.ed therefrom leave no reasonable doubt. Hudspeth v. State, 194 Ark. 576, 108 S.W. (2nd) 1085.

CALIFORNIA 286. *Crime against nature.* Every person who is guilty of the infamous crime against nature, committed with mankind or with any animal, is punishable by imprisonment in the state prison not less than one nor more than ten years.

287. *Penetration sufficient to complete the crime.* Any sexual penetration, however slight, is sufficient to complete the crime against nature.

288a. *Sex perversions.* Any person participating in the act of copulating the mouth of one person with the sexual organ of another is punishable by imprisonment in the state prison for not exceeding fifteen years.

Paragraph 290 provides for registration, fingerprinting, photographing, and giving information required by State Bureau of Criminal Identification for anyone convicted under the above and other acts.

COLORADO 48 64. *Crime against nature.* The infamous crime against nature, either with man or beast, shall subject the offender to be punished by imprisonment in the penitentiary for a term not less than one year, and such imprisonment may extend to life.

Only penetration per anum, and not per os, constitutes this crime. Koontz v. People 82 Colo. 589, 263 P. 19.
The above law was amended in 1939 to read: "Crime against nature. The infamous crime against nature . . . or any unnatural carnal copulation committed . . . per anus or per os or in any other way whatsoever shall subject the offender to be imprisoned in the penitentiary for a term of not less than one year and not more than fourteen years."

The solicitation of any unnatural copulation shall subject the offender to confinement in the county jail for not less than thirty days or more than two years.

CONNECTICUT 8544 *Bestiality and sodomy.* Any person who shall have carnal copulation with any beast, or who shall have carnal knowledge of any man, against the order of nature, unless forced or under fifteen years of age, shall be imprisoned in the State Prison not more than thirty years.

DELAWARE 5256 7. *Sodomy; penalty.* Whoever shall commit the crime against nature shall be deemed guilty of felony, and shall be fined not exceeding one thousand dollars, and shall be imprisoned not exceeding three years.

FLORIDA 800.01. *Crime against nature; punishment.* Whoever commits the abominable and detestable crime against nature, either with mankind or beast, shall be punished by imprisonment in the state prison not exceeding twenty years.

The crime includes all acts of bestiality, and is not limited to the common law concept of sodomy. Jackson v. State, 84 Fla. 646.

GEORGIA 26–5901. *Sodomy defined.* Sodomy is the carnal knowledge and connection against the order of nature, by man with man, or in the same unnatural manner with woman.

Evidence that defendant approached prosecutor at night, asked him if certain people were coming that way, placed his hand on prosecutor's shoulder and other hand on prosecutor's private parts, and said, "Let's go down in the alley yonder," and ran when others approached, is not sufficient to sustain charge of assault with intent to commit sodomy. 21 App. 505.

When evidence shows carnal knowledge between two men by mouth of one of them, both are guilty. 17 App. 825.

Per anus is not the only way of committing the crime. 17 App. 825.

26–5902. *Punishment of sodomy.* The punishment of sodomy shall be imprisonment at labor in the penitentiary for and during the natural life of the person convicted.

An attempt to commit sodomy is a misdemeanor, punishable by a fine not to exceed $1,000, and/or imprisonment not to exceed six months, at labor.

The crime of sodomy, in Georgia, cannot be committed, as defined, between two women; hence a person convicted on an indictment charging her with sodomy, both participants in the act being females, will be discharged on habeas corpus, on the ground that she is being illegally restrained of her liberty, in that the indictment on which she was convicted was null and void. 187/467 (200 S. E. 799) Thompson v. Aldredge, Sheriff.

Insertion of the male organ between legs or thighs of another person is not penetration within meaning of the law. Wharton v. State, 54 App. 439, 198 S.E. 823.

The felony of sodomy under 27–2501, must be punished by life imprisonment, except that, on the recommendation of the jury, approved by the presiding judge, the latter may reduce the crime to a misdemeanor and punish it as such.

IDAHO 18–6605. *Crime against nature. Punishment.* Every person who is guilty of the infamous crime against nature, committed with mankind or with animal, is punishable by imprisonment in the state prison not less than five years.

Included within the meaning of the law are all unnatural copulations committed per os or per anum. State v. Altwater, 29 Idaho 107.

The length of imprisonment in excess of five years is left entirely to the discretion of the court. In re Miller, 23 Idaho 403.

18–6606. *Crime against nature—Penetration—*Any sexual penetration, however slight, is sufficient to complete the crime against nature.

18–907. *Assault with intent to commit certain felonies.* Every person who assaults another with intent to commit rape, the infamous crime against nature, mayhem, robbery, or grand larceny, is punishable by imprisonment in the state prison not less than one year nor more than fourteen years.

ILLINOIS 37.548. *Infamous crimes—Disqualification.* Every person convicted of the crime of murder, rape, . . . sodomy, or other crime against nature . . . shall be deemed infamous, and shall forever thereafter be rendered incapable of holding any office of honor, trust or profit, of voting at any election, or serving as a juror, unless he or she is again restored to such rights by the terms of a pardon for the offense or otherwise according to law.

37.105. *Definiton—Punishment.* The infamous crime against nature either with man or beast, shall subject the offender to be punished by imprisonment in the penitentiary for a term of not less than one year and not more than ten years.

Husband and wife may commit crime against nature. Honselman v. People, 168 Ill. 172.

The insertion of the tongue does not constitute the crime against nature. People v. Smith, 258 Ill. 502.

37.106. *Emission.* It shall not be necessary to prove emission to convict any person of the crime against nature.

INDIANA 10–4221. *Sodomy.* Whoever commits the abominable and detestable crime against nature with mankind or beast; or whoever entices, allures, instigates or aids any person under the age of twenty-one (21) years to commit masturbation or self-pollution shall be deemed guilty of sodomy, and, on conviction shall be fined not less than one hundred dollars ($100) nor more than one thousand dollars ($1,000), to which may be added imprisonment in the state prison not less than two (2) years nor more than fourteen (14) years.

The crime of sodomy includes the offense of copulation by the mouth. Glover v. State 179 Ind. 459.

IOWA 705. *Sodomy—1. Definition—*Whoever shall have carnal copulation in any opening of the body except sexual parts, with another human being, or shall have carnal copulation with a beast, shall be deemed guilty of sodomy.

This may be committed by copulation in the mouth. State v. Ferris, 189 Iowa 505.

705.2. Any person who shall commit sodomy, shall be imprisoned in the penitentiary not more than ten years.

KANSAS 21–907. *Crime against nature.* Every person who shall be convicted of the detestable and abominable crime against nature, committed with mankind or with beast, shall be punished by confinement and hard labor not exceeding 10 years.

Proof of actual lecherous penetration per os sufficient. State v. Hurlbert, 118 Kan. 362.

KENTUCKY 436.050. *Sodomy: buggery.* Any person who commits sodomy or buggery, with man or beast, shall be confined in the penitentiary for not less than two nor more than five years.

LOUISIANA 740–89. *Crime against nature.* Crime against nature is the unnatural carnal copulation by a human being with another of the same or opposite sex or with an animal. Emission is not necessary, and, when committed by a human being with another, the use of the genital organ of one of the offenders of whatever sex is sufficient to constitute the crime.

Whoever commits the crime against nature shall be fined not more than two thousand dollars, or imprisoned, with or without hard labor, for not more than five years, or both.

MAINE Ch. 121. *Crimes against chastity, morality, and decency.* 3. *Crime against nature; penalty.* Whoever commits the crime against nature, with mankind or with a beast, shall be punished by imprisonment for not less than 1 year, nor more than 10 years.

MARYLAND 577. *Sodomy.* Every person convicted of the crime of sodomy shall be sentenced to the penitentiary for not less than one year nor more than ten years.

578. Every person who shall be convicted of taking into his or her mouth the sexual organ of any other person or animal, or who shall be convicted of placing his or her sexual organ in the mouth of any person or animal, or who shall be convicted of committing any other unnatural or perverted sexual practice with any other person or animal, shall be fined not more than one thousand ($1,000.00), dollars or be imprisoned . . . not exceeding ten years, or shall both be fined and imprisoned . . .

The indictment need only be framed in the statutory language, according to the law, and the particular perverted acts need not be specified.

MASSACHUSETTS 34. *Sodomy and buggery*. Whoever commits the abominable and detestable crime against nature, either with mankind or with a beast, shall be punished by imprisonment in the state prison for not more than twenty years.

35. *Unnatural and lascivious acts*. Whoever commits any unnatural and lascivious act with another person shall be punished by a fine of not less than one hundred nor more than one thousand dollars or by imprisonment in the state prison for not more than five years or in jail or the house of correction for not more than two and one half years.

MICHIGAN 750.158. *Crime against nature or sodomy*. Punishment—Any person who shall commit the abominable and detestable crime against nature either with mankind or with any animal shall be guilty of a felony, punishable by imprisonment in the state prison not more than 15 years.

750.159. *Emission need not be proved*—In any prosecution under the provisions of this chapter, it shall not be necessary to prove emission, and any sexual penetration, however slight, is sufficient to complete the crime specified in the next preceding section.

MINNESOTA 617.14. *Sodomy*. A person who carnally knows in any manner any animal or bird, or carnally knows any male or female person by the anus or by or with the mouth, or voluntarily submits to such carnal knowledge; or attempts sexual intercourse with a dead body, is guilty of sodomy, and is punishable with imprisonment in the state prison for not more than 20 years, and any sexual penetration, however slight, shall be sufficient to complete the crime.

A person on whom the crime of sodomy is committed is not an accomplice unless he consents to the act. State v. Schwartz, 215 Minn. 476.

MISSISSIPPI 2413. *Unnatural intercourse*—Every person who shall be convicted of the detestable and abominable crime against nature committed with mankind or with a beast, shall be punished by imprisonment in the penitentiary for a term of not more than ten years.

An indictment charging accused with having unnatural carnal intercourse with a woman by performing cunnilingus failed to show offense of sodomy, since penetration of the body is essential to the offense. State v. Hill, 179 Miss. 732.

MISSOURI 563.230. *The abominable and detestable crime against nature—penalty*.—Every person who shall be convicted of the detestable and abominable crime against nature, committed with mankind or with beast, with the sexual organs or with the mouth, shall be punished by imprisonment in the penitentiary not less than two years.

MONTANA 94-4118. *Crime against nature*. Every person who is guilty of the infamous crime against nature, committed with mankind or with any animal, is punishable by imprisonment in the state prison not less than five years.

In a prosecution for the infamous crime against nature (sodomy), courts should be assiduously on guard to warn the jury against yielding to the dictates of the intense prejudice naturally evoked by such a charge or convict upon slight evidence, since the charge is easily made, hard to prove, and still harder to disprove. State v. Keckoven, 107 Mont. 253.

94–4119. *Penetration sufficient to complete the crime.* Any sexual penetration, however slight, is sufficient to complete the crime against nature.

NEBRASKA 28–919. *Sodomy, defined; penalty.* Whoever has carnal copulation with a beast, or in any opening of the body except sexual parts with another human being, shall be guilty of sodomy and shall be imprisoned in the penitentiary not more than twenty years.

The crime includes both per os and per anum. Sledge v. State, 1 and 2 Neb. 350.

NEVADA 10141. *Crime against nature defined.* 194. The infamous crime against nature, either with man or beast, shall subject the offender to be punished by imprisonment in the state prison for a term not less than five years, and which may extend to life.

This section includes all unnatural acts in whatever form or by whatever means perpetrated, and an indictment charging that the accused did unlawfully commit "the infamous crime against nature" with a man, stating the nature of the act, was sufficient. In re Benites, 37 Nev. 145.

NEW HAMPSHIRE Ch. 449. *Offenses against chastity.* 9. *Lascivious acts.* Whoever commits any unnatural and lascivious act with another person shall be imprisoned not more than five years or fined not more than one thousand dollars, or both.

No specific law under the title of sodomy, buggery, crime against nature, or one of its legal synonyms.

NEW JERSEY 2:168–1. *Sodomy; punishment.* Sodomy, or the infamous crime against nature, committed with man or beast, shall be a high misdemeanor, and punished by a fine not exceeding one thousand dollars, or imprisonment at hard labor not exceeding twenty-one years, or both.

In a prosecution for sodomy, evidence of condition of rectum four months after offense was admissable to enable the jury to determine whether the condition of redness, irritation and dilation three days after the offense was abnormal and significant. State v. Pitman, 98 N.J. L626.
In the same case, evidence of the condition of the rectum of complaining witness three days after assault was admissable, the remoteness of the examination from the time of the offense merely affecting its probative force.

NEW MEXICO 41–704. *Sodomy—Penalty.*—Every person convicted of the abominable crime of sodomy, committed either with human being or any animal, on conviction thereof, shall be imprisoned for not less than one (1) year, or fined in any sum not less than one thousand dollars ($1,000), or by both.

The punishment provided for assault with intent to commit sodomy is imprisonment "for not more than one (1) year" or a fine "in any sum not exceeding one thousand dollars ($1,000), or by both. (41–705).

NEW YORK 690. *Sodomy* (third degree). A person who carnally knows any male or female person by the anus or by or with the mouth under circumstances not amounting to sodomy in the first degree or sodomy in the second degree is guilty of a misdemeanor.

Sodomy in the first degree involves intercourse by the anus or by or with the mouth without the consent of the other person, or when one of the persons is incapable of giving consent by reason of mental or physical weakness or immaturity, or when resistance is forcibly overcome, or when the resistance is prevented by fear of immediate and great bodily harm, or when it is prevented by stupor or weakness produced by an intoxicant, a narcotic, or an anaesthetic, or when the other person is in the custody of the law or unconscious. It is also first degree sodomy to carnally know "in any manner any animal or bird" or to attempt sexual intercourse with a dead body. Second degree sodomy involves a relationship with a person under the age of eighteen years, under conditions not amounting to first degree sodomy.

NORTH CAROLINA 14–177. *Crime against nature.*—If any person shall commit the abominable and detestable crime against nature, with mankind or beast, he shall be imprisoned in the state's prison not less than five nor more than sixty years.

This section includes all kindred acts of a bestial character whereby degraded and perverted sexual desires are sought to be gratified, the court ruled in State v. Griffin 175 N.C. 767. It includes all unnatural intercourse between male and male. State v. Fenner, 166 N.C. 247.

NORTH DAKOTA 12–2207. *Sodomy defined; punishment.* Every person who carnally knows in any manner any animal or bird, or carnally knows any male or female person by the anus or by or with the mouth, or voluntarily submits to such carnal knowledge, or attempts sexual intercourse with a dead body, is guilty of sodomy and shall be punished by imprisonment in the penitentiary for not less than one year nor more than ten years, or in the county jail for not more than one year. Any sexual penetration, however slight, is sufficient to complete the crime.

OHIO 13043. *Sodomy.* Whoever has carnal copulation with a beast, or in any opening of the body, except sexual parts, with another human being, shall be guilty of sodomy and shall be imprisoned in the penitentiary not more than twenty years.

The act of cunnilingus is not made a crime by the statutes of this state and is not within the purport of 13043. State v. Forquer, 74 App. 293.

OKLAHOMA 21–886. *Crime against nature.*—Every person who is guilty of the detestable and abominable crime against nature, committed with mankind or with a beast, is punishable by imprisonment in the penitentiary not exceeding ten years.

887. *Crime against nature, what penetration necessary.*—Any sexual penetration, however slight, is sufficient to complete the crime against nature.

"Mankind" includes male and female. Le Favour v. State 77 Okla. Cr. 383.

OREGON 23–910. *Sodomy.* If any person shall commit sodomy or the crime against nature, or any act or practice of sexual perversity, either with mankind or beast, or sustain osculatory relations with the private parts of any man, woman or child, or permit such relations to be sustained with his or her private parts, such person shall upon conviction thereof, be punished by imprisonment in the penitentiary not less than one year nor more than fifteen years.

PENNSYLVANIA 4501 *Sodomy.* Whosoever carnally knows in any manner any animal or bird, or carnally knows any male or female person by the anus or by or with the mouth, or whoever voluntarily submits to such carnal knowledge, is guilty of sodomy, a felony, and upon conviction thereof, shall be sentenced to pay a fine not exceeding five thousand dollars ($5,000), or to undergo imprisonment, by separate or solitary confinement at labor, not exceeding ten (10) years, or both.

4103. Carnal knowledge shall be deemed complete upon proof of penetration only.

In sodomy prosecution, penetration may be shown by circumstantial evidence, where such evidence is sufficient to satisfy the jury beyond reasonable doubt. Commonwealth v. Donahue, 7 A2d 13.

In a sodomy prosecution, the refusal to permit a physical examination of the defendant in open court was held not in error. Commonwealth v. Torr, 169 A 238, 111 Pa. Super. 178.

Consent of the prosecutor is no defense, but in such case his testimony requires corroboration. Commonwealth v. Smith, 3 Kulp 474.

4502. *Assault and solicitation to commit sodomy.* Whoever, unlawfully and maliciously, assaults another with intent to commit sodomy, or solicits, and incites another to permit and suffer such person to commit sodomy with him or her, is guilty of a felony, and upon conviction thereof, shall be sentenced to pay a fine not exceeding one thousand dollars ($1,000), or undergo imprisonment, by separate or solitary confinement at labor, not exceeding five (5) years, or both.

RHODE ISLAND. Ch. 610 12. Every person who shall be convicted of the abominable and detestable crime against nature, either with mankind or with any beast, shall be imprisoned not exceeding 20 years nor less than 7 years.

SOUTH CAROLINA 1439. *Buggery.* Whoever shall commit the abominable crime of buggery, whether with mankind or with beast, shall, on conviction, be deemed guilty of felony, and shall be imprisoned in the penitentiary for five years, and shall pay a fine of not less than five hundred dollars, or both, at the discretion of the court.

SOUTH DAKOTA 13:1716. *Crime against nature: penalty; construction.* Every person who is guilty of the detestable and abominable crime against nature committed with mankind or with a beast is punishable by imprisonment in the State Penitentiary not exceeding ten years.

Any sexual penetration, however slight, is sufficient to complete the crime against nature.

TENNESSEE 11184. *Crimes against nature.*—Crimes against nature, either with mankind or any beast, are punishable by imprisonment in the penitentiary not less than five nor more than fifteen years.

TEXAS Art. 524 (of Penal Code). *Sodomy.*—Whoever has carnal copulation with a beast, or in any opening of the body, except sexual parts, with another human being, or whoever shall use his mouth on the sexual parts of another human being for the purpose of having carnal copulation, or who shall voluntarily permit the use of his own sexual parts in a lewd or lascivious manner by any minor, shall be guilty of sodomy, and upon conviction thereof shall be deemed guilty of a felony, and shall be confined in the penitentiary not less than two (2) nor more than fifteen (15) years.

The above is a revision of an old law, which used the word *mankind* instead of *human being,* and did not specifically define the acts that made up the offense. It was held that woman was included under the term *mankind,* in Lewis v. State 36 Cr. R. 37.

If there was consent, the participant was an accomplice, and his testimony must be corroborated. Medis v. State 27 Cr. R. 194.

UTAH 103—Penal Code—7-7. Every person who assaults another with intent to commit rape, the infamous crime against nature, or mayhem is punishable by imprisonment in the state prison not less than one nor more than ten years.

103–51–22. *Sodomy.* Every person who is guilty of sodomy or any other detestable and abominable crime against nature, committed with mankind or with any animal with either the sexual organs or the mouth,

is punishable by imprisonment in the state prison not less than three years
nor more than twenty years.

Fellatio and cunnilingus represent the lowest and most debasing forms of sexual
perversion, it was held in re Ford's Estate 70 U. 456.
Emission not necessary to establish that sodomy is committed. State v. Peterson
81 U. 340.
Penetration per os is included in the statute as sodomy. State v. Peterson 81 U.
340.

VERMONT 8480. *Lewdness, penalty.* A person participating in the
act of copulating the mouth of one person with the sexual organ of
another shall be imprisoned in the State prison not less than one year nor
more than five years.
8478. *Lewdness.* A person guilty of open and gross lewdness and lascivious behavior shall be imprisoned not more than five years or fined
not more than $300.00.

VIRGINIA *Crimes against nature.*—If any person shall carnally know
in any manner any brute animal, or carnally know any male or female
person by the anus or by or with the mouth, or voluntarily submit to
such a carnal knowledge, he or she shall be guilty of a felony and shall
be confined in the penitentiary not less than one nor more than three
years.

Emission is not necessary for the crime against nature to have taken place. Commonwealth v. Thomas, 1 Va. Cas. 307.
Proof that accused had his head upon the stomach of another with the penis in
his hand is insufficient to prove carnal copulation in the mouth. Hudson v. Commonwealth, 141, Va. 525.

WASHINGTON 2456. *Crime against nature.* Every person who shall
carnally know in any manner any animal or bird; or who shall carnally
know any male or female person by the anus, or with the mouth or
tongue; or who shall voluntarily submit to such carnal knowledge; or
who shall attempt sexual intercourse with a dead body, shall be guilty
of sodomy and shall be punished by imprisonment in the state penitentiary for not more than ten years.

Proof of a man's taking hold of another's male organ of generation does not
tend to prove an attempt to commit sodomy as that is defined. State v. Ficklin
190 Wash. 168.

WEST VIRGINIA 6068 (61–8–13). *Crimes against nature.*—If any
person shall carnally know in any manner any brute animal, or carnally
know any male or female by the anus or by or with the mouth, or voluntarily submit to such carnal knowledge, he or she shall be guilty of a
felony, and, upon conviction thereof, shall be confined in the penitentiary
not less than one nor more than ten years.

WISCONSIN 351.40. *Sodomy*. Any person who shall commit sodomy, or the crime against nature, with mankind or beast shall be punished by imprisonment in the state prison not more than five years nor less than one year. Said crime may be committed by the penetration of the mouth of any human being by the organ of any male person as well as by the penetration of the rectum; proof of emission shall not be required.

WYOMING 9–520. *Sodomy*. Whoever commits the abominable and detestable crime against nature, by having carnal knowledge of a man or beast; or who being a male carnally knows any man or woman through the anus, or in any other manner contrary to nature; and whoever intices, allures, instigates or aids any person under the age of twenty-one (21) years to commit masturbation or self-pollution, is guilty of sodomy, and shall be imprisoned in the penitentiary not more than five (5) years or may be imprisoned in the county jail not more than twelve (12) months.

Masturbation or self-pollution includes the crime of cunnilingus, which is "any unnatural sexual gratification which tends to corrupt the morals." Young v. State 194 Ind. 221.

APPENDIX C

References and Sources

ALDRIDGE, JOHN W. *After the Lost Generation, a Critical Study of the Writers of Two Wars.* New York: McGraw-Hill, 1951.

ALLEN, CLIFFORD. *The Sexual Perversions and Abnormalities, a Study in the Psychology of Paraphilia.* 2nd ed.; New York: Oxford University Press, 1949.

ANOMALY. *The Invert and his Social Adjustment.* 2nd ed.; Baltimore: Williams and Wilkins, 1948.

BERGLER, EDMUND. *Neurotic Counterfeit-Sex: Impotence, Frigidity, "Mechanical" and Pseudosexuality, Homosexuality.* New York: Grune & Stratton, 1951.

BLOCH, IWAN. *The Sexual Life of our Time in its Relations to Modern Civilization.* New York: Rebman Co., 1920.

Book Review Digest, 1905 to 1950.

BOSS, MEDARD. *The Meaning and Content of Sexual Perversions.* 2nd ed.; New York: Grune & Stratton, 1949.

BROWN, FRED and RUDOLF T. KEMPTON. *Sex Questions and Answers: a Guide to Happy Marriage.* New York: Whittlesey House, 1950.

CARPENTER, EDWARD. *The Intermediate Sex: a Study of Some Transitional Types of Men and Women.* London: Allen & Unwin, 1941.

CARPENTER, EDWARD. *Intermediate Types Among Primitive Folk, a Study in Social Evolution.* 2nd ed.; London: George Allen & Unwin, 1919.

CARPENTER, EDWARD. *Love's Coming of Age.* New York: Mitchell Kennerley, 1919.

CHESSER, EUSTACE. *Sexual Behavior, Normal and Abnormal.* London and New York: Medical Publications, 1949.

CHEVALIER, JULIEN. *Une Maladie de la personnalité: l'inversion sexuelle.* Lyon: A. Storck, and Paris: G. Masson, 1893.

CHIDECKEL, MAURICE. *Female Sex Perversion: the Sexually Aberrated Woman as She Is.* New York: Eugenics Publishing Co., 1938.

DOLLARD, JOHN AND NEAL E. MILLER. *Personality and Psychotherapy: an Analysis in Terms of Learning, Thinking, and Culture.* New York: McGraw-Hill, 1950.

ELLIS, ALBERT. *The Folklore of Sex.* New York: Charles Boni, 1951.

ELLIS, HAVELOCK. *Studies in the Psychology of Sex.* Vol. 2: *Sexual Inversion.* 3rd ed.; Philadelphia: F. A. Davis Co., 1928.

Encyclopaedia Sexualis, a Comprehensive Encyclopaedia-Dictionary of the Sexual Sciences. Victor Robinson, editor. New York: Dingwall-Rock, 1936.

FORD, CLELLAN S. and FRANK A. BEACH. *Patterns of Sexual Behavior.* New York: Harper & Bros. and Paul B. Hoeber, 1951.

293

FREUD, SIGMUND. *A General Introduction to Psychoanalysis.* Garden City, N. Y.: Garden City Publishing Co., 1938.

FREUD, SIGMUND. *Leonardo da Vinci, a Psychosexual Study of an Infantile Reminiscence.* London: Kegan Paul, Trench, Trubner and Co., 1932.

FREUD, SIGMUND. *Three Contributions to the Theory of Sex.* New York: Nervous and Mental Disease Monographs, 1948. Also published under title *Three Essays on the Theory of Sexuality.* London: Imago Publishing Co., 1949.

GIDE, ANDRE. *Corydon.* New York: Farrar, Straus and Co., 1950.

GIDE, ANDRE. *The Journals.* 4 volumes; New York: Knopf, 1947–1951.

GUYON, RENE. *The Ethics of Sexual Acts.* New York: Knopf, 1948.

GUYON, RENE. *Sexual Freedom.* New York: Knopf, 1950.

HAMILTON, GILBERT VAN TASSEL, "Homosexuality as a Defense Against Incest," in *Encyclopaedia Sexualis, q. v.*

HENRY, G. W. *Sex Variants: a Study of Homosexual Patterns.* New York: Paul B. Hoeber, 1948.

HIRSCHFELD, MAGNUS. *Die Homosexualität des Mannes und des Weibes.* Berlin: L. Marcus, 1920.

HIRSCHFELD, MAGNUS. *Sexual Anomalies and Perversions.* London: Francis Aldor, 1944.

HIRSCHFELD, MAGNUS. *Sexual Pathology.* New York: Emerson, 1940.

Jahrbuch für sexuelle Zwischenstufen, 1899 to 1923.

KAHN, SAMUEL. *Mentality and Homosexuality.* Boston: Meador Publishing Co., 1937.

KIEFER, OTTO. *Sexual Life in Ancient Rome.* London: Routledge and Kegan Paul, 1950.

KINSEY, ALFRED C., WARDELL B. POMEROY AND CLYDE E. MARTIN. *Sexual Behavior in the Human Male.* Philadelphia: W. B. Saunders, 1948.

KRAFFT-EBING, R. V. *Psychopathia Sexualis.* New York: Physicians and Surgeons Book Co., 1925.

LEGMAN, G. "Fathers and Sons," in *On the Cause of Homosexuality.* New York: Breaking Point, 1950.

LEGMAN, G. *Love & Death; a Study in Censorship.* New York: Breaking Point, 1949.

LEWANDOWSKI, HERBERT. *Das Sexualproblem in der modernen Literatur und Kunst.* Dresden: Paul Aretz, 1927.

LEWIS, WYNDHAM. *The Art of Being Ruled.* London: Chatto and Windus, 1926.

LICHT, H. *Sexual Life in Ancient Greece.* London: Routledge and Kegan Paul, 1949.

LONDON, LOUIS S. and FRANK S. CAPRIO. *Sexual Deviations.* Washington, D. C.: Lincacre Press, 1950.

MANTEGAZZA, PAOLO. *The Sexual Relations of Mankind.* New York: Eugenics Publishing Co., 1935.

MOLL, ALBERT. *Libido Sexualis: Studies in the Psychosexual Laws of Love Verified by Clinical Sexual Case Histories.* New York: American Ethnological Press, 1933.

MOLL, ALBERT. *Perversions of the Sex Instinct: a Study of Sexual Inversion Based on Clinical Data and Official Documents.* Newark, N. J.: Julian Press, 1931.

NIN FRIAS, A. *Homosexualismo creador.* Madrid: Javier Morata, 1933.

PICTON, HAROLD. *The Morbid, the Abnormal and the Personal.* London: British Society for the Study of Sex Psychology, 1923.

PORCHE, FRANÇOIS. *L'Amour qui n'ose pas dire son nom.* Paris: Bernard Grasset, 1927.

POTTER, LA FORREST. *Strange Loves: a Study in Sexual Abnormalities.* New York: Robert Dodsley Co., 1933.

PRAZ, MARIO. *The Romantic Agony.* London: Oxford U. Press, 1933.

RAFFALOVICH, MARC-ANDRE. *Uranisme et unisexualité: étude sur différentes manifestations de l'instinct sexuel.* Lyon: A. Storck, and Paris: Masson, 1896.

REICH, WILHELM. *The Sexual Revolution: Toward a Self-Governing Character Structure.* New York: Orgone Institute Press, 1945.

STEKEL, WILHELM. *Bisexual Love: the Homosexual Neurosis.* Boston: R. G. Badger, 1922. Reprinted under title *The Homosexual Neurosis.* New York: Emerson Books, 1946.

SUMNER, WILLIAM G. *Folkways: a Study of the Sociological Importance of Usages, Customs, Mores, and Morals.* Boston: Ginn & Co., 1906.

SYMONDS, JOHN ADDINGTON. *A Problem in Greek Ethics, Being an Inquiry into the Phenomenon of Sexual Inversion.* London: Privately printed by the author, 1901.

SYMONDS, JOHN ADDINGTON. *A Problem in Modern Ethics, Being an Inquiry into the Phenomenon of Sexual Inversion.* London: Privately printed, 1896.

TARNOVSKII, V. M. *Anthropological, Legal and Medical Studies on Pederasty in Europe.* New York: Falstaff, 1933.

THOMPSON, CLARA. "Changing Concepts of Homosexuality in Psychoanalysis," *Psychiatry: Journal of the Biology and Pathology of Interpersonal Relations,* 10:183 (1947).

ULRICHS, CARL HEINRICH. *Ara Spei, Formatrix, Vindicta,* and other pamphlets. Published in Leipzig, 1864, 1865, etc., under the pseudonym of Numa Numantius.

WESTERMARCK, EDWARD. *The Origin and Development of the Moral Ideas.* 2nd ed.; London: Macmillan and Co., 1917, Chapter XLIII, "Homosexual Love."

WHITE, H. D. JENNINGS. *Psychological Causes of Homoerotism and Inversion.* London: British Society for Study of Sex Psychology, 1925.

APPENDIX D

A Check List of Novels and Dramas

Novels and dramas in which homosexuality is the basic theme, or in which it plays an important although minor rôle, are listed here. In those instances where I was unable to check the work personally or where I did not agree with the interpretation of an authority, I have so indicated.

Biographies and autobiographies (unless in the form of novels or dramas) have been omitted, because their inclusion would have necessitated the preparation of complete bibliographies on the lives and works of Tchaikowsky, Hölderlin, Andersen, Gide, Proust, Wilde, Whitman, Symonds, and many others. Such a bibliographical study is outside the scope of this book. Poetry has also been omitted, because of the large number of books in which homosexuality is the theme of a few poems, but not of the entire work.

All titles of foreign books are given in English if the works have been located in translation; otherwise, the titles are given in the original tongue. Dates of publication refer to the edition cited, which is the one located, and may not be either the first or the last.

This does not purport to be a comprehensive bibliography of novels and dramas on homosexuality, but it represents what I believe to be the most exhaustive effort at the compilation of such a bibliography that has yet been published.

ANDERSON, HELEN. *Pity for Women.* New York: Doubleday & Co., 1937.
An unhappy relationship between an older and a younger woman; the theme is overdone and somewhat hysterical.

ANDERSON, SHERWOOD. "Hands," in *Winesburg, Ohio.* New York: Modern Library.
A portrait of a man who has suffered because suspicion has fallen on him.

ARGIS, HENRI D'. *Gomorrhe.* Paris: Charles, 1889.
An untranslated French novel.

ARGIS, HENRI D'. *Sodome.* Paris: Piaget, 1888.
A well-known French novel, to which Paul Verlaine contributed an introduction.

BAKER, DOROTHY. *Trio.* Boston: Houghton Mifflin Co., 1943.
An unsympathetic portrait of a Lesbian who is a literary thief and a corrupter of youth.

BAKER, DOROTHY and HOWARD BAKER. *Trio.*
A drama, adapted from the novel, and first presented in New York on December 29, 1944. It has not been published, an omission which is no great loss to the literature of the theater.

BALZAC, HONORE DE. *The Girl with the Golden Eyes.* Translated by
Ernest Dowson. New York: Illustrated Editions, 1931; and numerous
other editions.
> The interpretation of this work as a story of Lesbianism has been given by
> Ellis, Chevalier, and others; however, it is not as clear as his *Vautrin*, an out-
> spoken drama on male homosexuality. There are a number of pertinent incidents
> and characters in *Père Goriot, Scenes of Parisian Life*, "Seraphita," etc.

BALZAC, HONORE DE. *Vautrin.* In various editions of the collected works
of Balzac.
> A drama; see above.

BARNES, DJUNA. *Ladies' Almanac.* Paris: Printed for the author by Imp.
Darantière, 1928.
> Never published in the United States; a book dealing with Lesbianism, written
> by a very talented author.

BARNES, DJUNA. *Nightwood.* New York: Harcourt, Brace & Co., 1937;
reprinted by New Directions, with introduction by T. S. Eliot.
> A beautiful and poetic novel whose very obscurity aids in capturing the spirit
> of a lonely world in which the characters are living. The story revolves around
> an all-female triangle.

BARR, JAMES. *Derricks.* New York: Greenberg, 1951.
> A volume of short stories; interesting variations and interpretations of the male
> homosexual theme.

BARR, JAMES. *Quatrefoil.* New York: Greenberg, 1950.
> A strong love between two naval officers brings forth grave conflict in the
> younger. The note of hope on which this novel ends is perhaps its finest con-
> tribution to the literature on the subject.

BARRES, MAURICE. *Le Jardin de Bérénice.* Paris: Perrin, 1891.
> A novel listed by Lewandowski.

BELLEMANS, HENRY. *Kings Row.* New York: Simon and Schuster, 1940.
> A friendship between two young men, one of whom is homosexual, forms an
> interesting section of this popular novel.

BELOT, ADOLPHE. *Mademoiselle Giraud, My Wife.* Chicago: Laird & Lee,
1891.
> A French novel cited by Havelock Ellis, Chevalier, and others; preface con-
> tributed by Emile Zola.

BENSON, ARTHUR CHRISTOPHER. *Memoirs of Arthur Hamilton.* London:
Paul Kegan, 1886; reprinted, New York: Mitchell Kennerley, 1907.
> A novel originally published in the form of a biography; reminiscences of
> homosexual episodes at Cambridge.

BINET-VALMER, G. *Le Gamin tendre.* Paris: Société du Mercure de
France, 1901.
> A novel cited by Nin Frías.

BINET-VALMER, G. *Lucien.* Paris: P. Ollendorff, 1910.
> The story of a homosexual who confesses to his father.

BIRABEAU, ANDRE. *Revelation.* New York: Viking Press, 1930.
A very fine story of a mother's discovery of the truth about a son who has just been killed; probably the best fictional portrait of a homosexual from the viewpoint of the mother.

BOURDET, EDOUARD. *The Captive.* New York: Brentano's, 1926.
A drama based on the triangle of a man, his wife, and a woman who is winning the latter's affections.

BOURGET, PAUL. *A Love Crime.* Paris and New York: Société des Beaux-Arts, 1905.
An English translation of a French novel mentioned by Havelock Ellis.

BOURJAILY, VANCE. *The End of My Life.* New York: Scribner's, 1947.
Homosexuality leads one of the characters in this book to destruction.

BOWEN, ELIZABETH. *The Hotel.* New York: Dial Press, 1928.
Jealousy and suspicion surround the friendship of a widow and a young girl in this novel.

BUECHNER, FREDERICK. *A Long Day's Dying.* New York: Alfred A. Knopf, 1950.
This is a novel which, in the opinion of Aldridge and Legman, has a homosexual theme basic to the entire book, but it will be difficult for many readers to share that evaluation.

BURNS, JOHN HORNE. *The Gallery.* New York: Harper & Bros., 1947.
A brilliant series of sketches related to the Second World War and American troops in Italy. The story "Momma" is probably the outstanding discription of a gay bar in modern literature.

BURNS, JOHN HORNE. *Lucifer with a Book.* New York: Harper & Bros., 1949.
A satire on private-school education, in which the affection between the teacher and pupil approaches sexual fulfillment, but meets inner resistance.

BURTON, RICHARD. *The Book of the Thousand Nights and a Night.* London: Kamashastra Society, 1885; New York: Limited Editions Club, 1934; New York: Heritage Press.
Burton's version of the *Arabian Nights* contains several stories on sodomy and pederasty and an essay on the subject which Burton prepared as an appendix. This material is to be found only in a few genuinely unexpurgated editions.

BUTTI, ENRICO A. *L'Automa.* Milan: Galli, 1892.
A work cited by London and Caprio, written by a man who is unknown in the English-speaking world, but was considered rather important in Italy.

CAIN, JAMES M. *Serenade.* New York: Alfred A. Knopf, 1937.
A story of how a woman's jealousy is aroused when her hold on a man is challenged by another male; a gripping novel, written in the style of the hard-boiled school, with an original variation of the triangle.

CAINE, HALL. *The Deemster.* Chicago: Rand, McNally & Co., 1888.
A novel mentioned by Lewandowski.

CAPOTE, TRUMAN. *Other Voices, Other Rooms*. New York: Random House, 1948.
The adolescent youth drifts toward a sexual relationship in an atmosphere of disillusionment, decadence, and sensitivity. A work of rich sensuousness, which would be a finer contribution to this literature were it not so ostentatiously overwritten.

CARCO, FRANCIS. *Jésus-la-Caille*. Paris: Fayard, 1930.
A story of male prostitution. The only editions which can be considered complete are those which contain *Les Malheurs de Fernande* (see below).

CARCO, FRANCIS. *Les Malheurs de Fernande*. Paris: L'Edition, 1918.
Originally written as the third part of *Jésus-la-Caille*, but issued as a separate book (see above).

CARPENTER, EDWARD. *Iolaüs, an Anthology of Friendship*. Boston: Charles E. Goodspeed, 1902.
An anthology in which material on homosexuality is not distinguished from that on other types of friendships.

CHANDLER, RAYMOND. *The Big Sleep*. New York: Alfred A. Knopf, 1939.
The homosexual is the murder victim in a hard-boiled detective story.

CHARLES-ETIENNE. *Notre-dame de Lesbos*. Paris: Librairie des Curiosités Littéraires, 1924.
A minor French novel on the Lesbian theme.

CLARKE, ASHLEY WALROND. *Jaspar Tristram*. London: William Heinemann, 1899.
A British novel reported by Havelock Ellis to treat of male homosexuality.

CLAUDEL, PAUL. *Tête d'or*. New Haven, Conn.: Yale University Press, 1919; in English.
A powerful poetic drama, in which the appeal for affection by Cébès to Simon is considered by many critics to be an expression of homosexuality.

COCTEAU, JEAN. *Le Livre blanc*. Paris: Editions du Signe, 1930.
Originally published anonymously, but with illustrations easily recognized to be by Cocteau, who later acknowledged authorship of this book.

COHEN, LESTER. *Oscar Wilde*. New York: Boni and Liveright, 1928.
A biographical drama.

COLETTE, S. G. and HENRY-GAUTHIER VILLARS (Colette and Willy). *The Indulgent Husband*. New York: Farrar, 1935.
There is a Lesbian theme in the witty and entertaining works of Colette, both those written alone and in collaboration with Willy. This book, in which it plays a major rôle, is a translation of *Claudine en Ménage;* other works in which it is apparent are *Claudine à Paris* and *Claudine Mariée*.

COLLI, NICCOLO DE. *Oscar Wilde*. Florence: Gruppo di cultura fiorentino degl'Isvici, 1933.
A drama in Italian.

COLOMA, LUIS. *Boy*. Milwaukee: Bruce Publishing Co., 1934.
Translation of a Spanish novel bearing the same title and mentioned by Lewandowski.

CONSTANTINE, MURRAY and MARGARET GOLDSMITH. *Venus in Scorpio*. London: John Lane, 1940.
An historical novel based on the life of Marie Antoinette, with suggestions of the probability of homosexuality in the accounts of her later adolescence.

COUPERUS, LOUIS. *Noodlot*. Amsterdam: L. J. Veen, 1890.
One of a group of novels by a major Dutch writer mentiond by Lewandowski and other critics.

COUVREUR, ANDRE. *Androgyne: les fantaisies du Professeur Tornada*. Paris: A. Michel, 1923.
A French novel by a minor writer.

DALE, ALAN (pseud. of Alfred J. Cohen). *A Marriage Below Zero*. New York: Dillingham & Co., 1889.
Mentioned by *Jahrbuch*.

DANE, CLEMENCE (pseud. of Winifred Ashton). *Regiment of Women*. New York: Macmillan Co., 1917.
Friendship and suggestion of Lesbianism among the teachers at a girls' school.

DARIEN, GEORGES. *Biribi*. Paris: A. Savine, 1890.
A novel of military life.

DARIEN, GEORGES and M. LAURAS. *Biribi*. Paris: E. Fasquelle, 1906.
Dramatic version of the novel by the same name.

DARIEN, GEORGES and EDOUARD DUBUS. *Les Vrais sous-offs*. Paris: A. Savine, not dated.
A reply to *Sous-offs* by Lucien Descaves.

DAUDET, LUCIEN ALPHONSE. *Le Chemin mort*. Paris: Flammarion, 19—(?).
A French novel mentioned by *Jahrbuch*.

DE FORREST, MICHAEL. *The Gay Year*. New York: Woodford Press, 1949.
An undistinguished novel on the gay life in New York.

DESCAVES, LUCIEN. *Sous-offs*. Paris: Tresse et Stock, 1889.
A book about homosexuality in the military service; attracted considerable attention at the time of its publication. An effort was made to suppress this novel, and the story of the fight against suppression is told in the 1892 edition.

DIDEROT, DENIS. *Memoirs of a Nun*. London: Routledge & Sons, 1928.
Translation of *La Réligieuse*, a well-known and popular French novel which depicts Lesbianism in an atmosphere of religion.

DOGNON, ANDRE DU. *Les Amours buissonières*. Paris: Editions du Scorpion, 1948.
An unimpressive story of promiscuity among male homosexuals.

DOGNON, ANDRE DU. *Le Monde inversé*. Paris: Editions du Scorpion, 1949.
Similar to above.

DOSTOEVSKY, FEODOR. "Nyelochka Nyezvanov" in *The Friend of the Family*. London: W. Heinemann, 1920.
This story is interpreted by Chevalier and others as dealing with Lesbianism. Such interpretations have generally been based on the French version, which is a rather free adaptation, entitled *Ame d'enfant* (Paris: Marpon et Flammarion, 1890).

DOWD, HARRISON. *The Night Air*. New York: Dial Press, 1950.
A story of a male homosexual in New York, against a background of theatrical and bohemian life.

EEKHOUD, GEORGES. *Escal-vigor*. Paris: Société du Mercure de France, 1899.
Eekhoud was one of the most important writers of his time to devote his literary output to homosexuality. Like his other books, *Escal-vigor* was concerned with the problems of the male invert and was one of the most popular novels on the subject during the late years of the nineteenth century. Other works by Eekhoud on this theme included *Mes communions*, *L'Autre vue*, *Le Cycle patibulaire*, and *Les Libertins d'Anvers*.

ENGSTRAND, STUART. *The Sling and the Arrow*. New York: Creative Age, 1947.
A novel, written like a clinical case history, about a married man who is gradually drifting toward homosexuality.

ESSEBAC, ACHILLE. *L'Elu*. Paris: Ambert, 1930.
Most popular of several novels on the subject of male homosexuality written by this author. Other novels on this theme by Essebac were *Dédé*, *Luc*, and *Partenz*.

FARRERE, CLAUDE. *Les Civilisés*. Paris: Flammarion, 1921.
A French novella mentioned by *Jahrbuch*.

FERRI-PISANI. *Les Pervertis*. Paris: Librairie Universelle, 1905.
Overt homosexuality among students.

FEYDEAU, ERNEST AIME. *La Comtesse de Chalis*. Paris: M. Lévy Frères, 1871.
A minor French novel on Lesbianism.

FIRBANK, RONALD. *Inclinations*. Reprinted in *Three Novels*. Norfolk: New Directions, 1951.
A story of a Lesbian passion, written by a man with a flair for delicate description. Firbank was a dilettante whose interest in homosexuality pervades his entire work.

FISHER, M. F. K. *Not Now but Now*. New York: Viking, 1947.
One of the four sections of this novel deals with the suspicion of Lesbianism surrounding a friendship.

FITZGERALD, F. SCOTT. *Tender Is the Night*. New York: Scribner's, 1934.
Although the homosexual theme is not a fundamental part of the construction of this novel, it plays a rôle of unique interest, because the man involved is an employee of the State Department. Thus Fitzgerald depicted a character some fifteen years before that person was "discovered" by the United States Senate.

FITZROY, A. T. *Despised and Rejected*. London: C. W. Daniel, 19–(?).
Male and female form a friendship in protection against a world in which they feel "despised and rejected" because of their sexual inclinations.

FLAUBERT, GUSTAVE. *Salammbô*. Paris: 1862; New York: E. P. Dutton, 1948; and numerous other editions.
Flaubert's classic is an historical romance laid in ancient Carthage and written after a remarkable archaeological study by the author. Many critics, such as Havelock Ellis, Chevalier, and others, consider it part of the literature on Lesbianism.

FRANK, WALDO. *The Dark Mother*. New York: Boni and Liveright, 1920.
The friendship between a young protagonist and a homosexual and the struggle of the former against the influence of the latter are depicted in a penetrating novel.

FREDERICS, DIANA. *Diana, a Strange Autobiography*. New York: Dial Press, 1939; reprinted by Citadel Press, New York.
A story told in the first person as the autobiography of a Lesbian.

FULLER, HENRY B. *Bertram Cope's Year*. Chicago: Ralph Fletcher Seymour, Alderbrink Press, 1919.
A novel of college youth by a distinguished American writer whose work was considered bold for its time, but on rereading appears extremely restrained.

GAUTIER, THEOPHILE. *Mademoiselle de Maupin*. Paris: 1835; New York: Modern Library; and many other editions.
The classic story of transvestism (female dressed as male), with the unique development of a man in love with a woman whom be believes to be a man.

GENET, JEAN. *Journal du voleur*. Paris: Gallimard, 1949.
One of the most significant writers in France, Genêt has made male homosexuality the central theme of his works. His books, unquestionably pornographic, offer a refreshing honesty when contrasted with the "delicate" treatment that the subject receives at the hands of so many writers.

GENET, JEAN. *Our Lady of the Flowers*. Paris: Morihien, 1949.
An English translation, not sold in the United States.

GENET, JEAN. *Pompes funèbres*. Paris: Morihien, 1949.
See note for *Journal du Voleur*.

GENET, JEAN. *Querelle de Brest*. Paris: Morihien, 1948.
See note for *Journal du Voleur*. One edition of this work contains remarkable illustrations, apparently by Jean Cocteau.

GIDE, ANDRE. *The Immoralist*. New York: Alfred A. Knopf, 1930.
A novel of conflict and conscience in a young man whose latent homosexuality is beginning to come to the fore. The illness and eventual death of the bride occur simultaneously with this awakening urge of the protagonist, complicating his own inner struggle and providing the material for one of the great books on this theme. Homosexuality is also apparent in most of Gide's other works, particularly *The Counterfeiters* and *Lafcadio's Adventures*.

GIDE, ANDRE. *Saül*. Paris: Editions de la Nouvelle Revue Française, 1922.
A drama based upon the Biblical story: considered by Gide to be one of his most significant contributions to homosexual literature.

GIRON, AIME and ALBERT TOZZA. *Antinoüs*. Paris: Ambert, 1904.
A novel mentioned by *Jahrbuch*.

GOODMAN, PAUL. *Parents' Day*. Saugatuck, Conn.: Five by Eight Press, 1951.
A poignant story, written with an understanding and sympathetic approach; the dilemma of a homosexual schoolteacher and his relationships with parents, students, and the administration of the school. In Goodman's other work, particularly *The Dead of Spring*, the homosexual theme is also evident.

GOURMONT, REMY DE. *Le Songe d'une femme*. Paris: Mercure de France, 1918.
A short French novel cited by *Jahrbuch*.

HALDANE, CHARLOTTE. *Man's World*. New York: George H. Doran Co., 1927.
Appears on the list of novels prepared by Nin Frías.

HALL, RADCLYFFE. *The Well of Loneliness*. New York: Covici, Friede, 1928; numerous reprints.
Probably one of the best known and most widely read books on Lesbianism. A passionate, eloquent, although sentimental plea for recognition and acceptance, and a glorified picture of love among Lesbians.

HARDY, THOMAS. *Desperate Remedies*. New York: Harper & Bros., 1896.
Although constituting but a single scene in the book, the conversation between Cytherea and Miss Adclyffe is one of the most outspoken descriptions of Lesbianism in English literature up to the twentieth century.

HELL, VIRGINIE. *Saphir ou le journal de Gilles*. Paris: Presses du Livre Français, 1949.
A light, minor novel dealing with a passionate love between two women.

HELLMAN, LILLIAN. *The Children's Hour*. New York: Alfred A. Knopf, 1934; also in several anthologies.
A powerful drama depicting the tragedy of gossip and suspicion which cast a shadow on the friendship of two women.

HEMINGWAY, ERNEST. "The Sea Change," "The Mother of a Queen," and "Homage to Switzerland," in *The Fifth Column and the First Forty-Nine Stories*. New York: P. F. Collier & Son, 1938; also in other collections.
A few of the numerous stories by Hemingway in which the male and the female homosexual themes—the latter in "The Sea Change"—are explored. Hemingway is one of the very few writers interested in both male and female inversion.

HERMANN, HANS. *Die Schuld der Väter*. Leipzig: Spohr, 189-(?).
A German novel mentioned by Raffalovich and numerous other writers.

HERNANDEZ CATA, ALFONSO. *El Angel de Sodoma*. Madrid: Mundo Latino, 1928.
A Spanish novel.

HESSE, HERMANN. *Narziss und Goldmund*. Berlin: S. Fischer, 1931.
The latent homosexual theme dominates a deep friendship of two young men in a religious atmosphere. The undertone of budding passion beneath the love of friends is seen in Hesse's other work, particularly *Demian*.

HICHENS, ROBERT S. *The Green Carnation*. New York: M. Kennerley, 1894.
A satire on the effeminate aesthete; probably directed at Oscar Wilde.

HÖLDERLIN, FRIEDRICH. *Hyperion*. Leipzig: P. Reclam, 187–(?).
A novel by one of Germany's significant poets of the nineteenth century; it is a story told in the form of correspondence and inspired by the Greek ideal.

IBARA, SAIKAKU. *Quaint Stories of Samurais*. Paris: Privately printed, 1928.
Short stories by a seventeenth-century Japanese writer, taken from a collection said to be known as *The Glorious Stories of Homosexuality*.

ISHERWOOD, CHRISTOPHER. *The Berlin Stories*. New York: New Directions, 1946.
A collection consisting of *The Last of Mr. Norris* (published in England under the title *Mr. Norris Changes Trains*) and *Goodbye to Berlin*, a series of sketches and stories. The theme of male homosexuality permeates the work of this brilliant writer; it is combined with satire, humor, and exceptionally well-drawn character development. In *The Memorial*, the more tragic and lonely aspects of the life are stressed, and in *Prater Violet* the undertones, subtle and somewhat difficult to perceive, are unquestionably present.

ISHERWOOD, CHRISTOPHER. *The Memorial: Portrait of a Family*. Norfolk: New Directions, 1946.
See above.

ISTRATI, PANAIT. *Kyra Kyralina*. New York: Alfred A. Knopf, 1926.
The fantastic adventures of a youth in the Near East, including his becoming the captive and favorite of a man of wealth. The book has a preface by Romain Rolland; Istrati attracted considerable attention on the Continent, although he has not had a strong influence in this country.

JACKSON, CHARLES. *The Fall of Valor*. New York: Rinehart & Co., 1946.
The awakening of the latent homosexuality in a married man, and the subsequent adventures and conflicts, are handled with finesse, but without deep psychological insight into this difficult theme.

JACKSON, CHARLES. *The Lost Weekend*. New York: Farrar & Rinehart, 1944.
This notable novel of alcoholism is the story of suppressed homosexuality, and the memories of homosexual adventures and desires return during the period of intoxication.

JACKSON, SHIRLEY. *Hangsaman*. New York: Farrar, Straus and Young, 1951.
An imaginary Lesbian romance takes place in the mind of a schizophrenic during a period of hallucinations.

JAMES, HENRY. *The Pupil*. London: Macmillan and Co., 1922. Published in the same volume with *What Maisie Knew* and *In the Cage*.

A study of the affection between a sickly pupil and a young tutor; the under-tones of erotic passion are not very clear, and perhaps were not intended by James, but the homosexual interpretation has been given to this work by such critics as Albert Guérard.

JONES, JAMES. *From Here to Eternity.* New York: Scribner's, 1951.
A description of the life and loves of the American soldier in World War II; includes several incidents involving the contacts of the soldiers with homosexuals.

KENT, NIAL. *The Divided Path.* New York: Greenberg, 1949.
A story of conflict in a young invert, his effort to adjust, his struggles against desires which he considers abnormal, and his search for a permanent relationship with another person. The novel avoids the hackneyed ending characteristic of this literature.

KIPLING, RUDYARD. *Stalky & Co.* Garden City, N. Y.: Doubleday, Page & Co., 1922.
This well-known novel is considered part of the literature of homosexuality by Lewandowski.

KOESTLER, ARTHUR. *Arrival and Departure.* New York: Macmillan Co., 1943.
The protagonist in this novel makes the most important decision of his life when he learns about a Lesbian relationship between two women whom he knows intimately.

LACRATELLE, JACQUES DE. *Marie Bonifas.* London and New York: G. P. Putnam's Sons, 1927; in English.
A young girl with masculine body and temperament becomes a recluse after being rebuffed in her search for love and after being ostracized in school and in society.

LAMARTINE, ALPHONSE DE. *Régina.* Paris: Imprimerie de Walder, 1858.
A short novel, generally interpreted as pertaining to Lesbianism. Although written by one of the great French romanticists, this work does not seem to have been translated into English.

LATOUCHE, HENRI DE. *Fragoletta.* Paris: Delloye, 1840.
A French novel cited by Raffalovich and Praz, and pertaining to female inversion.

LAWRENCE, D. H. "The Prussian Officer," in *The Portable D. H. Law-rence.* New York: Viking Press, 1947; also in numerous other collec-tions and anthologies.
One of the most powerful portraits of repressed homosexuality, and its relation-ship to hatred, brutality, and sadism.

LAWRENCE, D. H. *Women in Love.* New York: Viking Press, and various other editions.
A story of a deep friendship between two men who are in love with sisters and also with each other. In a minor way, the homosexual theme is subtly inter-woven into other works of Lawrence, particularly *Aaron's Rod* and *The Rainbow.*

LE CLERC, JACQUES. *Show Cases.* New York: Macy-Masius, 1928.
A series of short stories, told by one narrator, the themes of which are incest, nymphomania, and homosexuality.

LEHMANN, ROSAMOND. *Dusty Answer*. New York: Henry Holt and Co., 1927.

A work of extraordinary beauty in which the protagonist, an English schoolgirl, twice develops strong attachments, once to a student who is a Lesbian, and then to a man whose own sexual temperament prevents him from responding to the offer of love.

LEWIS, WYNDHAM. *The Apes of God*. New York: R. M. McBride & Co., 1932.

Both male and female inversion are portrayed in a satirical vein.

LOMBARD, JEAN. *L'Agonie*. Paris: A. Michel, 1926.

An historical novel about homosexuality in ancient Rome.

LORRAIN, JEAN. *Monsieur de Phocas*. Paris: A. Michel, 1929.

A work said to have been written under the influence of *The Picture of Dorian Gray;* the homosexual interpretation is given by Praz and Nin Frías.

LOTI, PIERRE. *Mon Frère Yves*. Paris: Calmann-Lévy, 1883.

This work, mentioned by Lewandowski, is by one of the best-known French writers of the nineteenth century. It is a story of the world-wide travels of a French sailor. No translation into English was located.

LOUŸS, PIERRE. *Aphrodite*. Numerous American editions.

Louÿs, one of the most prominent writers of France during the late nineteenth and early twentieth century, showed a continuous interest in Lesbianism throughout his work. Although *Aphrodite* is concerned with a deep heterosexual passion. the Lesbian theme is used as background, as in the author's *The Adventures of King Pausole*, whereas in his poetry, *The Songs of Bilitis*, it is the exclusive motif.

LUMET, LOUIS. *Les Cahiers d'un congréganiste*. Paris: E. Fasquelle, 1904.

Novel listed by *Jahrbuch*.

LUNE, JEAN DE LA. *Les Plantins*. Paris: Librairie française Genonceaux, 1903.

A novel listed by *Jahrbuch*.

LYS, GEORGES DE. *Une Idylle à Sedôm*. Paris: C. Dalou, 1889; reissued under title *La Vierge de Sedôm*. Paris: Offenstadt Frères, 1901.

A novel listed by *Jahrbuch*.

McINTOSH, HARLAN C. *This Finer Shadow*. New York: Lorac Books, 1941.

An unconvincing and overwritten story about a young man who drifts into homosexual circles in New York. The book received extravagant praise from John Cowper Powys.

McKENNA, STEPHEN. *Sonia, Between Two Worlds*. New York: George H. Doran Co., 1917.

An English novel mentioned by Lewandowski.

MACKENZIE, COMPTON. *Extraordinary Women*. New York: Macy-Masius, Vanguard Press, 1928.

A satirical and farcical portrait of Lesbianism; also available in an abridged edition. The theme of male homosexuality plays a minor but interesting rôle in the author's entertaining novel, *Vestal Fire*.

MAILER, NORMAN. *The Naked and the Dead.* New York: Rinehart, 1948.
The tension in this war novel between the lieutenant and the general is considered by Aldridge to be of homosexual origin. If this interpretation is accepted by the reader, the book demands comparison with D. H. Lawrence's treatment of a similar theme.

MAINDRON, MAURICE. *Saint-Cendre.* Paris: Editions de la Revue Blanche, 1898.
A novel mentioned by Praz; said to deal with Lesbianism.

MAIZEROY, RENE. *Le Boulet.* Paris: V. Havard, 1886.
One of a group of novels on homosexuality by this author that are mentioned by various critics. *Le Boulet* is cited by Raffalovich; *Les Amours défendues,* mentioned by Praz, is said to deal with Lesbianism; and *Deux amies,* mentioned by Lewandowski, apparently is on a Lesbian theme.

MANN, KLAUS. *Pathetic Symphony.* New York: Allen, Towne & Heath, 1948.
A novel based on the life of Tchaikowsky.

MANN, THOMAS. "Death in Venice," in *Stories of Three Decades.* New York: Alfred A. Knopf, 1946, and in numerous collections and anthologies.
One of the finest pieces of writing and character portrayal in the literature of homosexuality; the story of the attraction that an older man feels for a youth, and the inspiration that is drawn from this affection in an atmosphere free of guilt.

MARGUERITTE, PAUL. *Tous quatre.* Paris: E. Giraud, 1885.
A French novel cited by Raffalovich.

MARGUERITTE, VICTOR. *La Garçonne.* Paris: Flammarion, 1922.
An extremely popular novel in which the Lesbian theme is a symbol for the feminist movement and the struggle of woman for independence.

MARGUERITTE, VICTOR. *La Garçonne.* Paris: Flammarion, 1927.
A drama based on the novel of the same name.

MARTIN DU GARD, ROGER. *Un Taciturne.* Paris: Gallimard, 1932.
A French drama, powerfully written, with well-drawn characters; the story revolves around a man driven to extreme measures by the prospect of relinquishing the youth he loves.

MARX, HENRY. *Ryls, un amour hors de loi.* Paris: Ollendorff, 1924.
A French novel cited by Nin Frías.

MAUPASSANT, GUY DE. "La Femme de Paul," in *Oeuvres Complètes.* Paris: Librairie de France, 1934, I.
A poignant story, which is usually omitted from American and English editions of Maupassant's work; describes a man's reaction to his learning of a Lesbian relationship. The themes of transvestism, effeminacy, etc., are handled by Maupassant in several other stories: "Humiliation" and "Mademoiselle."

MAXWELL, WILLIAM. *The Folded Leaf*. New York: Harper & Bros., 1945.
A friendship and mutual dependency between two boys, hovering close to but
never developing into a sexual love; an extremely penetrating study of adolescence.

MAYNE, XAVIER. *Imre: A Memorandum*. Naples: The English Book-Press,
1908.
Cited by Havelock Ellis; not known to have been published in America or
England.

MEEKER, RICHARD. *The Better Angel*. New York: Greenberg, 1933.
The story of a brilliant young man who discovers early in life that he is "different," and who struggles to maintain his dignity in a hostile world.

MELVILLE, HERMAN. *Moby Dick*. New York: 1851; numerous reprints.
The homosexual element in this classic story of whaling has been discussed by
Maugham and other critics; it seems to me to be clear in the earlier parts of
the book. It would be difficult to impart any other interpretation to the scenes
in which Queequeg becomes intimate with Ishmael, particularly in the light
of Melville's other work: *Typee, Omoo,* and *Billy Budd*.

MENDES, CATULLE. *La Maison de la vieille*. Paris: Charpentier et Fasquelle,
1894.
A French novel cited by Raffalovich.

MENDES, CATULLE. *Méphistophéla*. Paris: E. Dentu, 1890.
One of the best known of the works of Mendès, a story of Lesbianism listed by
Havelock Ellis and Praz.

MERY, JOSEPH. *Monsieur Auguste*. Paris: Michel Lévy Frères, 1867.
Raffalovich and others cite this as a novel of male homosexuality.

MILTON, ERNEST. *To Kiss the Crocodile*. New York: Harper & Bros.,
1928.
The story of a young man who seeks to escape from the world because suspicion
falls upon him following disclosure of his presence at a party of homosexuals.
The party itself is one of the best descriptions of its type in the English language,
and the entire book is a *tour de force* of extraordinary beauty.

MIRBEAU, OCTAVE. *Sébastien Roch*. Paris: Bibliothèque Charpentier, 1905.
A French novel mentioned by Lewandowski and others.

MORITZ, KARL-PHILIPP. *Anton Reiser*. Heilbronn: Gebr. Henninger,
1886.
A psychological novel cited by Raffalovich.

MOTLEY, WILLARD. *Knock on any Door*. New York: Appleton-Century,
1947.
The story of a life, from choir boy to killer; a portrait of a gangster who on
the one hand picks up homosexuals in order to rob them, and on the other hand
develops a deep affection for a homosexual.

MOUREY, GABRIEL. *Lawn-tennis*. Paris: Tresse et Stock, 1891; in French.
A one-act play on the Lesbian theme.

MUSSET, ALFRED DE. *Gamiani, ou deux nuits d'excès.* Venice: 1853.

A short novel by one of the great French romanticists; interpreted by *Jahrbuch* and others as pertaining to homosexuality. An English translation, without publisher, date, or title, is listed in the catalogue of the Bibliothèque Nationale. The complete works of de Musset, both in French and in English, which I have examined did not contain this story.

NILES, BLAIR. *Strange Brother.* New York: Liveright, 1931; reprinted by Harris Publishing Co., 1949.

A sympathetic although over-sentimentalized account of a male homosexual; a theme to which the author was attracted in her accounts of prisoners on Devil's Island.

NORTAL, ALBERT and CHARLES-ETIENNE. *Les Adolescents passionés.* Paris: Curio, 1927.

A novel cited by Havelock Ellis.

OLIVIA. *Olivia.* New York: William Sloane Associates, 1949.

Lesbianism and schoolgirl affections are depicted in a thin novel.

PALGRAVE, F. G. *Hermann-Agha.* New York: Henry Holt, 1874.

Mentioned by *Jahrbuch.*

PAUL, ELLIOT H. *Concert Pitch.* New York: Random House, 1938.

A concert pianist discovers that a critic-sponsor has a passionate interest in him, in addition to a musical one. The novel has the usual fine qualities that mark the writings of Elliot Paul.

PELADAN, JOSEPHIN. *L'Androgyne.* Paris: Dentu, 1891.

A male writer who used a woman's pseudonym, Peladan, according to Praz, devoted his entire literary work to Lesbianism. Other books by him on this theme include *La Vertu suprême, Le Vice suprême, L'Initiation sentimentale,* and *A Coeur perdu.*

PELLAVICINO, FERRANTE. *Alcibiade, fanciullo a scuola.* Oranges: J. Wart, 1652.

A seventeenth-century Italian novel which attracted considerable attention; has been attributed to Aretino, although Pellavicino's authorship is today recognized. Also written by Pellavicino was *Il Prencipe hermafrodito* (1656). *Alcibiade* appears on the list of homosexual novels prepared by Lewandowski.

PEÑA, DAVID. *Oscar Wilde.* Buenos Aires: Sociedad Editorial, 1922.

A drama based on the life of Wilde.

PETERS, FRITZ. *Finistère.* New York: Farrar, Straus & Co., 1951.

A powerful novel depicting the search for affection of a homosexual youth, and the effect of the discovery of his secret on a group of family and friends. The background against which the protagonist turns to a male for love is probably the best portrait that fiction has yet offered of the genesis of inversion, and only a trite and unconvincing ending can be said to spoil what would otherwise be an outstanding contribution to this fiction.

PETRONIUS ARBITER. *The Satyricon.* Numerous translations and editions.

This Roman classic, generally published with the more erotic passages either deleted or untranslated, is often considered the oldest extant novel, and deals with overt male homosexuality. A translation has been ascribed to Oscar Wilde, but there is reason to believe that it was not done by Wilde. However, it has been published with the full text in English (New York: Privately printed, 1930).

PEYREFITTE, ROGER. *Special Friendships*. New York: Vanguard Press, 1950.
A portrait of a passionate attraction between two students at a religious school in France. Both for the quality of the writing, and for the penetrating study of the affections of adolescents, it deserves a permanent place in modern fiction.

PHILLIPS, THOMAS HAL. *The Bitterweed Path*. New York: Rinehart, 1949.
A story of the affection between an older and a younger man, into which the older man's son enters, to form an all-male triangle.

PIDANSAT DE MAIROBERT. *L'Observateur anglois*. London: J. Adamson, 1777–1778; in French. Republished under title *L'Espion Anglois*.
A lengthy eighteenth-century work, with many erotic passages; historians of French literature mention it for its treatment of homosexuality.

PLACE, SIDNEY (pseud. of X. M. Boulestin). *Les Fréquentations de Maurice*. Paris: Dorbon-Ainé, 191–(?).
A French novel, with London as the locale, and cited by Nin Frías.

PORTAL, GEORGES. *The Tunic of Nessus*. Paris: Les Editions Astra, 1939.
Published abroad in English, this is a translation of the author's *Un Protestant*. It is the story of the adventures, confessions, conflicts, and adjustments of a male homosexual.

PROUST, MARCEL. *Cities of the Plain*. New York: Albert & Charles Boni, 1927; numerous reprints.
This book makes up one section of Proust's long novel, *Remembrance of Things Past*—memories of the author, his search and struggle to recall detail, to analyze with minute perception, and to portray upper-class French society. The entire work of Proust is imbued with male homosexuality, starting almost from the opening pages of *Swann's Way*, the first section of his long novel. *Cities of the Plain*, however, is devoted to the subject almost exclusively, although Gide and others felt that Proust had given a more sympathetic study of inversion in earlier parts of his work. In addition, *The Captive* and *The Sweet Cheat Gone*, concerned with the narrator's love for Albertine, are believed by many critics to be novels of concealed homosexuality, with Albertine a man rather than a woman.

RACHILDE (MME. MARGUERITE VALLETTE). *Les Hors nature*. Paris: Société du Mercure de France, 1897.
Cited by Porché, Nin Frías, and others.

RACHILDE (MME. MARGUERITE VALLETTE). *Monsieur Vénus*. New York: Covici, Friede, 1929.
Cited by Symonds, London and Caprio, and others; however, Praz found more sadism and sexlessness in the characters than Lesbianism.

REBOUX, PAUL. *Le Jeune amant*. Paris: E. Flammarion, 1913.
A novel, listed by Lewandowski.

REDNI, JAN DE. *Le livre du désir et de la cruelle volupté*. Paris: Edition Française, 1906.

An historical novel; the author has written several other works on classical themes with a homosexual interest, as books on Sappho, etc.

REGNIER, HENRI DE. *La Pécheresse*. Paris: Mercure de France, 1920.
A novel listed by Lewandowski, who also cites the author's stories, *Couleur du Temps*.

REID, FORREST. *The Garden God*. London: D. Nutt, 1906.
A story of two boys, cited by Havelock Ellis.

RENAULT, MARY. *The Middle Mist*. New York: William Morrow and Co., 1945.
A Lesbian relationship does not interfere with the usual pursuits of life and love. An interesting novel, published in England under the title *Friendly Young Ladies*.

RICE, CRAIG. *Having Wonderful Crime*. New York: Simon and Schuster, 1944.
A mediocre mystery story with a Lesbian theme.

RICTUS, JEHAN. *Fil de fer*. Paris: L. Michaud, 1908.
A novel cited by *Jahrbuch*.

ROCHESTER, JOHN WILMOT, 2nd Earl of. *Sodom*. Antwerp (?): 1684; reprinted in Paris: Verlag von H. Welter, 1904, and bound with *Kryptadia*, IX, 1905.
A drama, generally attributed to the second Earl of Rochester, although authorship was denied. It is an amusing, pornographic, satirical attack on the reign of Charles II, written in heroic couplets. Of the 1684 edition, no copies are known; republication of this work by the editors of *Kryptadia* was evidently from a manuscript, which is said to be in existence today.

ROLAND-MANUEL, SUZANNE. *Le Trille du diable*. Paris: Editions des Deux Rives, 1946.
A lengthy novel about Lesbians.

ROLFE, FREDERICK WILLIAM (Baron Corvo). *Don Tarquino*. London: Chatto, 1929.
One of a group of novels by Baron Corvo, all of which are of interest in the study of this literature.

ROLLAND, ROMAIN. *Jean Christophe in Paris*. New York: H. Holt and Co., 1925.
A work mentioned by Nin Frías for its handling of the homosexual theme.

(ANONYMOUS). *Le Roman d'un inverté-né*; in Laupts' *L'Homosexualité et les types homosexuels*. Paris: Vigot frères, 1910.
The confessions of a homosexual; the story of a man in deep conflict with himself. This was originally written as a letter to Emile Zola. Has been published in German in Raffalovich's book, *Der Uranismus*.

ROSTAND, MAURICE. *Le Procès d'Oscar Wilde*. Paris: Flammarion, 1934.
A drama by a great French playwright, based on the trials of Oscar Wilde.

ROUSSIN, ANDRE. *Les Œufs de l'autruche.* Monaco: Editions du Rocher, 1950.
A contemporary French drama.

ROYDE-SMITH, NAOMI. *The Island.* New York: Harper & Bros., 1930.
A story of the effect that a love for another girl has on the life of a woman. There is never a frank statement of the Lesbian problem in this book; in fact, it is evaded by the author, yet its existence seems undeniable. In an earlier novel, *The Tortoiseshell Cat,* the writer also approached and touched upon the Lesbian theme.

SACHER-MASOCH, LEOPOLD VON. *Venus in Furs.* Paris: C. Carrington, 1902; also available in other editions and in various translations.
The classic work on masochism is considered part of the literature of homosexuality by Chevalier, London and Caprio, and others.

SARTRE, JEAN-PAUL. *The Age of Reason* and *The Reprieve.* New York: Alfred A. Knopf, 1947.
These novels form the first two parts of a trilogy, entitled *The Roads to Freedom.* Although the homosexual is never the central character nor his problems the central situation, he is a symbol, being one of a group of the displaced, the disillusioned, the uprooted. For Sartre, these people are seeking new values in a world which they have rejected and which in turn has rejected them. The homosexual theme was also apparent in the author's drama, *No Exit.*

SCHLUMBERGER, JEAN. *Heureux qui comme Ulysse.* Paris: Privately published, 1906.
A novella, cited by *Jahrbuch.*

SCULLY, ROBERT. *The Scarlet Pansy.* New York: Royal Publishers, not dated.
The low-point of the homosexual novel; a crude and poorly disguised effort at transposition of sex.

SMOLLETT, TOBIAS G. *The Adventures of Roderick Random.* London: 1748; numerous reprints, usually under the title *Roderick Random.*
Although constituting only one chapter of this classic, the meeting of Roderick with Lord Strutwell is probably the earliest portrait of a homosexual in any English fiction that has survived.

STADION, EMMERICH GRAF VON. *Schatten im Licht.* Wien: Prochaska, 1882.
A novel mentioned by Krafft-Ebing.

STEIN, GERTRUDE. *Things as They Are.* Pawlet, Vt.: Banyan Press, 1950.
A beautiful story, written in 1903 but first published posthumously; depicts love in an all-female triangle.

STERNHEIM, CARL. *Oskar Wilde.* Potsdam: Kiepenheuer, 1925.
A drama based on the life of Wilde.

STEVENSON, EDWARD IRENÆUS PRIME-. *Left to Themselves.* New York: Hunt and Eaton, 1891.

One of a group of novels by this author that are on the *Jahrbuch* list; others include *A Great Patience, Many Waters,* and *Weed and Flour. Left to Themselves* is described as a story of two young men.

STOKES, LESLIE and SEWELL STOKES. *Oscar Wilde.* London: M. Secker and Warburg, 1937.
A drama based on the life of Wilde.

STONE, GRACE ZARING. *The Grotto.* New York: Harper & Brothers, 1951.
The struggle of a mother against her son's homosexuality. Neither the mother nor the author shows any psychological insight into the problem.

STURGIS, HOWARD OVERING. *Tim.* London and New York: Macmillan, 1891.
A novel about schoolboys, cited by Havelock Ellis.

TELLIER, ANDRE. *Twilight Men.* New York: Greenberg, 1931.
One of the earliest American novels in which the protagonist is an overt homosexual and the subject is treated in a forthright manner.

THOMAS, WARD. *Stranger in the Land.* Boston: Houghton Mifflin Co., 1949.
Male homosexuality in a small town; the sympathetic approach is ineffective because of the sensational portrayal of the evils of blackmail.

TYLER, PARKER and CHARLES HENRY FORD. *The Young and Evil.* Paris: Obelisk Press, 1933.
Unpublished (and said to be unpublishable) in America, this novel has been described by men of letters who have read it as "frankly pornographic and of unquestioned literary merit."

VANBRUGH, JOHN. *The Relapse.* London: 1697; reprinted in various editions of Vanbrugh's work, and in several anthologies.
A play that is mentioned by many writers as pertaining to homosexuality; actually, there is a portrait of an overt homosexual, but he is a minor character, and the main development of the drama does not revolve around him. *The Relapse* is interesting in this literature because it was one of the few examples of overt homosexuality to be portrayed on the stage previous to the twentieth century.

VIDAL, GORE. *The City and the Pillar.* New York: E. P. Dutton, 1948.
The dilemma of the homosexual in modern society is portrayed against a background of the gay life into which he drifts in Hollywood and New York. The hackneyed ending in violence detracts from a book which in places rises above the mediocre.

VIDAL, GORE. *The Season of Comfort.* New York: E. P. Dutton, 1949.
The conflicts and adjustments of a bisexual youth.

WAHL, LOREN. *The Invisible Glass.* New York: Greenberg, 1950.
The homosexual as a member of a minority group is portrayed by placing a white Army officer in a Negro regiment in Italy. This is a well-knit novel, which shows deep understanding of the similarities and differences between the two minority questions, but the usual ending in violence is particularly unfortunate because it has extreme anti-homosexual implications which were probably neither intended nor understood by the author.

WAUGH, ALEC. *The Loom of Youth*. New York: George H. Doran Co., 1920.
A novel about education, listed by Lewandowski.

WAUGH, EVELYN. *Brideshead Revisited*. Boston: Little, Brown and Co., 1945.
An Army captain reminisces about a family he had known intimately; one of the members of the family is a homosexual whose adventures, sexual and religious, are depicted with humor and understanding.

WEIRAUCH, ANNA ELISABET. *The Outcast*. New York: Greenberg, 1933; reprinted by Willey Book Co., 1948.
The life of the central character in *The Scorpion* (see below) is continued in this novel, which ends with the heroine's renunciation of Lesbianism.

WEIRAUCH, ANNA ELISABET. *The Scorpion*. New York: Greenberg, 1932; reprinted by Willey Book Co., 1948.
A story of the early life of a Lesbian.

WILBRANDT, ADOLF VON. *Fridolin's Mystical Marriage*. New York: W. S. Gottsberger, 1884.
A rather restrained novel of male homosexuality, built around the theme of the intermediate sex.

WILDE, OSCAR. *The Picture of Dorian Gray*. New York: Modern Library; and numerous other editions.
The homosexuality is thinly concealed in Wilde's famous novel.

WILDE, OSCAR. *The Portrait of Mr W. H.* New York: Mitchell Kennerley, 1921.
A fictional essay interpreting the sonnets of Shakespeare in the light of the Bard's passion for a young actor.

WILHELM, GALE. *Torchlight to Valhalla*. New York: Random House, 1938.
A girl turns to a woman for love, after her effort to find love with a man fails. This is the work of a writer with keen insight and an ability to draw characters with an economy of words.

WILHELM, GALE. *We Too Are Drifting*. New York: Random House, 1935.
There is superb writing in this short novel of a three-cornered all-female relationship, with its frustrations, its jealousies, and its compensations.

WILLINGHAM, CALDER. *End as a Man*. New York: Vanguard Press, 1947.
A bitter attack on military education, including a description of homosexuality among the students.

WYLIE, PHILIP. *The Disappearance*. New York: Rinehart & Co., 1951.
A fantasy in which two worlds, one consisting only of men, the other only of women, suddenly come into existence. It is in the woman's world that the puritanical morality clashes with the drive for sexual satisfaction. In *Opus 21*, by the same author, there is an interesting development of an incident involving Lesbianism.

ZOLA, EMILE. *Nana*. New York: Modern Library; and numerous editions.

This French classic has some unmistakable passages on Lesbianism, a subject to which Zola gave attention in *La Curée*, in the opinion of London and Caprio, and in his tri-city trilogy, *London, Rome,* and *Paris,* according to Lewandowski.

ZWEIG, ARNOLD. *Claudia*. New York: Viking Press, 1930.

A novel consisting of a series of loosely related sketches, in one of which a man tells his wife about an adolescent relationship with another boy.

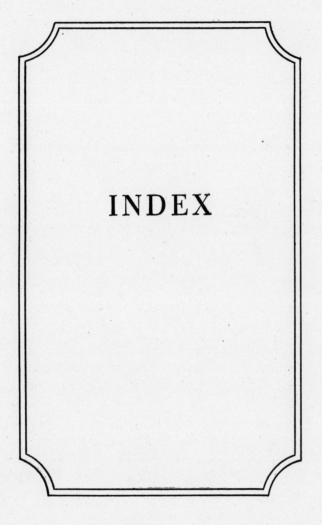

INDEX

Index